M          F          A


VS


N          Y          C

*The Two Cultures of American Fiction*

*Edited by Chad Harbach*

M  F  A
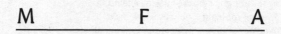

VS

N  Y  C
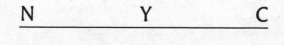

*n+1 / Faber and Faber*
*New York*

n+1/Faber and Faber
Faber and Faber, Inc., is an affiliate of Farrar, Straus and Giroux
18 West 18th Street, New York 10011

Owing to limitations of space, all acknowledgments for permission to reprint
previously published material can be found on pages 311–312.

Library of Congress Cataloging-in-Publication Data
MFA vs NYC: the Two Cultures of American Fiction / edited by Chad
    Harbach. — First edition.
        pages   cm
        ISBN 978-0-86547-813-8 (pbk.) — ISBN 978-0-374-71227-3 (ebook)
        1. Authors and publishers—United States. 2. Fiction—Authorship.
    3. Authorship—Vocational guidance. 4. Creative writing (Higher
    education)—United States. 5. Fiction—Publishing—United States.
    I. Harbach, Chad, editor of compilation.

PN155.M45 2014
808.02—dc23

                                                        2013048115

Designed by Dan O. Williams
Production by Dayna Tortorici

www.nplusonemag.com
www.twitter.com/nplusonemag · www.facebook.com/nplusone
www.fsgbooks.com
www.twitter.com/fsgbooks · www.facebook.com/fsgbooks

10  9  8  7  6  5  4  3  2

# Contents

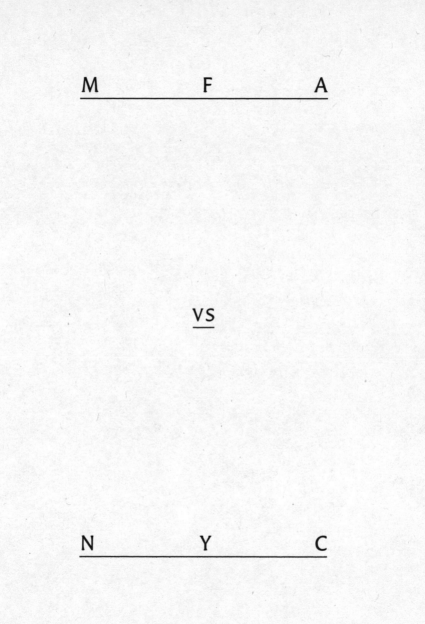

M    F    A

VS

N    Y    C

# Introduction
## Chad Harbach

In late 2010, the essay that gives this book its name was published in *n+1* Issue 10. Afterward, I received quite a bit of mail. Many of my correspondents (and coeditors) professed to have found the essay extremely depressing. Two friends living abroad, one in Istanbul and the other in London, each wrote to say that, having read my essay, they felt pretty disinclined to return to the United States. (They have both since returned.) A young woman from Korea sent several long and anguished letters about how lonely I'd made her feel.

My essay proceeded from a few simple observations: First, that graduate and undergraduate creative writing programs have expanded with wild speed in the past three decades. Second, that this expansion has drawn more writers than ever before inside the university system, so that teaching rivals publishing as a percentage of writers' income. And third, that this has created two centers of gravity for American fiction: "MFA," which is dispersed throughout our university towns, and "NYC," which hews close to Manhattan's trade publishing industry. From there I tried to trace some of the social and literary consequences of this two-headed system—one in which the two heads are always chatting and bickering and buying each other drinks.

What was so depressing? In part, it may have been not the essay's conclusions but its goal: that is, to consider the fiction writer less as an utterly free artistic being, with responsibilities only to posterity and eternal truth (or whatever), and more as a person constrained by circumstance—a person who needs money, and whose milieu influences the way she lives, reads, thinks, and writes. A person whose work is shaped by education and economy and a host of other pressures, large and small.

A sociological approach can go too far, of course; because the writer is free on the page, and the same circumstances (not that any two people have ever lived under precisely the same circumstances) can produce an infinity of different work. But the pressures exist, always, and this book attempts to talk about them. *MFA vs NYC* is a book about fiction writers, and fiction writers have always existed in a messy middle ground between art and aspiration, on the one hand, and on the other, the grungy, annoying, sometimes debilitating details of reality. *How much does it cost?* is a key question in Austen and Balzac and Chekhov and Joyce and Wharton and Fitzgerald and Raymond Carver and Rebecca Curtis and many in between. It's not part of the job or constitution of the novelist or the short-story writer to shun the material details of the conditions within which we live our lives. The very best American novel gets under way, in its very first sentence, because its broad-shouldered narrator has "little or no money in [his] purse." So he goes to see a pair of crotchety retiree investors, who haggle over his pay, settle on a very low number, and put him on a boat.

The best way to approach this book, I think, is as a kind of jointly written novel—one whose composite heroine is the fiction writer circa 2014. Her voyage is a long one, and she has her frailties: her concentration is fragile, she wakes up too late and checks her email too often, she drinks too much coffee in the morning and too much wine at night. But she is always working, working, working, trying both to pay her rent and to put the way the world feels into words. Most often these tasks seem utterly incompatible; sometimes they convene and then separate again.

Our heroine, as most writers today do, attends college as a matter of course. From then forward, she may intersect with the university at many points, whether for a day or a decade, as she moves into and out of its orbit as an MFA student, PhD candidate (whether in creative writing or another discipline), adjunct instructor, guest lecturer, visiting fellow, and part-time or tenured MFA professor.

This has always existed, this affiliation between the writer and the university. Donald Hall and Ezra Pound put the case very succinctly in 1962.

HALL: Now the poets in America are mostly teachers. Do you have any ideas on the connection of teaching in the university with writing poetry?

POUND: It is the economic factor. A man's got to get in his rent somehow.

But as the creative writing industry expands, the affiliation becomes ever stronger. It also becomes more maligned. The MFA has many detractors, and many of them greatly overstate their case, harking back to a time when every writer was a wine-chugging Hemingway firing a homemade rifle at a rabid shark from the back of a speeding ambulance. (Nobody ever uses Edith Wharton, or any woman,

Chad Harbach

as an example of an author untainted by degrees, though until recently women were much less likely to be degreed.) "MFA writing" is supposed to be sedulous, dutiful, and uninspired. And much of it is—most of it is. The problem with this argument is that these adjectives describe the vast majority of the writing that has been done in the history of the planet, but they often fail to describe the books written by graduates of MFA programs.

The MFA's defenders tend to be more knowledgeable about what actually happens in a creative writing classroom, but the return comes back with as much tricky spin as the initial serve. These defenders are generally people paid to inhabit such classrooms, and thus tend toward the rosy admissions-office view of a system that clearly has problematic elements, both pedagogic and, in its very American way of charging large numbers of students large sums to pursue a dream achievable by a few, economic.

One purpose of this book, then, is to offer a more multifarious and nuanced view of the MFA program than has previously been offered. Eric Bennett provides a foundational (and personal) history of the program that started it all, the Iowa Writers' Workshop; Fredric Jameson and Elif Batuman situate the workshop and the writing it produces within larger currents of literary history; Carla Blumenkranz describes, through the figure of Gordon Lish, the complicated personal dynamics of the workshop. And a host of students and teachers, present and past—George Saunders, Maria Adelmann, David Foster Wallace, Alexander Chee, Diana Wagman, Keith Gessen, and Eli S. Evans—depict and analyze their own experience on both sides of the seminar table.

New York City, of course, is the other polestar of our heroine's life—even if she stays far away from it, it never falls far from her

6

thoughts. Perhaps she moves to the city after college but finds her day job uncongenial to her progress as a writer, and absconds to a university town with cheaper rents. Or she attends college in the city, grows accustomed to the overwhelming niceness of Brooklyn (that's why so many writers live there: it's nice), and decides the rent is worth it. At some point she sells a book to a publishing house, perhaps for a sum that seems an incredible windfall—and then, as Emily Gould describes, she spends it with incredible speed, partly on clothes that go out of style, but mostly on taxes and rent.

Or our heroine never moves to New York at all, but engages with it through her book (*if* she sells her book), and primarily through the people—agent, editor, publicist—who shepherd her book through publication. Agents Jim Rutman and Melissa Flashman, editor Lorin Stein, and publicist Jynne Martin attempt to elucidate the strange and unpredictable process by which a manuscript becomes a book and a book becomes popular. One conclusion is that the people who work in publishing and the people who publish tend to begin in much the same place, with the same ambitions, and follow branching paths. Another is that the old Hollywood mantra—*nobody knows anything*—holds true for books as well.

This rubric of two cultures, I think, makes for useful descriptions of material, social, and intellectual life for young and youngish American writers. It also, like any useful rubric, leaves stuff out. San Francisco and Los Angeles, for instance. Minneapolis. Any small local movement that arises. Internet writing—that's a big one, though much internet writing seems either to emanate from New York or be oriented toward it. And, as Darryl Lorenzo Wellington describes, the swelling field of self-publishing, in which the writer would be sovereign but generally winds up in thrall to Amazon. There are many

Chad Harbach

outsiders to the system—many of whom want in, others of whom wish to remain forever out.

In the end, of course, a writer can be ruined by school—by a too-great desire to emulate her peers or please her teachers. She can be ruined by the publishing industry—by trying to anticipate what the masses, or Manhattan editors, want to buy. She can be ruined by her poverty, or her parents. Or she can find her way. +

# MFA vs NYC

## Chad Harbach

In his 2009 book *The Program Era: Postwar Fiction and the Rise of Creative Writing*, Mark McGurl describes how American fiction has become inseparable from its institutional context—the university—as particularly embodied in the writing workshop. The book is remarkable in many respects, not least for McGurl's suggestive readings of a host of major American writers. In terms of the intellectual history of the writing workshop, *The Program Era* marks a turning point after which the MFA program comes to seem somehow different than it did previously. It feels, reading McGurl, as if the MFA beast has at last been offered a look in the mirror, and may finally come to know itself as it is.

This may seem paradoxical, or backward: writing programs, after all, have long existed as an object of self-study for the people who actually attend or teach in them, usually in the form of satire—David Foster Wallace's "Westward the Course of Empire Takes Its Way," Francine Prose's *Blue Angel*, that movie with the Belle & Sebastian soundtrack, and on and on. But (to borrow one of McGurl's many ideas) the program writer, even if he's been both student and professor, always wants to assume, and is to some extent granted, outsider status by the university; he's always lobbing his flaming bags of prose over the ivied gate late at night. Then in the morning he puts on a tie and walks through the gate and goes to his office. In the university, the fiction writer nevertheless manages not to think of himself as of the university.

McGurl interrupts this unselfconsciousness by filing a full and official report from across the hallway: from the English Department proper, forcing the aspiring novelist to look across that hallway and notice a bunch of graduate students and professors sitting there, in identical offices, wielding identical red pens. *You're like me now!* is one of the cheerful subtexts of *The Program Era*—a literary critic's pointing out that the creative writer is just as institutionally entangled as the critic has long been acknowledged to be. Or, more charitably put (for McGurl is perpetually charitable), that the fiction writer, at last, can cease fretting about how free and wild he is and get to work.

But what kind of work? One good outcome of McGurl's analysis would be to lay to rest the perpetual hand-wringing about what MFA programs do to writers (e.g., turn them into cringing, cautious, post-Carverite automatons). Because of the universitization of American fiction that McGurl describes, it's virtually impossible to read a particular book and deduce whether the writer attended a program. For one thing, she almost certainly did. For another, the workshop as a form has bled downward into the colleges, so that a writer could easily have taken a lifetime's worth of workshops as an undergraduate, à la Jonathan Safran Foer. And even if the writer has somehow never heard of an MFA program or set foot on a college campus, it doesn't matter, because if she's read any American fiction of the past sixty years, or met someone who did, she's imbibed the general idea and aesthetic. We are all MFAs now.

On the flip side (as McGurl can't quite know, because he attended "real" grad school), MFA programs themselves are so lax and laissez-faire as to have a shockingly small impact on students' work—especially shocking if you're the student and paying $80,000 for the privilege. Staffed by writer-professors preoccupied with their own work or their failure to produce any, freed from pedagogical urgency by the tenuousness of the link between fiction writing and employment, and populated by ever-younger, often immediately postcollegiate students, MFA programs today serve less as hotbeds of fierce stylistic inculcation, or finishing schools for almost-ready writers (in the way of, say, Iowa in the 1970s), and more as an ingenious partial solution to an eminent American problem: how to extend our already protracted adolescence past twenty-two and toward thirty, in order to cope with an oversupplied labor market.

Two years spent in an MFA program, in other words, constitute a tiny and often ineffectual part of the American writer's lifelong engagement with the university. And yet critics continue to bemoan the mechanizing effects of the programs, and to draw links between a writer's degree-holding status and her degree of aesthetic freedom. *Get out of the schools and live!* they urge, forgetting on the one hand how much of contemporary life is lived in the shadow of the university, even if beyond its walls; and on the other hand how much free living an adult can do while attending two classes per week. It's time to do away with this distinction between the MFAs and the non-MFAs, the unfree and the free, the caged and the wild. Once we do, perhaps we can venture a new, less normative distinction, based not on the writer's educational background but on the system within which she earns (or aspires to earn) her living: MFA or NYC.

There were 79 degree-granting programs in creative writing in 1975; today, there are 1,269! This explosion has created a huge source of financial support for working writers, not just in the form of lecture fees, adjunctships, and temporary appointments—though these abound—but honest-to-goodness jobs: decently paid, relatively secure compared with other industries, and often even tenured. It would be fascinating to know the numbers—what percentage of the total income of American fiction writers comes from the university, and what percentage from publishing contracts—but it's safe to say that the university now rivals, if it hasn't surpassed, New York as the economic center of the literary fiction world. This situation—of two complementary economic systems of roughly matched strength—is a new one for American fiction. As the mass readership of literary fiction has peaked and subsided, and the march of technology sends the New York publishing world into spasms of perpetual anxiety, if not its much-advertised death throes, the MFA program has picked up the financial slack and then some, offering steady payment to more fiction writers than, perhaps, have ever been paid before.

Everyone knows this. But what's remarked rarely if at all is the way this balance has created, in effect, two literary cultures (or, more precisely, two literary fiction cultures) in the United States: one condensed in New York, the other spread across the diffuse network of provincial college towns that spans from Irvine, California, to Austin, Texas, to Ann Arbor, Michigan, to Tallahassee, Florida (with a kind of wormhole at the center, in Iowa City, into which one can step and reappear at *The New Yorker* offices on 42nd Street). The superficial differences between these two cultures can be summed up charticle-style: short stories vs novels; Amy Hempel vs Jonathan Franzen; library copies vs galley copies; *Poets & Writers* vs *The New York Observer*; *Wonder Boys* vs *The Devil Wears Prada*; the Association of Writers and Writing Programs conference vs the Frankfurt Book Fair; departmental parties vs publishing parties; literary readings vs publishing parties; staying home vs publishing parties. But the differences also run deep. Each culture has its own canonical works and heroic figures; each has its own logic of social and professional advancement. Each affords its members certain aesthetic and personal freedoms while restricting others; each exerts its own subtle but powerful pressures on the work being produced.

Of course the two cultures overlap in any number of obvious ways, some of them significant. The NYC writer most probably earned an MFA; the MFA writer, meanwhile, may well publish her books at a New York house. There are even MFA programs in New York, lots of them, though these generally partake of the NYC culture. And many writers move back and forth between the MFA and NYC worlds, whether over the course of a career or within a single year. A writer like Deborah Eisenberg, who spends half the year in New York and half at the University of Virginia; whose early stories were published to acclaim in *The New Yorker* but who subsequently became known (or unknown) as a "writer's writer"—that is, a workshop leader's writer; whose fiction, oddly, never appears anymore in New York–based magazines but who writes frequently for *The New York Review of Books* and publishes new books to raves from a variety of New York organs, shows in how many ways a writer can slip between these two cultures before winding up perfectly poised between them.* And yet what's so striking is how

---

* In 2012, Eisenberg moved from Virginia to Columbia University.

Chad Harbach

distinct the cultures do, in fact, feel and how distinctly they at least pretend to function. On the level of individual experience, each can feel hermetic, and the traveler from one to the other finds herself in an alien land. The fact that it's possible to travel without a passport, or to be granted dual citizenship, makes them no less distinct.

The model for the MFA fiction writer is her program counterpart, the poet. Poets have long been professionally bound to academia; decades before the blanketing of the country with MFA programs requiring professors, the poets took to the grad schools, earning PhDs in English and other literary disciplines to finance their real vocation. Thus came of age the concept of the poet-teacher. The poet earns money as a teacher; and, at a higher level of professional accomplishment, from grants and prizes; and, at an even higher level, from appearance fees at other colleges. She does not, as a rule, earn money by publishing books of poems—it has become almost inconceivable that anyone outside a university library will read them. The consequences of this economic arrangement for the quality of American poetry have been often bemoaned (poems are insular, arcane, gratuitously allusive, et cetera), if poorly understood. Of more interest here is the economic arrangement proper, and the ways in which it has become that of a large number of fiction writers as well.

As the fiction writer-teacher becomes the norm, the fiction MFA also becomes an odd hybrid. On the one hand, MFA programs are still studio based: luxuries of time during which both serious and dilettantish people can develop their artistic skills outside the demands of the market. In this way, the programs aspire to a kind of immanent (and convenient) ideal; it doesn't matter whether the student publishes now or in ten years or never, whether her degree ever earns her a penny, as long as she serves her muse. On the other hand, as available teaching jobs multiply, MFA programs become increasingly preprofessional. They provide, after all, a terminal degree in a burgeoning field. And (the ambitious student rightly asks) why not enter that field straightaway? After all, there are actual jobs available for MFA holders, while the other humanities stagnate and overall unemployment hovers around 10 percent.

Thus the fiction writer's MFA increasingly resembles the poet's old PhD; not in the rigors of the degree itself—getting an MFA is so *easy*—but in the way it immerses the writer in a professional academic network. She lives in a college town, and when she turns her gaze forward and outward, toward the future and the literary world at large, she sees not, primarily, the New York cluster of editors and agents and publishers but, rather, a matrix of hundreds of colleges with MFA programs, potential employers all, linked together by *Poets & Writers*, AWP, and summertime workshops at picturesque make-out camps like Sewanee and Bread Loaf. More links, more connections, are provided by the attractive, unread, university-funded literary quarterlies that are swapped between these places and by the endowments and discretionary funds that deliver an established writer-teacher from her home program to a different one, for a well-paid night or week, with everybody's drinks expensed. This system of circulating patronage may have some pedagogical value but exists chiefly to supplement the income of the writer-teacher and, perhaps more important, to impress on the students the more glamorous side of becoming—of aspiring to become—a writer-teacher.

For the MFA writer, then, publishing a book becomes neither a primary way to earn money nor even a direct attempt to do so. The book instead serves as a credential. Just as the critic publishes her dissertation in order to secure a job in an ever-tightening market, the fiction writer publishes her book of stories, or her novel, to cap off her MFA. There is an element of liberation in this, however complex; the MFA writer is no longer at the whim of the market—or, rather, has entered a less whimsical, more tolerant market. The New York publishing houses become ever more fearful and defensive, battened down against the encroachments of other "media," old and new and merely imagined—but the MFA writer doesn't have to deal with those big houses. And if she does get published by one, she doesn't need a six-figure advance. On the whole, independent and university presses (as for the poet and the critic) will do just fine. The MFA writer is also exempt from publicity to a large extent—she still checks her Amazon ranking obsessively, as everyone does, but she can do so with a dollop of humor and not as an inquiry into professional survival. Instead she enters into the professor's publish-or-perish bargain, in which the writing of future books, no matter how they sell, results in professional advancement and increasing security. Is this not artistic freedom of a quiet and congenial sort? Could not books be written here in the university, all sorts of different books, that could never be written from within the narrow confines of the New York publishing world?

Yes, but. The MFA writer escapes certain pressures only to submit to others. Early in her career, for instance, she is all in a rush to publish—first to place stories in the quarterlies, and then to get some version of her MFA thesis into print, by hook or by crook, in order to be eligible for jobs. While the NYC writer might be willing to toil obscurely for a decade or more, nourishing herself with the thought of a big psychic and financial payoff that might never come, the MFA writer is not. She has no actual physical New York to cling to, no parties to attend; if her degree is finished but her book is not, she's purely a cast-out from the world in which she wishes to move. This can encourage the publication of slight and sometimes premature books, books that might give readers, and the writer herself, the wrong idea of what she can do.

Then, later in the career, comes the more obvious pressure not to publish at all—she has, after all, become a professor, and a professor gets paid to profess. One escapes the shackles of the corporate publishing apparatus only by accepting those of the departmental administration, and of one's students, at which point the trade-off can come to seem like a bait and switch—although as the MFA system matures, its aspirants no doubt become more clear-eyed about what awaits them.

The MFA system also nudges the writer toward the writing of short stories; of all the ambient commonplaces about MFA programs, perhaps the only accurate one is that the programs are organized around the story form. This begins in workshops, both MFA and undergraduate, where the minute, scrupulous attentions of one's instructor and peers are best suited to the consideration of short pieces, which can be marked up, cut down, rewritten and reorganized, and brought back for further review. The short story, like the ten-page college term paper, or the twenty-five-page graduate paper, has become a primary pedagogical genre form.

It's not just that MFA students are encouraged to write stories in workshop, though this is true; it's that the entire culture is steeped in the form. To learn how to write short stories, you also have to read them. MFA professors—many of them story writers themselves—recommend story collections to their students. MFA students recommend other collections to one another; they also, significantly, teach undergraduate creative writing courses, which are built almost exclusively around short works. In classes that need to divide their attention between the skill of reading and the craft of writing (and whose popularity rests partly on their lack of rigor), there's no time for plowing through novels. Also, scores of colleges now have associated literary journals, which tend overwhelmingly to focus on the short story; by publishing in as many of these as possible, a young writer begins building the reputation that will eventually secure her a job as a teacher-writer, and an older writer sustains her CV by the same means.

Thus the names that reverberate through the MFA system, from the freshman creative writing course up through the tenured faculty, tend to be those of story writers. At first glance, this may seem like a kind of collective suicide, because everyone knows that no one reads short stories. And it's true that the story, once such a reliable source of income for writers, has fallen out of mass favor, perhaps for a reason opposite to that of the poem: if in the public imagination poetry reeks suspiciously of high academia—the dry, impacted arcana of specialists addressing specialists—then the short story may have become subtly and pejoratively associated with low academia—the workaday drudgery of classroom exercises and assignments. The poet sublimates into the thin air of the overeducated PhD; the story writer melts down into the slush of the composition department. Neither hits the cultural mark. A writer's early short stories (as any New York editor will tell you) lead to a novel, or they lead nowhere at all.

But there's a dialectical reversal to be found here, in which the story/novel debate reveals itself to be just one aspect of the MFA/ NYC cultural divide, and in which the story might even be winning. One of the clearest signs of that divide is the way that different groups of writers are read, valued, and discussed in the two different "places"—one could, for instance, live a long, full life in New York without ever hearing of Stuart Dybek, a canonical MFA-culture story writer who oversaw the Western Michigan program for decades before moving on to Northwestern. A new Gary Shteyngart novel, meanwhile, will be met with indifference at most MFA programs. Entire such NYC and MFA rosters could be named. In effect, parallel and competing canons of contemporary literature have formed—and when it comes to canon formation, New York, and therefore the novel, may be at a disadvantage.

New York can't be excelled at two things: superstardom and forgetfulness. And so the New York "canon," at any given moment, tends to consist of a few perennial superstars—Roth, DeLillo, Pynchon, Auster—whose reputations are secure at least until they die, and beneath whom circulate an ever changing group of acclaimed young novelists—Joshua Ferris, Nicole Krauss, Rivka Galchen, Jonathan Safran Foer—and a host of midcareer writers whose names are magnified when they put out a book and shrink in between. Reputation in this world depends directly on the market and the publishing cycle, the reviews and the prizes, and so all except those at the very top have little reason to hope for a durable readership. The contemporary New York canon tends to be more *contemporary* than *canon*—it consists of popular new novels, and previous books by the authors of same.

The MFA canon works differently. The rapid expansion of MFA programs in recent decades has opened up large institutional spaces above and below: above, for writer-professors who teach MFA students; below, for undergraduate students who are taught by MFAs (and by former MFAs hired as adjuncts). All told, program fiction amounts to a new discipline, with a new curriculum. This new curriculum consists mainly of short stories, and the short fiction anthologies commonly used in introductory courses become the primary mechanism by which the MFA canon is assembled and disseminated.

A quick glance at some of the most popular anthologies shows the rough contours of the program canon. *The Vintage Book of Contemporary American Short Stories* (1994), edited by Tobias Wolff, honors the dirty realists and their successors with a dedication to Raymond Carver, an introduction that begins, in classic dirty-realist fashion, "A few years ago I met a wheat farmer from North Dakota . . . ," and stories by Carver, Ann Beattie (University of Virginia), Richard Bausch (Memphis), Richard Ford (Trinity College, Dublin), Tim O'Brien (Texas State–San Marcos), and Jayne Anne Phillips (Rutgers), as well as Dybek (Northwestern), Joy Williams (Wyoming), Robert Stone (Yale), Mary Gaitskill (until recently, Syracuse), Barry Hannah (Mississippi, before his death), Ron Hansen (Santa Clara), Jamaica Kincaid (Claremont McKenna), Edward P. Jones (George Washington), Joyce Carol Oates (Princeton), Mona Simpson (Bard), Denis Johnson (currently unaffiliated), and Wolff's Stanford colleague John L'Heureux. *The Scribner Anthology of Contemporary Short Fiction* (2007) retains a dozen of Wolff's picks, and adds a new generation of post-dirty, ethnically diverse writers: Amy Bloom (Wesleyan), Peter Ho Davies (Michigan), Junot Díaz (MIT), et al. Ben Marcus's *Anchor Book of New American Short Stories* (2004) rounds out the picture, overlapping with Scribner but not Vintage, adding still younger writers, and emphasizing recent contributions to the anti-dirty, explicitly stylized or stylish tradition—for instance, Aimee Bender (USC), Gary Lutz (Pitt-Greensberg), and Mary Caponegro (Bard).*

---

* Since the original publication of this essay, a few of these writers have changed affiliations: Richard Bausch to Chapman University; Richard Ford to Columbia; and Robert Stone to Texas State–San Marcos.

Via these anthologies—and via word of mouth and personal appearance—a large and somewhat stable body of writers is read by a large number of MFAs and an even larger number of undergrads, semester in and semester out. Thus the oft-scorned short story may secure a more durable readership than the vaunted novel. While Denis Johnson won a National Book Award in 2007 for his novel *Tree of Smoke* and Junot Díaz, a Pulitzer in 2008 for his novel *The Brief Wondrous Life of Oscar Wao*, these writers' reputations and readerships may rely more heavily on their single, slim volumes of stories, *Jesus' Son* and *Drown*, both of which are reliably anthologized and have entered the consciousness of a whole generation of college students.

One could even suggest that, in the absence of a contemporary American canon produced by the critics in the English department (that one consists only of Toni Morrison), the writers in the MFA program have gone ahead and built their own—as well as the institutional means to disseminate, perpetuate, and replenish it. This canon centers on short works, and distinguishes itself from the New York canon in other ways. While it still avails one to be a white guy in NYC, at least at the top of the market where Franzen, DeLillo, and Roth reside (and where the preferred ethnic other remains the Jewish male), the MFA canon has a less masculine tone, and a more overt interest in cultural pluralism. And while the New York list updates itself with each new copy of the *Times Book Review*, the MFA canon dates back, with pointed precision, to 1970—the year of the earliest story in both the Vintage and Scribner anthologies. NYC remembers the seventies not at all, and the eighties only for the coke, but the MFA culture keeps alive the reputations of great (Ann Beattie), near-great (Joy Williams), and merely excellent writers whom publishing has long since passed by.

Chad Harbach

The year 1970, not coincidentally, also marks the beginning of the careers of many of the eminent writers who emerged from the MFA heyday, and who now hold the most distinguished chairs in the MFA culture. Thus the MFA canon is a living canon not just by definition—it is, after all, "contemporary" literature—but because the writers who constitute it are constant presences on the scene and active shapers of the canon's contents. They teach (however reluctantly); they advise; they anthologize; they travel from program to program to read. A writer's university becomes an automatic champion of her work, and as her students disperse to jobs at other schools, so does the championing. The writer doesn't assign her own work—she doesn't have to—but she assigns that of her friends, and invites them to speak. It will be interesting to see what happens when this group of older writers dies (they are unlikely to give up their jobs beforehand); whether the MFA canon will leap forward, or back, or switch tracks entirely, to accommodate the interests, private and aesthetic, of a younger group of writer-teachers. Perhaps (among other possibilities) the MFA culture will take a turn toward the novel.

As the MFA fiction writer moves toward the poetic/academic model, the NYC writer moves toward the Hollywood model. Not because fiction writers earn their keep as screenwriters (a few do, but that was by and large an earlier era; MFA/NYC could be said to have replaced NYC/LA as an organizing cultural rubric) but because New York publishing increasingly resembles the Hollywood world of blockbuster-or-bust, in which a handful of books earn all the hype and do humongous business; others succeed as low-budget indies; and the rest are released to a shudder of silence, if at all. Advances skew to the very high and the pitifully low, and the overall economics of the industry amplify and reinforce this income gap, as the blockbuster novelist not only sells her book to an actual film studio—thus stepping out of the shadow world into the true bright one—but also parcels out lucrative translation rights to foreign markets. The advance multiplies; the money makes money. And—what's better than money—people will actually read the book.

Thus the literary-corporate publishing industry comes to replicate the prevailing economic logic, in which the rich get richer and the rest live on hope and copyediting. As with any ultracompetitive industry, like professional basketball or hedge funds, exceptional prestige accrues to the successes, and with some reason. The NYC writer has to earn money by *writing* (or else consider herself a failure on her own terms), which gives her a certain enlarged dignity and ambition. It also imposes certain strictures. First off, as already mentioned, it demands that the writer write novels.

Second, and perhaps most important, to be an NYC writer means to submit to an unconscious yet powerful pressure toward readability. Such pressure has always existed, of course, but in recent years it has achieved a fearsome intensity. On the one hand, a weakened market for literary fiction makes publishing houses less likely than ever to devote resources to work that doesn't, like a pop song, "hook" the reader right away. On the other, the MFA-driven shift in the academic canon has altered the approach of writers outside the university as well as those within. Throughout the latter half of the last century, many of our most talented novelists—Nabokov, Gaddis, Bellow, Pynchon, DeLillo, Wallace—carved out for themselves a cultural position that depended precisely on a combination of public and academic acclaim. Such writers were readable enough to become famous yet large and knotty enough to require professional explanation—thus securing an afterlife, and an aftermarket, for their lives' work. Syntactic intricacy, narrative ambiguity, formal innovation, and even length were aids to canonization, feeding the university's need for books against which students and professors could test and prove their interpretive skills. Canonization, in turn, contributed to public renown. Thus the ambitious novelist, writing with one eye on the academy and the other on New York, could hope to secure a durable readership without succumbing (at least not fully) to the logic of the blockbuster. It was a strategy shaped by, and suited to, the era of the English department, which valued scholarly interpretation over writerly imitation, the long novel over the short story. (And when it came to white males imagining themselves into the canon, it helped that the canon was still composed mostly of white males.)

The death of David Foster Wallace could be said to mark the end of this quasi-popular tradition, at least temporarily. What one notices first about NYC-orbiting contemporary fiction is how much sense everyone makes. The best young NYC novelists go to great lengths to write comprehensible prose and tie their plots neat as a bow. How one longs, in a way, for endings like that of DeLillo's first novel, *Americana*, where everyone just pees on everyone else for no reason! The trend toward neatness and accessibility is often posited to be the consequence of the workshop's relentless paring. But for NYC writers—despite their degrees—it might be better understood as the result of fierce market pressure toward the middlebrow, combined with a deep authorial desire to communicate to the uninterested. The NYC writer knows that to speak obliquely is tantamount to not speaking at all; if anyone notices her words, it will only be to accuse her of irrelevance and elitism. She doesn't worry about who might read her work in twenty years; she worries about who might read it *now*. She's thrown her economic lot in with the publishers, and the publishers are very, very worried. Who has both the money to buy a hardcover book and the time to stick with something tricky? Who wants to reread Faulknerian sentences on a Kindle, or scroll back to pick up a missed plot point? Nobody, says the publisher. And the NYC novelist understands—she'd better understand, or else she'll have to move to Cleveland.

It helps, too, to write long books; to address large-scale societal change and engage in sharp but affable satire of same; and to title the work with sweeping, often faintly nationalist simplicity: *Mason & Dixon*, say, or *American Pastoral* (American anything, really—*Psycho*, *Wife*, *Rust*, *Purgatorio*, *Subversive*, *Woman*). This is not to belittle these books, a few of which are excellent, but to point out that their authors are only partly at liberty (*American Liberty!*) to do otherwise. However naturally large the NYC novelist's imagination, it is shaped by the need to make a broad appeal, to communicate quickly, and to be socially relevant in ways that can be re-created in a review. The current archetype of this kind of novel also happens to be the best American novel of the young millennium—Jonathan Franzen's *Freedom*. (Franzen, famously, offered an unfortunately ahistorical account of the novelist's difficult relationship to difficulty in a 2002 essay about William Gaddis.) Having written, in *The Corrections*, a clear and lyrical long novel that brought large social and political forces to bear on domestic life, Franzen followed it with an even longer and clearer novel that brings even larger social and political forces to bear on domestic life. He could hardly have done anything else. *Freedom* is the most simply written of his books and also the most complex and best; it grapples with the most unspeakable of contemporary political problems—overpopulation—in a rivetingly plainspoken way. The novelist who converts heroic effort into effortless prose has been a standard figure since Flaubert, but in Franzen this project comes to seem like something else, something more momentous and telling if not aesthetically superior—something, perhaps, like the willed effort of the entire culture to create for itself a novel that it still wants to read.

In short, the writer who hopes to make a living by publishing—whether wildly successful like Franzen, more moderately so, or just starting out—is subject to a host of subtle market pressures, pressures that might be neutral in their aesthetic effects, but which enforce a certain consistency, and a sort of Authorial Social Responsibility. Regardless of whether reading comprehension and attention spans have actually declined, the publishers think they have, and the market shapes itself accordingly. The presumed necessity of "competing for attention" with other media becomes internalized, and the work comes out crystal clear. The point is not that good books go unpublished—to the contrary, scores of crappy literary novels continue to get snapped up by hopeful editors. The point is that market forces cause some good books to go unnoticed, and even more—how many more?—to go unwritten.

And the NYC writer, because she lives in New York, has constant opportunity to intuit and internalize the demands of her industry. It could be objected that just because the NYC writer's editor, publisher, agent, and publicist all live in New York, that doesn't mean that she does, too. After all, it would be cheaper and calmer to live most anywhere else. This objection is sound in theory; in practice, it is false. NYC novelists live in New York—specifically, they live in a small area of west-central Brooklyn bounded by DUMBO and Prospect Heights. They partake of a social world defined by the selection (by agents), evaluation (by editors), purchase (by publishers), production, publication, publicization, and second evaluation (by reviewers) and purchase (by readers) of NYC novels. The NYC novelist gathers her news not from *Poets & Writers* but from the *Observer* and Gawker; not from the academic grapevine but from publishing parties, where she drinks with agents and editors and publicists. She writes reviews for *Bookforum* and the Sunday *Times*. She also tends to set her work in the city where she and her imagined reader reside: as in the most recent novels of Shteyngart, Ferris, Galchen, and Foer, to name just four prominent members of *The New Yorker*'s 20-under-40 list.

None of this amounts to a shrewd conspiracy, as mystified outsiders sometimes charge, but it does mean that the NYC writer participates in the publishing and reviewing racket to an unnerving extent. She is an unabashed industry expert. Even if years away from finishing her first novel, she constantly and involuntarily collects information about what the publishing industry needs, or thinks it needs. Thus the congeniality of Brooklyn becomes a silky web that binds writers to the demands of the market, demands that insinuate themselves into every detail and email of the writer's life. It seems like a sordid situation. Then again, the publishing industry has always been singularly confused, unable to devote itself fully to either art or commerce, so perhaps the influence works both ways; perhaps the NYC writer, by keeping the industry close, hopes also to keep it honest, and a little bit interested in the art it champions.

What will happen? Economically speaking, the MFA system has announced its outsize ambitions, making huge investments in infrastructure and personnel, and offering gaudy salaries and propitious working conditions to secure top talent. The NYC system, on the other hand, presents itself as cautious and embattled, devoted to hanging on. And a business model that relies on tuition and tax revenue (the top five MFA programs in 2011, according to *Poets & Writers*, are part of large public universities); the continued unemployability of twentysomethings; and the continued hunger of undergraduates for undemanding classes, does seem more forward-looking than one that relies on overflow income from superfluous books by celebrities, politicians, and their former lovers. It was announced recently that Zadie Smith—one of the few writers equipped by fame to do otherwise—has accepted a tenured position at NYU, presumably for the health insurance; perhaps this marks the beginning of the end, a sign that in the future there will be no NYC writers at all, just a handful of writers accomplished enough to teach in NYC. New York will have become—as it has long been becoming—a place where some writers go for a *Wanderjahr* or two between the completion of their MFAs and the commencement of their teaching careers. No one with "literary" aspirations will expect to earn a living by publishing books; the glory days when publishers still waffled between patronage and commerce will be much lamented. The lit-lovers who used to become editors and agents will direct MFA programs instead; the book industry will become as rational—that is, as single-mindedly devoted to profit—as every other capitalist industry. The writers, even more so than now, will write for other writers. And so their common ambition and mission and salvation, their profession—indeed their only hope—will be to make writers of us all. +

M     F     A

# Applying

For my first year they offered me a fellowship. I think it was $10,000
for the year. And I was such an idiot, I had never conceptualized having
$10,000. *What am I going to do, do I need to get someone to help me manage all
this money?* It turned out I definitely did not need a money manager.
   **Eli S. Evans, University of Arizona, 2004**


I'd already started college in Russia when my family and I emigrated
to the States in 1992. In Russia engineering is basically what you do, so
I'd started in computers. I transferred to the University of Pittsburgh,
got my degree in information sciences, and spent six and a half years
doing software development. Writing was always my dream, but in
Russia I was told to put it aside, you can never do this for real as a profession. So I would always tell myself I was going to try on my own.
But doing it on your own can be incredibly discouraging—you write a
page and read it over and you're disgusted at how bad it is. So when I
was living in Boston and working in IT, I started taking adult ed classes.
They were for people who had jobs during the day, but they were
taught by very serious writers. I was working at a start-up, which means
you go to work and don't really know when you're going to come home,
so I would get up at 5:30 a.m. to write for an hour or two before going
to work. Eventually I needed more time. I needed to focus more—I was
working in these little snippets and I wanted something more serious.
So I started to look into MFA programs.
   **Ellen Litman, Syracuse University, 2004**

# A Mini-Manifesto

## George Saunders

### 1

Saying that "Creative writing programs are bad" is like saying "College football teams are bad" or "Book clubs are bad" or "Emergency rooms are bad." All it takes is one good example to disprove the generality.

### 2

Most critiques I read of creative writing programs or writing in the academy are kicking entities that don't actually (in my experience) exist. The trope about CW students not reading, or being encouraged to be sort of ahistorical and New Agey—I don't see that. I really don't. And I travel to a lot of MFA programs. Everywhere I go, people are reading, and reading deeply, and not just contemporary fiction either. And people seem to realize they are part of a tradition, and had better know that tradition if they hope to further it. Likewise the trope about "producing writers who all write alike." That trope is so well known that it is a cliché, such a cliché that I don't know a single CW teacher who is not aware of it and on the watch for it. (It could be argued that anytime you get ten to forty people together and have a core group of teachers, some homogenization is going to happen, but, in a sense, isn't that what culture is? The establishment of a standard and then a resulting attempt to mimic that standard, followed by a passionate revolt against that stupid repressive reactionary standard, which is then replaced by a lovely innovative pure new standard, et cetera?) (It's also possible that the perception of homogeneity is a function of the fact that, as CW programs expand so that every town has fifteen of them, more average writers are being let in [see no. 11, below] and so what we are really seeing is a bunch of average writers doing what average writers are supposed to do, which is write average. It might also be possible that, in any generation, there are only about two writers who are really great anyway, and it takes time to sort that out, and meanwhile the books keep flying off the presses.)

3

As in all things, we have to look at particulars. If someone says, "Creative writing programs are bad," I think we want to ask: "Which one?" And: "When?"

4

I would feel weird if my students were going into mad debt to study with me. At Syracuse, we give 100 percent remitted tuition and about $15,000 a year, which a person can (sort of, approximately) live on in Syracuse. In any event, nobody's leaving here with, you know,

$80,000 in student loans. So this changes the dynamic dramatically. I feel good about teaching here, I feel like it's honest. If we can help someone along their personal trajectory, great. If not, well, the person is only three years older than he or she was. It's not so high-stress, which creates a more pro-art atmosphere. And I think we're pretty honest about our limitations, and our role, and the need for students to take charge of their own artistic development and resist the potentially infantilizing effects of "being accepted" and being back in school and all of that—that is, the tendency to surrender agency to the program.

5

I try constantly to be lobbing out thoughts on the potential dangers of the thing we are doing—that is, the perils of the workshop model. There are many. But if you admit them and lay them on the table, I think they lose a lot of their power. So I try pretty often to say: How are we doing here? Is there something in the way we're looking at these stories that might be forbidding certain possibilities? Are we actually talking crap here? Being reductive? And to ask: What, of all this stuff I'm saying, might actually be helping you? What's just obnoxious? What do you want more of, what do you want less of? I think this is important, in the same way that you'd want your doctor to have a proper level of skepticism about the scientific method.

6

The numbers are important. We admit six students a year in fiction and have basically three fiction people teaching here, with one floating semester-long line a year for a guest writer. That's a pretty good ratio and it means we absolutely know our students. We know them personally and we care about them, and so this presents an incredible range of so-called "teaching moments." Say I've had X in three classes, and have had a number of good and intimate conferences with X, about the work but also maybe about the personal dynamics behind the work, and I know something about X's process, and about what X has and hasn't read/liked, and I also know what X hates about his/her work, where he/she blocks up . . . that's valuable information. And if you're paying attention you can sometimes find out-of-the-classroom moments to do little tweaks, little pushes, little confusions that might help a dam break or whatever. But this can only happen—or happens more often—when you have a manageable number of students.

7

There are, alas, a lot of problems with aspects of the creative writing program idea, but my contention is that as long as a person (and the program itself) is mindful of these things, they can become part of the very things the workshop is talking about. For example, let's say we're talking about the twentieth-century American short story collection. We might, in talking about Flannery O'Connor, find ourselves wondering if the standard workshop mode of discussion is too rational to really explain the glories of her work. That is, does the "normal" workshop approach really come to terms with the level of extrarationality in her work and, if not, how might we change that, or at least stay alert to that possibility? This all seems to me to be fair game.

## A Mini-Manifesto

<u>8</u>

It's important, I think, to see the whole MFA thing as a pretty freaky but short-term immersion. You are not going to be doing this workshop crap forever. You are doing it to get a little baptism by fire, purge yourself of certain habits (of sloth, of under-revision, of the sin of thinking you've made a thing clear when you haven't) and then you are going to run away from the whole approach like your pants are on fire, and not look back, but return to that sacred land where your writing is private and you don't have to defend or explain it one bit. If you need that immersion and think it would help, go for it. If not, not. And don't apply just because you think it's the thing to do or is a "good career move" or everyone else in your school is doing it. Apply when you really feel you need . . . something: shelter or focus or good readers or just some time out of the capitalist shitstorm.

<u>9</u>

If someone wants to go to a CW program, then goes to a CW program and it sucks, she probably won't die from it. And she might at least feel: Well, I took my chance.

<u>10</u>

It's important to remember that a CW program is neither necessary nor sufficient. That is: you don't have to go through one to write a beautiful book, and going through one will not assure that you will write a beautiful book. And: no teacher in any CW program that I know of has ever claimed the contrary of the two statements above (that is, that going through a CW program is necessary or sufficient).

11
—

There are probably too many CW programs. I say this because, if we accept that talent in writing basically resembles the classic bell curve—with a very few really amazing writers at the far end and some real stinkers at the near end, and a bunch of pretty good/average writers in the big bump in the middle—then it would be a little weird if the twin vertical lines demarcating the range we label "Accepted to Grad School" get so widely spaced that the range includes the whole middle section—if, that is, any good/average writer can get in. This is the same as saying, I suppose, that there are tons more writers in grad school than there will ever be spaces on the bookshelf for, or teaching jobs for, or whatever.

12
—

There is something gross about a culture telling a bunch of people who are never going to be artists that they maybe are, even if only by implication. This might argue for, you know, shutting down a few programs. But who's going to do that? And why would we? Or, you know, why would "they"? Most of them are making money. And, from the young artist's point of view: "Hey, give me a chance! I'm not one of the average ones! I'm not! This is all I've ever wanted to do!" Which seems fair enough.

13
—

It's important to remember that the ability of a teacher to know "who's got it" is pretty wobbly. Especially when you are working with young writers, who can grow exponentially in just a few months.

A Mini-Manifesto

This means, therefore, that acceptance/rejection is not all that meaningful. Well, I mean, obviously it's meaningful to the person being accepted or rejected. But it's not 100 percent diagnostic. There are definitely going to be people who get rejected and go on to write wonderful books. Every year, at every school. So this puts a certain onus on the young (applying) writer: don't think acceptance/rejection is (necessarily) a dealbreaker or dealmaker. It's not. (And as a corollary, I'd say it's very important for the teacher of writing to have a little internal mantra that goes: "Well, I could be wrong. How should I know? I've been wrong before." One thing I don't like is when a writing teacher plays seer. You know: "I've seen a lot of young writers come down the pike, and you, Ferdinand, have got It. Mel doesn't. Mel thinks he does, but Mel—oh, poor Mel. Shoot, here he comes.")

14

We all love the idea of, you know, Tolstoy and Chekhov and Gorky exchanging manuscripts and passionate letters of critique and so on (or Ginsberg/Kerouac or Hemingway/Fitzgerald, whoever), and so maybe the goal would be for one's CW community to look something like that: a bunch of artists, living simply and honestly, cutting out the crap, trying to construct a happy little petri dish, forming intense friendships that center around, but are not limited to, art, and that continue on through the rest of their lives.

15

I was once doing some screenwriting with a kind of famous producer and expressed some hesitation about writing a scene the way he was suggesting. "I just think it might be a little cheesy if it was, you know, filmed wrong," I said.

"Ah," he said. "Here's an idea: how about we don't film it wrong?"

The same applies for CW programs. If they suck when we do it wrong, let's try to not do it wrong. +

# Applying

I came to an MFA somewhat accidentally. I was very interested in writing, but the idea of sitting in a classroom for two years with other twenty-four-year-olds in Randomtown, USA, wasn't of particular interest to me. What happened instead, also somewhat by accident, was that I started working at *The New Yorker*. First as an editorial assistant, and then I was made an editor when I was twenty-five. At that point I wasn't going to leave to go to an MFA. But I was writing poems, and I had been writing fiction also. It was my conviction that I could write the poems on my own and turn them into a book. But as anyone who works in publishing knows, your job takes up a lot of time and energy. You have to be really fierce about it. You have to devote your night hours to your work. So I found myself at a place where I had a bunch of poems, but I wasn't growing as much as I could have as a writer.

I had this quasi-manuscript and wanted to finish it. I wanted to work with someone. A friend of mine—she was a medical student at NYU, and writing a lot of poems—mentioned this program she was doing at Warren Wilson where you go for ten days a year. You're assigned a mentor whom you work with throughout the semester. And I thought: This is what I've been looking for. I didn't care about the degree—I did it for that mentorship.

**Meghan O'Rourke, Warren Wilson, 2005**

When I was in college, I knew I wanted to get an MFA. I remember consulting with my mentor Rob Cohen at that point, and he said, "Give it some time; take some time off." Anyway, I went back and forth—I was going to apply right after college but ended up taking two years off. And that's a conversation that I have with my students now, and I'm glad that I took those two years off and that's what I tell them to do too.

**Eleanor Henderson, University of Virginia, 2005**

# Basket Weaving 101

## Maria Adelmann

I remember the two postcollege years I spent in New York as one long day in a windowless room. I shared an office with four other people and a printer that emitted heat like a radiator. I decorated the space above my desk with little quotes and scraps from glossy magazines, reminders of the life I wasn't living. Each day when I arrived at work, I'd place the novel I was currently reading at the corner of my desk—it was my beacon of light, my reward. Books were how I measured my days and how I endured them.

After finishing college, I had gone straight to a full-time job in New York. I knew I wanted to write, but I didn't think I wanted an MFA—it seemed silly to get a degree in something so personal and, in theory, unteachable. Besides, I needed money, I needed to act like an adult, I needed to feel the pressure of the "real world." I figured I could earn money by day and write by night.

By day, I was a Visual Merchandising Creative Manager for a clothing company. I dressed mannequins and drew illustrations that detailed how stores should fold clothes and set up displays. I had thought the word "creative" meant I would be doing something fun. For a few months, it did seem fun. Then it got old.

And by night? By night I was asleep.

At the height of my short career, I was making $55,000 a year but spending sixty hours a week at or commuting to the office. I had two friends, peers from my windowless office. Tasks became repetitive. And to what purpose was I working? To sell crappy clothes? I started listening to books on tape at work, pretending it was music. I wrote down a quote from *The Picture of Dorian Gray* and pinned it to my bulletin board: "Experience . . . is merely the name men give to their mistakes." Women, too.

I began planning my escape. If I switched to a part-time job that allowed more time to build a creative life, I would take a severe pay cut and lose my health insurance. I recalled a college writing professor once saying that a story I'd written might earn me a spot in a competitive MFA program, and that such programs often paid tuition and living expenses. I used the printer in my office to make an eleven-by-seventeen spreadsheet about MFA programs, their requirements, and the funding they offered. I applied to eighteen fiction programs, which cost me about $1,000. I chose fiction not because it was my preferred genre—I was more interested in just about every other genre, including poetry, nonfiction, and screenwriting—but because I had an appropriate writing sample and could conjure up the necessary recommendation letters. I was not going to spend another year in New York.

I was accepted to seven programs and wait-listed at a few more. I decided on the University of Virginia, which offered a $16,000 fellowship in the first year, followed by a teaching salary of about $10,000 during the second and third years. The $40,000 "pay cut" from Visual Merchandising didn't weigh on me at all—my new salary left me in a friendlier tax bracket, my student loans could be deferred without interest because I was in school again, and everything in Virginia cost less than in New York. (My car insurance payment, for example, decreased by $100 a month.) And I'd been living extremely frugally in New York—putting nearly $800 a month in my savings, and sending another $1,000 to pay off college loans.

I actually spent more money in Virginia going out than I had in New York—suddenly I had time and friends. I drank. A lot. I even blew $1,000 on a hazy, one-week bender in Tennessee. I ate out—more often than in New York, but very cheaply. In 2010, I ate dinner at IHOP on twenty-one Thursdays, for the 50 percent student discount. In 2011, I spent thirty Tuesdays at a local restaurant that had a $5 dinner special. Usually I ordered the burger, but sometimes I preferred the salmon sandwich.

Throughout my MFA, I never held a steady second or summer job, though many of my classmates did. I budgeted carefully, occasionally dipped into my savings, and filled in the gaps with odd jobs. I scored tests for Educational Testing Services, taught at a community writing center, helped UVA freshmen enroll in classes, house- and pet-sat for professors, edited grants for the university hospital, and won a few writing prizes. I could do most of these gigs when, where, and how I wanted. (Over three years, I only spent some two hundred hours actually *at* a job outside my house—about the time I spent at work in a single month in New York.)

When I first arrived in Charlottesville, people seemed to move in slow motion, and graduate school made me feel lazy. I could spend an entire day in bed reading David Hasselhoff's god-awful autobiography or making a dress out of *Star Wars* sheets because I wasn't in the mood for real "work"—which, I realize, is a serious misnomer, because work is something you get paid for. Writers talk a lot about "gestation," about letting stories brew. Especially writers with funding.

Yes, many of us MFA-ers were rounding into our thirties while making 10:00 p.m. IHOP runs for dinner, eating eggs that didn't look quite right, as if they came from some other kind of bird, maybe a pigeon. I lived in a questionable neighborhood (literally on the wrong side of the tracks—freight trains ran right through the yard), in a government-subsidized house that had a mouse problem and a possibly related plumbing problem. One weekend, the kitchen filled with shit; I found a dead mouse at the bottom of my trashcan and a lizard in my mousetrap. None of this was very different from New York—just replace the lizard with a cockroach—but living off canned beans and pigeon eggs for the sake of art seemed somehow cooler and riskier as a New Yorker than as a . . . graduate student.

Once my brother, an engineer, asked what I was writing. "Short stories?" he responded. "Didn't you write those in, like, fifth grade? That would be like if I went to graduate school for addition and subtraction." When I told my dad I had written a novella, he was similarly skeptical. "Novella?" he said. "That chocolate spread?"

I might have made more money off chocolate spread, as novellas are notoriously unsellable. But that is the beauty of the MFA—we were given the opportunity to follow our whims.

A sharply dressed New York agent in black heels visited the MFA program to tell us, somewhat hostilely, why our future books wouldn't sell (because no one reads short stories, because Jonathan Franzen already wrote that novel, because no one cares about your road trip). We looked back at her in shock, like children who had just been told that Santa is dead. In a way, the MFA had preserved our innocence about literature and publishing, and thus allowed us to discover what we wanted to write instead of urging us to write what would sell or was trendy.

I didn't use any of my time in the MFA program schmoozing, most likely because I'm socially awkward, but also because it wasn't on my mind. Maybe that was stupid of me, but it also shows you the headspace of the MFA, a very different headspace from that of New York, where I was once told by a young woman who worked in publishing that I should stop being shy and start making connections because I had "a pretty enough face to sell a book."

I didn't use all, or even most, of my time in the MFA program writing. I became at peace with gestation or laziness or whatever it was. There were long, dry periods where I hardly put pen to paper (finger to key), but I managed to fill my time with inexpensive pleasures. I spent a week hiking the Appalachian Trail. I ran three half-marathons. I made detailed board games and intricate Halloween costumes. I cross-stitched the entire cast of *The Royal Tenenbaums*. I collected copious data about myself and drew up reports. I made YouTube videos that never went viral. I painted pictures of my bookshelves. I went to local historical sites. I hung out with friends in the middle of the day—we painted our faces, swapped clothes, went strawberry and apple picking, baked and delivered holiday cookies.

Friends were a surprise asset of the MFA program. I found an immediate support system of like-minded peers. We were bound together, like a congregation or an AA group, by something more powerful than ourselves—not the degree or even the writing, but the craving to create on our own terms. We were all skeptical of "the system" (most systems) and thus of the MFA itself. We feared becoming notorious "MFA-style writers," robots churning out technically perfect but emotionally dead stories. Would we get so beat down by

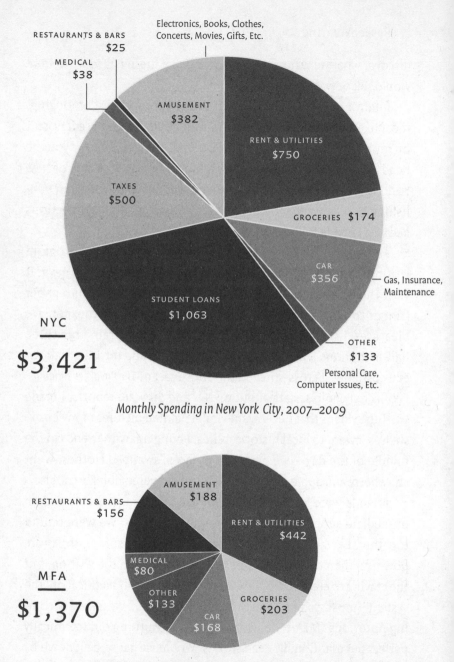

RESTAURANTS & BARS
$25

MEDICAL
$38

Electronics, Books, Clothes,
Concerts, Movies, Gifts, Etc.

AMUSEMENT
$382

RENT & UTILITIES
$750

TAXES
$500

GROCERIES  $174

CAR
$356

Gas, Insurance,
Maintenance

STUDENT LOANS
$1,063

NYC

$3,421

OTHER
$133

Personal Care,
Computer Issues, Etc.

*Monthly Spending in New York City, 2007–2009*

AMUSEMENT
$188

RESTAURANTS & BARS
$156

RENT & UTILITIES
$442

MEDICAL
$80

OTHER
$133

MFA

$1,370

CAR
$168

GROCERIES
$203

*Monthly Spending in Charlottesville, Virginia, 2009–2012*

Ann Beattie (whose workshop, *The New York Times* had recently told us, was "like a bloodbath") that we would give up writing for good?

Most of us had enrolled in an MFA program for the same reason—we were looking for a way out, an escape, either from the roller coaster of fluctuating income cobbled together from part-time employment or from the full-time jobs that had left us with little energy to write. We had been drawn to the MFA by its quantifiable benefits—time, money—but it turned out that the unquantifiable support was worth a great deal to us, too.

You might think the MFA program allowed too much free time. For example, you might look closely at my paintings of books—I re-created more than seventy spines and twenty-five covers, each with meticulously painted letters—and wonder if I could've found something more productive to do. I'm not so sure. Is it so naive of me to believe that the best work is completed outside the market, from a place of personal passion? How can I help but quote Thoreau?

> I too had woven a kind of basket of a delicate texture, but I had not made it worth any one's while to buy them. Yet not the less, in my case, did I think it worth my while to weave them, and instead of studying how to make it worth men's while to buy my baskets, I studied rather how to avoid the necessity of selling them.

During the MFA, I wove a lot of crappy baskets. I wrote 347 drafts resulting in 26 full stories, not all of which were good. My best story took the most drafts—48. Thank god I didn't have to try to sell them.

When I was on a roll, I would spend several days and nights in a row writing. I would venture from my room only occasionally, zombie-like and unable to speak, in great need of protein. I'd eat black beans from the can while standing in the pantry. "She must be writing," my roommates would whisper as I staggered back to my room. Some of my best work was composed over these focused, manic bouts. I cannot imagine another place where a person can take a week off from life, simply because she has an idea.

Over the course of two years, I workshopped 17 of my stories and gathered 172 critiques from 20 different sources. This is too much advice from too many people, but if I was lucky I could tune in to one or two readers who offered advice that felt relevant. Admittedly, it could be difficult to ignore the background noise. As a group, we were conscious of the need to be kind and give positive feedback, but nonetheless, comments could be hurtful, and professors could play favorites. Sometimes the glut of contradictory praise and criticism felt like a flashlight shining directly into my eyes, offering so much light that I couldn't see a thing. A third year of workshop would have been exhausting, and after an unpleasant thesis defense at the end of my second year, I didn't write for many months. But now that I'm back at it, I often long not just for an honest reader, but for a deadline.

Our bad stories taught us what to do better next time—though we tried not simply to eliminate our "imperfections" but also to cultivate them. Some of the greatest writers have managed to transform their "flaws" into the best components of their style. But before flaws look like style, they look like flaws, and you write a lot of bad, unsellable stories. (Sometimes even your good stories are unsellable.)

Some of my "baskets," irregular as they may have been, did turn out to be unexpectedly profitable. During a particularly bad bout of writer's block (or, as the doctor put it, major depressive disorder), I gave myself a project that wouldn't require any heavy thought but would both get me out of bed and save me money on Christmas presents. I turned my book paintings into note cards by scanning the pictures digitally and printing them onto card stock. Figuring out precisely how to do this was much more complicated than I'd first imagined, and for a while I could be found at the twenty-four-hour Kinko's at an array of odd times. Eventually I realized I would need a better print shop to produce the cards as I really wanted them. This required ordering in bulk, so I decided to try to sell the extra cards at local book- and stationery stores and on Etsy. My big break came when Anthropologie discovered them online and ordered sixteen thousand. I never dreamed, during the idle-seeming weeks I'd spent painting books, that those paintings would sustain me financially, and yet they earned me more than $10,000 in less than a year. Now, when I'm not making as much money as I should be, I email a bunch of bookstores hoping for card orders—and I usually get several.

I tried my hand at the business end of writing, too, submitting to over a hundred literary magazines and contests during my final year of the MFA. I received almost the same number of rejections, some encouraging feedback, and just enough acceptances and winnings to keep me sated emotionally, if not financially.

I graduated from UVA some months ago. They mailed my diploma in a tube to my mom's house in New Jersey. I just saw it for the first time yesterday, because I am here, in my childhood bedroom, with all of my belongings, writing this essay. I could have stayed in Virginia, or looked for a full-time job just about anywhere—I still have some money saved up. But I'd rather sell book cards, pick up odd jobs from time to time, and keep the freedom to follow my intuitions. I never know in advance which of my baskets will turn out to be valuable, financially or otherwise, but some of them will. The important thing is to keep making baskets. My MFA program may not have mirrored the "real world" (thank goodness for that), and it may not have taught me how to make money, but it did teach me what my time is worth. +

# Applying

The World Trade Center attacks happened two or three weeks after I started college. I felt like what I was doing—working odd jobs for minimum wage, going to school—suddenly felt shallow. I was working full time and partying all the time and still pulling straight As. It seemed like one big joke. I started to explore the option of enlisting—I suppose it was really idealistic and naive of me, but I enlisted. I was still dedicated, though, to finishing my English degree. Over the course of my tours of duty, two in Afghanistan and two in Iraq, I completed my degree with American Military University, an online school. I wish I could have finished school in a more traditional way, but at the time it was really impossible. I did the same thing with my MFA. The military would pay for it; I wouldn't have to invest any money. It made sense to do it online, to enter a no-residency program while the military was paying, and that's what I did.

**Matthew Hefti, National University, 2013**

In 1982, I was living in New York City. I was thirty-three and a waiter at a fancy restaurant, making quite a bit of money and writing a little on the side. I always told everybody that I was a writer, but I was doing way too many drugs and drinking and staying up way too late to be a good writer. Through a series of synchronistic things, I ended up getting accepted to the Columbia MFA program. I was now paying $25,000 for an education, so I figured I'd better get serious.

**Tom Spanbauer, Columbia University, 1986**

# The Pyramid Scheme

## Eric Bennett

Did the CIA fund creative writing in America? The idea seems like the invention of a creative writer. Yet once upon a time (1967, to be exact), Paul Engle, the director of the Iowa Writers' Workshop, received money from the Farfield Foundation to support international writing at the University of Iowa. The Farfield Foundation was not really a foundation; it was a CIA front that supported cultural operations, mostly in Europe, through an organization called the Congress for Cultural Freedom.

Seven years earlier, at the height of his game, Engle had approached the Rockefeller Foundation—a real foundation—with big fears and grand plans. "I trust you have seen the recent announcement that the Soviet Union is founding a University at Moscow for students coming from outside the country," he wrote. This could only mean that "thousands of young people of intelligence, many of whom could never get University training in their own countries, will receive education . . . along with the expected ideological indoctrination." Engle denounced rounding up students in "one easily supervised place" as a "typical Soviet tactic." He believed that the United States must "compete with

51

that, hard and by long time planning"—by, well, rounding up foreign students in an easily supervised place called Iowa City. Through the University of Iowa, Engle received $10,000 to travel in Asia and Europe to recruit young writers—left-leaning intellectuals—to send to the United States on fellowship.

It's an accepted part of the story of creative writing in America that Iowa started it. The Iowa Writers' Workshop emerged in the 1930s and powerfully influenced the programs that followed. The second-wave programs, around fifty of which appeared in the 1960s, were founded by Iowa graduates. Third- and fourth- and fifth-wave programs, also Iowa scions, have kept coming ever since. So, yes: Iowa.

But it's also an accepted part of the story that creative writing programs arose spontaneously: creative writing was an idea whose time had come. Writers wanted jobs, and students wanted fun classes. In the 1960s, with Soviet satellites orbiting, American baby boomers matriculating, and federal dollars flooding into higher education, colleges and universities marveled at Iowa's success and followed its lead. To judge by the bellwether, creative writing programs worked. Iowa looked great: famous writers taught there, graduated from there, gave readings there, and drank and philandered and enriched themselves and others there.

Yet what drew writers to Iowa was not the innate splendor of a spontaneously good idea. What drew writers to Iowa is what draws writers anywhere: money and hype, which tend to be less spontaneous than ideas.

So where did the money and the hype come from?

Much of the answer lies in the remarkable career of Paul Engle, the Workshop's second director, a do-it-yourself cold warrior whose accomplishments remain mostly covered in archival dust. For two decades after World War II, Iowa prospered on donations from conservative businessmen persuaded by Engle that the program fortified democratic values at home and abroad: it fought Communism. The Workshop thrived on checks from philanthropic foundations such as the Rockefeller Foundation, which gave Iowa $40,000 between 1953 and 1956—good money at the time. It also attracted support from the Asia Foundation (another channel for CIA money) and the State Department as the years went by.

W. Averell Harriman became an Iowa partisan as well. Harriman had been Roosevelt's ambassador to the Kremlin during World War II and Truman's ambassador to the United Kingdom. After the war he administered the Marshall Plan from Paris, and in the 1950s he served as governor of New York. He also made a couple of plausible bids for the Democratic nomination for President, contrasting his commitment to winning hearts and minds with the Eisenhower administration's atomic saber-rattling. He influenced Engle's view of foreign policy, wrote checks to Iowa, and, when Engle later traveled on the Rockefeller grant, gave him diplomatic access to U.S. embassies across Asia.

As for the hype, it followed the money and attracted more of it, as hype does. Publishing moguls Henry Luce and Gardner Cowles conceived of themselves as fighting a battle of ideas, as they contrasted the American Way of Life with the gray Soviet nightmare on the pages of their newspapers and glossy magazines. Luce published *Time* and *Life*, Cowles published *Look* and several midwestern newspapers, and both loved to feature Iowa: its embodiment of literary individualism, its celebration of self-expression, its cornfields.

Knowing he could count on such publicity, Engle staged spectacles in Iowa City for audiences far beyond Iowa City. He read memorial sonnets for the Iowa Dead at a dedication ceremony for the new student union. He convened a celebration of Baudelaire with an eye toward the non-Communist left in Paris. He organized a festival of the sciences and arts. *Life* and *Time* and *Look* transformed these events into impressive press clippings, and the clippings, via Engle's tireless hands, arrived in the mailboxes of possible donors.

In 1954, Engle became the editor of the O. Henry Prize collection, and so it became his task to select the year's best short stories and introduce them to a mass readership. Lo and behold, writers affiliated with Iowa began to be featured with great prominence in the collection. Engle marveled at this, the impartial fruits of his judging, in fund-raising pitches to the Rockefeller Foundation, the Asia Foundation, and the State Department.

The Iowa Workshop, then, attained national eminence by capitalizing on the fears and hopes of the cold war. But the creative writing programs founded in Iowa's image did not, in this respect, resemble it. No other program would be celebrated on the glossy pages of *Look* and *Life*. No other program would receive an initial burst of underwriting from Maytag and U.S. Steel and Quaker Oats and *Reader's Digest* and Iowa Electric Light & Power and Amana Refrigeration and Merchants National Bank and Iowa National Mutual Insurance and Averell Harriman. No other program would attract such interest from the Asia Foundation, the State Department, and the CIA. And the anticlimax of the creative writing enterprise must derive at least in part from this difference.

There, in the paragraphs above, is blood squeezed from the stone of a dissertation. If, in 2006, as a no-longer-quite-plausibly aspiring novelist beached on the shores of academe, you're struggling against the bleakness of the dissertation as a genre, you'll do your best to work the CIA into yours. You'll want to write a heroic dissertation—or at least a novelistic one. You'll read books about soft diplomacy during the cold war, learn about the Farfield Foundation, and search for its name, on an abject hunch, in the forty boxes of the Papers of Paul Engle at the Special Collections Library at the University of Iowa. You'll exhaust those archives and also the ones at Palo Alto (where Wallace Stegner founded the Stanford program) and Tarrytown (home of the Rockefeller archives), tracing the relationship between creative writing and the cold war. But even as you do, you'll wonder about your motives.

Because you yourself attended the Iowa Writers' Workshop before deciding to enter a PhD program. At Iowa, you were disappointed by the reduced form of intellectual engagement you found there and the narrow definition of what counted as "literary." The Workshop was like a muffin tin you poured the batter of your dreams into. You entered with something undefined and tantalizingly protean and left with muffins. You really believe this. But you can also see yourself clearly enough: unpublished, ambitious, obscure, ponderous. In short, the kind of person who writes a dissertation.

Were you right to be frustrated by the ethos of Iowa City, or are you merely a frustrated novelist? Were there objective grounds for your sense of creative stultification, or did the Workshop simply not love you enough? Was the whole idea of your dissertation a guerrilla raid on the kind of recognition you couldn't attain by legitimate means? And did the CIA really have much to do with it?

At the Iowa Writers' Workshop between 1998 and 2000, I had the option of writing fiction in one of four ways.

First, I could carve, polish, compress, and simplify; banish myself from my writing as T. S. Eliot advised and strive to enter the gray, crystalline tradition of modernist fiction as it runs from Flaubert through early Joyce and Hemingway to Raymond Carver (alumnus) and Alice Munro. Marilynne Robinson (teacher) did this in her 1980 novel *Housekeeping*. Denis Johnson (alumnus), played devil to Robinson's angel in *Jesus' Son*. Frank Conroy (director, 1987–2005), had this style down cold—and it is cold. Conroy must have sought it in applications, longing with some kind of spiritual masochism to shiver again and again at the iciness of early Joyce. Such lapidary simplicity becomes psychedelic if you polish it enough. Justin Tussing (class ahead of me) mastered it in his prismatic novel, *The Best People in the World*. Chris Offutt (alumnus and teacher) combined linguistic, intellectual, and actual poverty in *Kentucky Straight*. I myself, feeling the influence, revised sentences into pea gravel.

Second, and also much approved, I could work in a warmer vein—the genuinely and winningly loquacious. During my years at Iowa, Ethan Canin (my favorite teacher) set the example here, writing charismatically chatty prose that, like the man himself, exhibited the gross health of the fortunate and tenderhearted. Your influences, if you tended this way, were F. Scott Fitzgerald, John Irving, or anybody else whose sentences unwind with glowing ease. Cheever loomed as an undisputed great. Curtis Sittenfeld, in the class below mine, displayed this style and charm and unassuming grace in *Prep* and *American Wife*. Adam Haslett (class ahead of me) made it funny and sad in *You Are Not a Stranger Here*. Marilynne Robinson's recent novels, *Gilead* and *Home*, turn toward this manner from the adamantine beauty of *Housekeeping*.

Third, you could write what's often called "magical realism." Joy Williams (alumna, teacher) and Stuart Dybek (alumnus, teacher) helped to shape a strain of fable-making passed down to my classmates from Kafka and Schulz and Calvino or their Latin American heirs. Sarah Shun-lien Bynum was writing *Madeleine Is Sleeping*; Sarah

Braunstein was developing the sensibility she'd weave into *The Sweet Relief of Missing Children*; Paul Harding was laying the groundwork for the enchanting weirdness of his Pulitzer Prize–winning *Tinkers*.

These first three categories were the acceptable ones. But category four involved writing things that in the eyes of the Workshop appeared weird and unsuccessful—that fell outside the community of norms, that tried too hard. The prevailing term for ambitious pieces that didn't fit was "postmodernism." The term was a kind of smackdown. At Workshop potlucks, a guy on an enviable fellowship bellowed "FOU-cault SCHMOO-koh." Submitting a "postmodern" story was like belching in class.

But what is a postmodern story? In those years Robinson was already in the *Norton Anthology of Postmodern American Fiction*, as were Jayne Anne Phillips (alumna) and Bobbie Ann Mason, model citizens of the MFA nation. Joy Williams and Stuart Dybek were certainly not Victorians nor modernists nor bestsellers. What was it that you weren't supposed to do?

At the time I considered Sigmund Freud and François Rabelais my favorite novelists. At the time I understood that they were not novelists. Later I understood that I was being annoying. But I thought then, and still think now, that, like late-era Borders, the three-headed Iowa canon frustrated as much as satisfied a hunger for literature that got you thinking. Iowa fiction, published and unpublished, got you *feeling*—it got you seeing and tasting and touching and smelling and hearing. It was like going to an arboretum with a child. You want exactly that from life, and also more.

People at Iowa love to love Prairie Lights, the local independent bookstore. In Prairie Lights I found myself overwhelmed by the literature of the senses and the literature of the quirky sensing voice. I wanted heavy books from a bunch of different disciplines; on hermeneutics, on monetary policy, on string theory, on psychoanalysis, on the Gospels, on the strange war between analytic and continental philosophers, on sexual pathology. I was twenty-three. I knew I wanted to write a novel of ideas, a novel of systems, but one also with characters, and also heart—a novel comprising everything, not just how icicles broken from church eaves on winter afternoons taste of asphalt (but that, too). James Wood did not yet loom over everything, but I wanted to make James Wood barf. At Prairie Lights, I would have felt much better buying the work of Nathan Englander (alum) if it had been next to that of Friedrich Engels. I felt there how I feel in bars that serve only wine and beer.

This aversion to novels and stories of full-throttle experience, erudition, and cognition—the unspoken proscription against attempting to write them—was the narrowness I sensed and hated. The question I wanted to answer, as I faced down my dissertation, was whether this aversion was an accidental feature of Iowa during my time, or if it reflected something more.

In July 2007 I returned to Iowa City for the first time since graduating. It's one of my favorite places in the United States, and I'd always envied both those classmates who published quickly, earning a right to linger around the Workshop after their time, and those who felt no shame about lingering despite failing to publish. I sublet an apartment above a pizza restaurant I used to love and spent quiet nights at bars I had rowdy memories of. But the main business was research. Each day from nine to five I visited the Papers of Paul Engle in the university library, and in four weeks watched Engle's life pass three times: once in the letters he sent, once in the letters he received, and once in newspaper and magazine clippings. Three separate times, as the decades slipped by, I watched a broad, supple mind in tune with its era harden into a tedious one, trying to attach old phrases and concepts to a world that no longer existed. I was haunted and smitten. As only an ambitious and frustrated person can fall in love with an ambitious and frustrated person, I fell in love with Engle. His career was a long slow slide from full-throated poetic aspiration into monochromatic administrative greatness—a modern story if there ever was one.

At the beginning of the month I didn't know what I was looking for, exactly. At the end I had a list of unlikely names, a file of ideological quotations, and the smoking gun of the CIA connection. Later, after gathering secondary sources and digesting the primary ones, I would have my thesis: that the cold war not only underwrote the discipline but also gave it its intellectual shape. This was the linchpin of the story, and it would take a long time to develop. That summer I was mostly just mesmerized by a biography.

Engle's life, at least for a while, exuded pure romance and adventure: a boyhood in a midwestern city still redolent of the frontier; a father who trained horses; an adolescence during the heady years of American modernism; a coming-of-age at the beginning of the Depression; the receipt of laurels for his poetry by his early twenties (he won the Yale Series of Younger Poets prize in 1932); travels in Europe as a Rhodes Scholar; the witnessing of Nazi rallies in Munich; celebrity back home for *American Song*, a collection of brawny, patriotic blank verse published in 1934 and touted on the front page of *The New York Times Book Review* by a conservative reviewer; his undignified, typically American, and only half-successful attempt to befriend Stephen Spender, Cecil Day-Lewis, and W. H. Auden at Oxford in the 1930s, when those poets were striking poses as exciting young communists; his conversion to communism; his adoption of the role of the strapping American vernacular savant in the face of English reticence and snobbery; passionate letters to his future wife back home; a honeymoon in Russia; a homecoming so much less exciting than the voyage out; a U.S. lecture tour; a job teaching at his alma mater, the University of Iowa; the strangely anticlimactic war years, including an unsuccessful bid to serve in the OSS; the panicked recantation of his communist sympathies in the dawning days of the House Un-American Activities Committee; a marriage not long in its happiness; two daughters; the gradual assumption of the helm of the Iowa Writers' Workshop; the inexorable diminishment of his prospects as a poet; and the birth, in the iciest years of the cold war, of an institutional vision that would transform American literature.

Engle longed, above all, for poets to move nations. His poems say it, and his papers do. I doubt he had a happier moment in his life than when he addressed Americans from NBC in London in 1934. "We stand on the thin and moving edge of our history," he crackled distantly to his countrymen, "where it bends down on one side to the irretrievable past and, on the other, swings outward to the flat plain of the future." What was he talking about? He probably didn't know exactly. Soon Engle would make the communist conversion; soon after, he would convert back. His youthful exuberance could fit itself to the ideology nearest at hand. Sway, image, ethos, and glory attracted him: the raw power of words. In *American Song*, in 1934, when he was still a darling of the conservatives, he envisioned the American poet launching poetry into the sky like a weapon:

America, great glowing open hearth,
In you we will heat the cold steel of our speech,

## The Pyramid Scheme

Rolling it molten out into a mold,
Polish it to a shining length, and straddling
The continent, with hands that have been fashioned,
One from the prairie, one from the ocean, winds,
Draw back a brawny arm with a shout and hurl
The fiery spear-shaft of American song
Against the dark destruction of our doom
To burn the long, black wind of the years with flame.

What did this even mean? It meant that the poetic and the public, the personal and the national, could still fuse in the right words. It was a dream that, after 1939, would vanish almost as quickly as Communism in America.

When Engle got back from England, the figure of T. S. Eliot—his hard poems, his oblique criticism, his antagonism to dialectical materialism—had long since embarked on its path to ascendancy on American campuses. The United States, the last power standing, would need some high culture of its own, and Eliot set the tone. The New Critics, his handmaidens, were waiting to infiltrate the old English faculties. Within ten years, modernism would win an unadulterated victory, and difficult free verse would sit alongside epics and sonnets on the syllabi. The day would belong to Robert Lowell, writing as a latter-day metaphysical. Engle—in his commitment to soaring iambic lines, to the legacy of Stephen Vincent Benét, to the open idiom that had so recently remained viable—would look like a has-been.

But it was not in Engle's character to stand still or look back. His gut told him something that most educated citizens would have to learn from sociologists: that the postwar era belonged to institutions. The unit of power was no longer the great man but the vast bureaucracy. Eliot had done the police in different voices; if you assumed the lyrical "I," it sounded hushed, tiny, tragically diminished, none of which appealed to a mind as brawny and sunny as Engle's. The unit of power was no longer the poem.

But it could be the poet as a concept, a figure, a living symbol—and therefore, implicitly, the institution that handled and housed the poet. Engle began working long hours at Iowa. His new poems, when he wrote them, merely burnished his credentials as an administrator, patriot, and family man. Many were sonnets, earnestly passé, and his audience included political patrons, present or prospective. (Harriman received flattering sonnets; after Kennedy was assassinated, and despite the advice of candid, unimpressed first readers, Jackie Kennedy received memorial sonnets.) Between the mid-1940s and the early 1960s, Engle transformed the Writers' Workshop from a regional curiosity into a national landmark. The fiery spear-shaft of American song would take the form of an academic discipline. The fund-raising began.

Engle constantly invoked the need to bring foreign writers to Iowa so they could learn to love America. That was the key to raising money. If intellectuals from Seoul and Manila and Bangladesh could write and be read and live well-housed with full stomachs amid beautiful cornfields and unrivaled civil liberties, they would return home fighting for our side. This was what Engle told midwestern businessmen, and midwestern businessmen wrote big checks.

Engle, leaning heavily on the ideas that Harriman expressed in *Foreign Affairs* and *The Atlantic Monthly*, believed that young radicals in places like India and Pakistan would choose the American Way if only they saw its best side. *The New Yorker*, reporting on Engle's travel grant from the Rockefeller Foundation, mocked "his wish to capture and import a

Japanese poet rather than his book of *haiku*, a Sumatran novelist rather than his searing depiction of social conditions on upland rubber plantations." But the snarkiness implied that Engle didn't know what he was doing. Engle knew exactly what he was doing.

Engle borrowed tactics from the CIA long before their check arrived in 1967. At the time, the Agency sponsored literature and fine arts abroad through the Congress for Cultural Freedom to convince the non-Communist left in the U.K. and Europe that America was about more than Mickey Mouse and Coca-Cola. The CCF underwrote *Encounter* magazine and subsidized subscriptions to American literary journals for intellectuals in the Eastern bloc. Some of the CIA guys were old Iowa graduates from the early 1950s—including the novelists John Hunt and Robie Macauley—and Engle probably first connected with the CIA through Hunt.

By the mid-1960s, Engle had lost interest in the domestic workshop, and so lost control of it. He let it go its own way and founded the International Writing Program with the help of the Chinese novelist Hualing Nieh, who would become his second wife. In retrospective accounts, Engle presented this founding as a sudden idea, a spontaneously good one. But it marked the culmination of the logic of twenty years of dreaming.

When I was at Iowa, Frank Conroy, Engle's longest-running successor, did not name the acceptable categories. Instead, he shot down projects by shooting down their influences. He loathed Barth, Pynchon, Gaddis, Barthelme. He had a thing against J. D. Salinger that was hard to explain. To go anywhere near Melville or Nabokov was to ingest the fatal microbes of the obnoxious. Of David Foster Wallace he growled, with a wave of his hand, "He has his thing that he does."

Conroy hated what he called "cute stuff," unless it worked, but it tended never to work. Trying to get cute stuff to work before a sneering audience is like trying to get an erection to work before a sneering audience. Conroy's arsenal of pejoratives was his one indulgence in lavish style. "Cockamamie," he'd snarl. "Poppycock." Or "bunk," "bunkum," "balderdash." He could deliver these quaint execrations in tones that made H. L. Mencken sound like Regis Philbin.

Conroy would launch his arsenal from his seat at the head of the table. His eyebrows were hedges out from which his eyes glowered like a badger's. He would have hated that metaphor. His eyelashes remained handsomely dark in contrast to his white hair and sallow complexion. He loved one particular metaphor that likened the crying of a baby to the squeaking of a rusty hinge.

His force of personality exceeded his sweep of talent—and not because he wasn't talented. By the time I met him he had entered the King Lear stage of his career. He was swatting at realities and phantoms in a medley of awesome magnificence and embarrassing feebleness. His rage and tenderness were moving. I adored him. He was a thunderstorm on the heath of his classroom, and you stepped into his classroom to have your emotions buffeted for two hours. Nothing much was at stake, but it sure seemed like it. He was notoriously bad at remembering the names of students. If he called you by your name it was like seeing your accomplishments praised in the newspaper. "Should we sit where we sat last week," I asked during the second week of class, "so you can remember our names?" "Sit down, Eric," he said.

What did Conroy assault us in service of? He wanted literary craft to be a pyramid. He drew a pyramid on the blackboard and divided it with horizontal lines. The long stratum at the base was grammar and syntax, which he called "Meaning, Sense, Clarity." The next layer, shorter and higher, comprised the senses that prose evoked: what you tasted, touched, heard, smelled, and saw. Then came character, then metaphor. This is from memory: I can't remember the pyramid exactly, and maybe Conroy changed it each time. What I remember for sure is that everything above metaphor Conroy referred to as "the fancy stuff." At the top was symbolism, the fanciest of all. You worked from the broad and basic to the rarefied and abstract.

Although you could build a pyramid without an apex, it was anathema to leave an apex hovering and foundationless. I'll switch metaphors, slightly, since Conroy did too. The last thing you wanted was a castle in the air. A castle in the air was a bad story. There was a ground, the realm of the body, and up from it rose the fiction that worked. Conroy presented these ideas as timeless wisdom.

His delivery was one of a kind, but his ideas were not. They were and are the prevailing wisdom—the almost ubiquitous wisdom. Within today's MFA culture, the worst thing an aspiring writer can do is bring to the table a certain ambitiousness of preconception. All the handbooks say so. "If your central motive as a writer is to put across ideas," Steve Almond says, "write an essay." Stephen Koch warns that writers should not be too intellectual. "The intellect can *understand* a story—but only the imagination can *tell it*. Always prefer the concrete to the abstract. At this stage it is better to *see* the story, to *hear* and to *feel* it, than to think it." Koch quotes others: a writer must not "think about the plot of the novel" but "think about specific situations," aiming "at making pictures, not notes" (John Braine), and: "Do not think. Dream" (Richard Bausch). According to Anne Lamott, literature issues from divine ignorance. "Very few writers really know what they are doing until they've done it."

Eric Bennett

Since the 1980s, the textbook most widely assigned in American creative writing classes has been Janet Burroway's *Writing Fiction*. Early editions (there are now eight) dared students to go ahead and try to write a story based on intellectual content—a political, religious, scientific, or moral idea—rather than the senses and contingent experience. Such a project "is likely to produce a bad story. If it produces a bad story, it will be invaluably instructive to you, and you will be relieved of the onus of ever doing it again. If it produces a good story, then you have done something else, something more, and something more original than the assignment asks for." The logic is impeccably circular: if you proceed from an idea, you'll write a bad story; if the story's good, you weren't proceeding from an idea, even if you thought you were.


Creative writing pedagogues in the aftermath of World War II, without exception, read *Partisan Review*, *The Kenyon Review*, *The Hudson Review*, and *The Sewanee Review*. They breathed the intellectual air of New Critics, on the one hand, and New York intellectuals on the other. These camps, formerly enemy camps—Southern reactionaries and Northern socialists at each other's throats in the 1930s—had by the '50s merged into a liberal consensus that published highly intellectual, but at the time only newly "academic," essays in those four journals, all of which, like Iowa, were subsidized by the Rockefeller Foundation. John Crowe Ransom, who believed in growing cotton and refused to apologize for slavery, found common ground with Lionel Trilling, who believed in Trotsky—but how?

The consensus centered on a critique of instrumental reason as it came down to us from the Enlightenment—a reaction against the scientific rationality that led to Hiroshima and Nagasaki, the bureaucratic efficiency that made the death camps in Poland possible, and the materialism behind the increasingly sinister Soviet regime. Ransom and his fellow southerners had developed their ideas in the 1920s as agrarian men of letters resentful of the specter of northern industrialism. Meanwhile, Trilling and his fellow socialists were reeling from all that had discredited the Popular Front: the purge of the old Bolsheviks in the late 1930s, the Soviet conduct of the Spanish Civil War, the nonaggression pact that the Soviets signed with the Nazis in 1939, and so on. These were chastened radicals who believed in the avant-garde and saw in totalitarianism the consequences of pure ideas unchecked by the irrational prerogatives of culture. So the prewar left merged with the prewar right. Both circles thought that the way to avoid the likes of Nazism or Stalinism in the United States was to venerate and fortify the particular, the individual, the situated, the embedded, the irreducible. The argument took its purest form in Hannah Arendt's essays about the concentration camps in *Partisan Review*.

You probably can see where this is going: one can easily trace the genealogy from the critical writings of Trilling and Ransom at the beginning of the cold war to creative writing handbooks and methods then and since. The discipline of creative writing was effectively born in the 1950s. Imperial prosperity gave rise to it, postwar anxieties shaped it. "*Science*," Ransom argued in *The World's Body*, "gratifies a rational or practical impulse and exhibits the minimum of perception. Art gratifies a perceptual impulse and exhibits the minimum of reason." He admired the Imagist poets writing before World War I who traded vacuous Victorian sentimentalism for hard objects, the stuff of the perceiving mind. Totalitarianism, by the 1930s, had replaced Victorian sentimentalism as the target, but the underlying problem was the same: airy conceptions that blinded people to hard realities. In *The Liberal Imagination* Trilling celebrated Hemingway and Faulkner for being "intensely at work upon the recalcitrant stuff of life." Life was recalcitrant because it resisted our best efforts to reduce it to intellectual abstractions, to ideas, to ideologies.

Engle versified Ransom's notions in the 1950s, and no doubt taught them. In *Poems in Praise* he celebrated Robert Frost for turning "from Plato's pure ideal / To drink the cold spring of the real, / Proving by his devoted act / Enchantment of the daily fact." It was daily facts that would make the literature that fortified the Free World: nuts and bolts, bread and butter, washing machines sold by Maytag executives who wrote checks to Iowa. William Carlos Williams, as far as Engle was concerned, was distinguished by his success along these lines:

> No vagueness for him as a poet—always the bright
> particulars, as a doctor works with the definite
> fever, bone, fear. No universals for him apart
> from the precise thing—not the general color of red,
> but that exact geranium in its tin can, rusted and red.

Universals called to mind Auschwitz and the Comintern. Idiosyncratic details were the very essence of irreducible personhood.

To Wallace Stegner, who directed the influential Stanford program throughout the 1950s, a true writer was "an incorrigible lover of concrete things," weaving stories from "such materials as the hard knotting of anger in the solar plexus, the hollowness of a night street, the sound of poplar leaves." A novelist was "a vendor of the sensuous particulars of life, a perceiver and handler of things," an artist "not ordinarily or ideally a generalizer, not a dealer in concepts."

## The Pyramid Scheme

From Trilling and Ransom and Arendt to Engle and Stegner, and from them to Conroy and Almond and Koch and Braine and Bausch and Lamott and Burroway, the path is not long. And yet that path was erased quickly. Raymond Carver, trained by writers steeped in anti-Communist formulations, probably didn't realize that his short stories were doing ideological combat with a dead Soviet dictator.*

Of course, it's more than brute inertia; when institutions outlive their animating ideologies, they get converted to new purposes. Over the past forty years, creative writing's small-is-beautiful approach has served it well, as measured by the discipline's explosive growth while most of its humanities counterparts shrink and cower. The reasons for this could fill many essays. For one thing, creative writing has successfully embedded itself in the university by imitating other disciplines without treading on their ground. A pyramid resembles a pedagogy—it's fungible, and easy to draw on the board. Introductory math and physics professors like to draw diagrams too, a welcome analogy for a discipline wishing both to establish itself as teachable and to lengthen its reach into the undergraduate curriculum, where a claim of pure writerly exceptionalism won't cut it. Specialization is also crucial, both for credibility's sake and to avoid invading neighboring fiefdoms, and today's creative writing department specializes in sensory and biographical memory. The safest material is that which the philosophers and economists

---

* The above quotations from Koch, Lamott, Burroway, Engle, and Trilling also appear in my essay "Creative Writing and the Cold War University" in *A Companion to Creative Writing*, ed. Graeme Harper, which presents the scholarly version of this argument.

Eric Bennett

and sociologists have no claim on, such as how icicles broken from church eaves on winter afternoons taste of asphalt.*

And it's easier to teach Meaning, Sense, and Clarity than old literature and intellectual history. Pyramid-building fosters the hope that we can arrive at the powerful symbol of a white whale, not by thinking it up ahead of time, but by mastering the sensory details of whaling. "Don't allegorize Calvinism," Conroy could have barked at me, "describe a harpoon and a dinghy!"

The thing to lament is not only that we have a bunch of novels about harpoons and dinghies (or suburbs or bad marriages or road trips or offices in New York). The thing to lament is also the dead end of isolation that comes from describing the dead end of isolation—and from using vibrant literary communities to foster this

---

* In *The Program Era*, Mark McGurl posits ethnic and socioeconomic identity as main sources of academic specialization within the academic discipline of creative writing. In the chemistry department, you fabricate new molecules; in the creative writing department, you give voice to an undocumented American experience. This seems right to me, and well formulated, but McGurl's account, which really gets rolling in its analysis of the post-sixties era, neglects the philosophical continuity between the first two decades of the cold war and what came after. Betty Friedan borrowed her conceptions of frustrated selfhood from psychological analyses of death camps (as Darra Mulderry has pointed out), and in general the venerated individuality of the 1950s, theorized in reaction to the traumas of World War II, belonged to white males only because *everything* belonged to them—not because the theory called for it, and in fact, quite the contrary. Until the 1960s, creative writing programs entailed an inclusive ideology whose time had not yet come; then its time came (and accounts, I think at least in part, for the boom). The universal white male subject, of vital interest for his difference from every other white male subject in the face of Auschwitz and the Gulag, stopped having to be white and male. This was a much bigger change for the admissions office than for the novelists and poets teaching writing. Creative writing programs (as suggested by Wallace Stegner's heroically progressive journalism in the 1940s and Paul Engle's heartfelt encouragement of Gwendolyn Brooks, also in the 1940s) were early bastions of multicultural and sexual inclusion—as much as they could be within an academy largely segregated by race and gender.

phenomenon. In our workshops, we simply accept it as true that larger structures of common interest have been destroyed by the atomizing forces of economy and ideology, and what's left to do is be faithful to the needs of the sentence.

To have read enough to feel the oceanic movement of events and ideas in history; to have experienced enough to escape the confines of a personal provincialism; to have distanced yourself enough from your hang-ups and pettiness to create words reflecting the emotional complexity of minds beyond your own; to have worked with language long enough to be able to wield it beautifully; and to have genius enough to find dramatic situations that embody all that you have lived and read, is rare. It's not something that every student of creative writing—in the hundreds of programs up and running these days—is going to pull off. Maybe one person a decade will pull it off. Maybe one person every half century will *really* pull it off.

Of course we live in an age that cringes at words like "greatness"—and also at the notion that we're not all great. But ages that didn't cringe at greatness produced great writing without creative writing programs. And people who attend creative writing programs for the most part wish to write great things. It's sick to ask them to aspire but not to aspire *too much*. An air of self-doubt permeates the discipline, showing up again and again as the question, "Can writing be taught?"

Faced with this question, teachers of creative writing might consider adopting (as a few, of course, already do) a defiant rather than resigned attitude, doing more than supervising the building of the bases of pyramids. They might try to get beyond the senses. Texts worth reading—worth reading now, and worth reading two hundred years from now—coordinate the personal with the national or international; they embed the instant in the instant's full context and long history. It's what the *Odyssey* does and what *Middlemarch* does and what *Invisible Man* does and what Jonathan Franzen and Marilynne Robinson's recent novels try to do. But to write like this, you're going to have to spend some time thinking. +

# The Fictional Future
## David Foster Wallace

*This is a section of the essay "Fictional Futures and the Conspicuously Young," which was published in* The Review of Contemporary Fiction *in 1988, one year after Wallace's graduation from the University of Arizona MFA program and the publication of* The Broom of the System.

It's in terms of economics that academic Creative Writing Programs* offer their least ambiguous advantages. Published writers (assuming they themselves have a graduate writing degree) can earn enough by workshop teaching to support themselves and their own fiction without having to resort to more numbing or time-consuming employment. On the student side, fellowships—some absurdly generous—and paid assistantships in teaching are usually available to almost all students. Programs tend to be a sweet deal.

---

* These words are capitalized because they understand themselves as capitalized. Trust me on this.

David Foster Wallace

And there are more such programs in this country now than any-where anytime before. The once lone brow of the Iowa Workshop has birthed first-rate creative departments at places like Stanford, Houston, Columbia, Johns Hopkins, Virginia, Michigan, Arizona, et cetera. The majority of accredited American IHEs now have at least some sort of formal academic provision for students who want vocational training in fiction writing. This has all happened within the last fifteen years. It's unprecedented, and so are the effects of the trend on young U.S. fiction. Of the Conspicuously Young writers I've mentioned above,* I know of none who've not had some training in either a graduate or undergraduate writing department. Most of them hold MFAs. Some are, even as we speak, working toward a degree called a "Creative PhD." Never has a "literary generation" been so thoroughly and formally trained, nor has such a large percentage of aspiring fiction writers eschewed extramural apprenticeship for ivy and grades.

And the contributions of the academy's rise in American fiction go beyond the fiscal. The workshop phenomenon has been justly credited with a recent "renaissance of the American short story," a renaissance heralded in the late '70s with the emergence of writers like the late Raymond Carver (taught at Syracuse), Jayne Anne Phillips (MFA from Iowa), and the late Breece Pancake (MFA from Virginia). More small magazines devoted to short literary fiction exist today than ever before, most of them either sponsored by programs or edited and staffed by recent MFAs. Short-story collections, even by relative unknowns, are now halfway viable economically, and publishers have moved briskly to accommodate trend.

---

* Ed: These include Jay McInerney, David Leavitt, Tama Janowitz, Lorrie Moore, and Wallace himself.

The Fictional Future

More important for young writers themselves, programs can afford them time, academic (and parental!) legitimacy, and an environment in which to Hone Their Craft, Grow, Find Their Voice,* et cetera. For the student, a community of serious, like-minded persons with whom to exchange ideas has pretty clear advantages. So, in many ways, does the fiction class itself. In a workshop, rudiments of technique and process can be taught fairly quickly to kids who might in the past have spent years in New York lofts learning basic tricks of the trade by trial and error. A classroom atmosphere of rigorous constructive criticism helps toughen young writers' hides and prepare them for the wildly disparate responses the world of real readers holds in store. Best of all, a good workshop forces students regularly to formulate consistent, reasoned criticisms of colleagues' work; and this, almost without fail, makes them far more astute about the strengths and weaknesses of their own fiction.

Still, I think it's the Program-sword's other edge that justifies the various Establishments' present disenchantment with CY fiction more than anything else. The dark side of the Program trend exists, grows; and it's much more than an instantiation of the standard academic lovely-in-theory-but-mangled-in-practice conundrum. So we'll leave aside nasty little issues like departmental politics, faculty power struggles that summon images of sharks fighting for control of a bathtub, the dispiriting hiss of everybody's egos in various stages of inflation or deflation, a downright unshakable publish-or-perish mentality that equates appearance in print with talent or promise. These might be particular to one student's experience. Certain problems inherent in Programs' very structure and

---

* On these, too: they are to Programs what azan are to mosques.

purpose, though, are not. For one thing, the pedagogical relation between fiction professor and fiction student has unhealthiness built right in. Writing teachers are by calling writers, not teachers. The fact that most of them are teaching not for its own sake but to support a separate and obsessive calling has got to be accepted, as does its consequence: every minute spent on class and department business is, for Program staff, a minute not spent working on their own art, and must to a degree be resented. The best teachers seem to acknowledge the conflict between their vocations, reach some kind of internal compromise, and go on. The rest, according to their capacities, either suppress the resentment or make sure they do the barely acceptable minimum their primary source of income requires. Almost all, though, take the resentment out in large part on the psyches of their pupils—for pupils represent artistic time wasted, an expenditure of a teacher's fiction-energy without fiction-production. It's all perfectly understandable. Clearly, though, feeling like a burden, an impediment to real art-production, is not going to be conducive to a student's development, to say nothing of his enthusiasm. Not to mention his basic willingness to engage his instructor in the kind of dynamic back-and-forth any real creative education requires, since it's usually the very-low-profile, docile, undemanding student who is favored, recruited, supported, and advanced by a faculty for whom demand equals distraction.

In other words, the fact that creative writing teachers must wear two hats has unhappy implications for the quality of both MFA candidates and the education they receive in Programs. And it's very unclear who if anyone's to blame. Teaching fiction writing is darn hard to do well. The conscientious teacher must not only be both highly critical and emotionally sensitive, acute in his reading and articulate about his acuity: he must be all these things with regard to precisely those issues that can be communicated to and discussed in a workshop group. And that inevitably yields a distorted emphasis on the sorts of simple, surface concerns that a dozen or so people can talk about coherently: straightforward mechanics of traditional fiction production like fidelity to point-of-view, consistency of tense and tone, development of character, verisimilitude of setting, et cetera. Faults or virtues that cannot quickly be identified or discussed between bells—little things like interestingness, depth of vision, originality, political assumptions and agendas, the question whether deviation from norm is in some cases OK—must, for sound Program-pedagogical reasons, be ignored or discouraged. Too, in order to remain both helpful and sane, the professional writer/ teacher has got to develop, consciously or not, an aesthetic doctrine, a static set of principles about how a "good" story works. Otherwise he'd have to start from intuitive scratch with each student piece he reads, and that way the liquor cabinet lies. But consider what this means: the Program staffer must teach the practice of art, which by its nature always exists in at least some state of tension with the rules of its practice, as essentially an applied system of rules. Surely this kind of enforced closure to further fictional possibilities isn't good for most teachers' own literary development. Nor is it at all good for their students, most of whom have been in school for at least sixteen years and know that the way the school game is played is: (1) Determine what the instructor wants; and (2) Supply it forthwith. Most Programs, then, produce two kinds of students. There are those few who, whether particularly gifted or not, have enough interest and faith in their fiction instincts to elect sometimes to deviate from professors' prescriptions. Many of these students are shown the door, or drop out, or gut out a couple years during which the door is always being pointed to, throats cleared, Fin. Aid unavailable. These turn out to be the lucky ones. The other kind are those who, the minute fanny touches chair, make the instructors' dicta their own—whether from insecurity, educational programming, or genuine agreement (rare)—who row instead of rock, play the game quietly and solidly, and begin producing solid, quiet work, most of which lands neatly in Dreary Camp #3, nice, cautious, boring Workshop Stories, stories as tough to find technical fault with as they are to remember after putting them down. Here are the rouged corpses for Dr. Gass's graveyard. Workshops like corpses. They have to. Because any class, even one in "creativity," is going to place supreme value on not making mistakes. And corpses, whatever their other faults, never ever screw up.*

I doubt whether any of this is revelatory, but I hope it's properly scary. Because Creative Writing Programs, while claiming in all good faith to train professional writers, in reality train more teachers of Creative Writing. The only thing a Master of Fine Arts degree actually qualifies one to do is teach . . . Fine Arts. Almost all present fiction professors hold something like an MFA. So do most editors of literary magazines. Most MFA candidates who stay in the Business will go on to teach and edit. Small wonder, then, that older critics feel in so much current CY fiction the tweed breeze that could signal a veritable storm of boredom: envision if you dare a careful, accomplished national literature, mistake-free, seamless as fine linoleum; fiction

---

* Only considerations of space and legal liability restrain me from sharing with you in detail the persistent legend, at one nameless institution, of the embalmed cadaver cadged from the medical school by two deeply troubled young MFA candidates, enrolled in a workshop as their proxy, smuggled pre-bell into the seminar room each week, and propped in its assigned seat, there to clutch a pencil in its white fist and stare straight ahead with an expression of somewhat rigid good cheer. The name of the legend is "The Cadaver That Got a B."

preoccupied with norm as value instead of value's servant; fiction by academics who were taught by academics and teach aspiring academics; novel after critique-resistant novel about tenure-angst, coed-lust, cafeteria-schmerz.

Railing against occluded subject matter and tradition-tested style is one thing. A larger issue is whether Writing Programs and their grinding, story-every-three-weeks workshop assembly lines could, eventually, lower all standards, precipitate a broad-level literary mediocrity, fictional equivalents of what Donald Hall calls "The McPoem." I think, if they get much more popular, and do not drop the pose of "education" in favor of a humbler and more honest self-appraisal—a form of literary patronage and an occasion for literary community—we might well end up with a McStory chain that would put Ray Kroc to shame. Because it's not just the unhealthy structure of the Program, the weird creative constraints it has to impose on instructors and students alike—it's the type of student who is attracted by such an arrangement. A sheepheaded willingness to toe any line just because it's the most comfortable way to survive is contemptible in any student. But students are just symptoms. Here's the disease: in terms of rigor, demand, intellectual and emotional requirement, a lot of Creative Writing Programs are an unfunny joke. Few require of applicants any significant preparation in history, literature, criticism, composition, foreign languages, art, or philosophy; fewer still make attempts to provide it in curricula or require it as a criterion for graduation.

Part of this problem is political. Academic departments of Creative Writing and "Straight Literature" tend to hold each other in mutual contempt, a state of affairs that student, Program, and serious-fiction audience are all going to regret a lot if it continues to obtain. Way too many students are being "certified" to go out there and try to do meaningful work on the cutting edge of an artistic discipline of whose underpinnings, history, and greatest achievements they are largely ignorant. The obligatory survey of "Writers Who Are Important to You" at the start of each term seems to suggest that Homer and Milton, Cervantes and Shakespeare, Maupassant and Gogol—to say nothing of the Testaments—have receded into the mists of Straight Lit; that, for far too much of this generation, Salinger invented the wheel, Updike internal combustion, and Carver, Beattie, and Phillips drive what's worth chasing. Forget Allan Bloom gnashing his teeth at high school students who pretend to no aspirations past an affordable mortgage—we're supposed to want to be writers, here. We as a generation are in danger of justifying Eliot at his zaniest if via a blend of academic stasis and intellectual disinterest we show to the dissatisfaction of all that culture is either cumulative or it is dead, empty on either side of a social Now that admits neither passion about the future nor curiosity about the past. +

# Classmates

I didn't see my own experience, working in ordnance in Iraq and Afghanistan, as necessarily markedly different from my classmates'. I did see it as markedly different from that of someone who gets a traditional MFA at a studio program for two or three years, and only sees other MFA students and spends his entire time devoted to that. Spending time in the army in Iraq and Afghanistan sounds intense from an outsider's perspective, but a guy working in an inner-city school in Los Angeles who's going through the program at the same time as me, he has his own day-to-day experiences that are pretty intense. The MFA is only a part of his whole life, he's trying to live his life but also be a writer.

**Matthew Hefti**

I think, a lot of the time, MFA programs are just like big social meet-ups. At mine, a lot of people made friends and started sleeping with each other and everybody went out and got drunk every Wednesday, but nobody produced any great art in the end. You could tell who the serious people were, who was actually going to succeed. Then there were the people who were just using it as a way to meet people. I used to say that MFA stood for Mostly Fucked Around, which was often true.

**Kristin McGonigle, The New School, 2004**

You get very close to the people in your year. For a lot of the students, they were the oddball in their group at college or wherever they lived, they didn't have a community of writers, and now suddenly they're in this small ocean of writers in the middle of nowhere. Everybody goes to this bar called the Fox Head. It's really smoky and small and cheap. The first night you're in the Fox Head, you look out the window and see this store called John's across the street, and someone invariably asks, "You see those steps over there? When Raymond Carver was a student he would sit there with Cheever, when Cheever was teaching, and they'd wait for John's to open so they could buy bottles of booze." And you're like, no way! That's right across the street! That's one of the little legends that you hear pretty much immediately, all those famous drinking things. I lived right by the hospital in that story "Emergency" from *Jesus' Son*. There's a giant sign across the hospital, EMERGENCY, and every time you see that, you think of Denis Johnson.

**Lee Klein, Iowa Writers' Workshop, 2006**

The Workshop was a very masculine environment in my day. Women were pretty much token students, and there were no female teachers. So it was really competitive in class, then you'd go out drinking afterward. I wasn't much of a drinker, but I'd be observing everything while other people were getting smashed. There were some people at the university who were doing drugs pretty heavily, but I think that in the Workshop the primary drug was booze. The writers you were trying to imitate at the time were still Faulkner and Fitzgerald and Hemingway, all drunkards, so a lot of people seemed to think that being drunk was part of the lifestyle.

**Mark Dintenfass, Iowa Writers' Workshop, 1968**

# My Parade
## Alexander Chee

When I'm identified as a fiction writer at parties, the question comes pretty quickly. Did you go to school for it? someone asks. Yes, I say. Where? they ask, because I don't usually offer it.

I went to the Iowa Writers' Workshop, I say.

Over the years, I've received two standard reactions when I say this. The first is a kind of incredulity: the person acts as if he or she has met a very rare creature. Some even challenge me, as if this is the sort of thing people lie about (and some probably do, though that makes me sad). Some ask if I mean the famous school for writers—and there are other writing programs in the state of Iowa, excellent ones, but I know they're referring to the Workshop, and so I say yes, though instantly I feel as if I have been made an impostor, hiding in the clothes of a great man.

The second reaction is condescension, as if I have admitted to a terrible sin. To these people, I'm to be written off. Nothing I do could disprove what they now believe of me. All my successes will be chalked up to "connections"; all my failures will prove the dangers of overeducation. If they ever like a book of mine they will say, "It's okay as MFA fiction goes."

I suppose this is just part of the price I pay for having been one of those people, the doubting kind, sure that it was all bullshit.

I got my first glimpse of Iowa City when I moved to San Francisco after graduating college. I made the friend I was driving with take the Iowa City exit from I-80, and we pulled into the truck stop.

"I just want to look at it, in case I decide to go to school here," I said. This seemed safe to say sarcastically, like saying I wanted to look at the White House because I was going to be President one day. I got out, pumped some gas into the car, looked around at the truck stop and said to her, "It looks terrible. Let's go." And we laughed as we drove away.

Even then, the moment haunted me, a vague premonitory knock—*Someday you'll eat those words*. But I pushed it away. It was impossible for me to go to Iowa. I would never go, I told myself. And they would never let me in.

At the college my youthful self had left behind, I'd studied fiction writing and essay writing, and the three teachers I'd spoken to about my future offered strong opinions. Mary Robison warned of studying writing too much. "No one is doing anything like what you do," she said. "You don't want to mess that up by taking too many classes." Kit Reed was dismissive. "Don't waste your time. You just need to write, you don't need the program. There's nothing there you need. Just go write."

Only Annie Dillard made the case for an MFA. "You want to put off the real world as long as possible," she said. "You'll write and read and be around other serious young writers."

## My Parade

Two against one.

The real world I moved to was San Francisco during the AIDS crisis, which was well under way when I arrived. My time there felt more like a preview of the end of the world—especially after the earthquake that brought down part of the Bay Bridge. My activist friends from college were all moving to the Bay Area, getting apartments together, going to rallies, protests, marches, direct actions, street theater. I saw the AIDS activism and queer politics movement emerging as a response to the fight of my generation, and I joined with the seriousness of a soldier. My friends and I were people who knew AIDS could kill us all, and we were fighting against those who believed it would kill only gay people. To this day I can't tell you if we were trying to remind them of our humanity, or their own.

I would stay two years in San Francisco, then move to New York in the summer of 1991, for the love of a man who lived there.

When I arrived in New York, I had a job waiting for me, courtesy of a bookstore I'd worked at in San Francisco, A Different Light. They had a New York store as well, and arranged an employee transfer. My new bosses set me to work cataloging the contents of a warehouse in Queens that had belonged to a mail-order gay and lesbian bookstore that A Different Light had acquired at auction. After the chaos of San Francisco, New York wasn't much quieter, but this job was—it was like going to sit in a padded room every day, a room padded with books.

If I went to San Francisco with the seriousness of a soldier, I left with a soldier's bitterness. I had seen friends beaten by the police and hospitalized, or arrested and denied their AIDS medication under the pretext that they were taking drugs. I had been profiled by the police, suspected of plotting against them. One of the organizations I belonged to had asked me to find out if my then boyfriend was a police plant. This, I think, hastened the end of our relationship, though I don't think he ever knew he was under suspicion. At least, he never found out from me.

It was nice, then, to sit in a quiet room every day, surrounded by books. And there were thousands of them, books I knew alongside books I'd never heard of, spilling off the shelves and out of boxes. They ranged from pulp pornography paperbacks to Vita Sackville-West first editions to the works of the Violet Quill group. Slowly I became aware that for me, a young gay writer who wanted to write, well, every-thing—poetry, fiction, essays—this was an education. The catalog I was creating was a catalog of what kinds of gay writing had succeeded and failed—what the culture allowed and what it did not.

My literary heroes were mostly women writers and thinkers—Joy Williams, Joan Didion, Anne Sexton, June Jordan, Sarah Schulman, Audre Lorde, Cherrie Moraga, Christa Wolf—and much of this writing was political as well as literary. I hoped, like them, to find a way to fuse my work with my belief in the possibility of a better, more radicalized world. Their work was in this room, as well as that of their predecessors and teachers—Muriel Rukeyser, for example, whom I discovered there, and still love.

For every writer like Gore Vidal, Gertrude Stein, James Baldwin, or Susan Sontag, there were so many others no one had heard of. The fame of the well-known writers seemed to me a protection against the void, and worthy of study. Especially as two of my literary heroes, the artist David Wojnarowicz and the filmmaker Derek Jarman, were quite publicly dying of AIDS, and I knew, from the work I'd been doing, that nothing was likely to save them.

## My Parade

Back in San Francisco, a certain Beat poet used to come into the store and move his books from the poetry section in the back up to the new-books table. After he left, we'd move them back. Sometimes I let them stay awhile; other times his pettiness angered me. But here in this room, I understood. Fame seemed like a terrible, even a stupid thing to want, but it also could protect you from vanishing forever, especially if you were a gay writer, already disadvantaged when it came to publication, much less posterity.

The question was—as always—how do you become famous?

The best and only honorable way, to my mind, was to write things people wanted to read. In my own small way, I'd made some progress on that front since arriving in New York. An editor at a publishing house invited me to lunch, because he was interested to find out whether I had a novel in me or not, based on a travel feature I'd written—I had begun writing for magazines. I was also interested in this question of whether I had a novel in me, and I showed up to that lunch cocky, with blue hair and a ripped T-shirt. My tweed-jacketed new friend smiled in the dark pub as he sipped his water, and we somehow got onto the topic of the Iowa Writers' Workshop. Underneath my performance of assured sarcasm and San Francisco queer punk cockiness, I took mental notes as he told me stories about Michael Cunningham, one of the few male writers I admired (I held male writers in very low esteem then). Cunningham's story "White Angel," which had appeared in *The New Yorker* and was a part of his novel *A Home at the End of the World*, was the stark marker against which I measured my own ambitions. The story I remember best is how Cunningham would go running at Iowa and smoke Gauloises cigarettes afterward by the track, and how this led the other students to call him "French Cigarette."

"After we graduated, we all moved back to New York," the editor said. This I especially stored away as important: all these writers from New York heading to the Midwest to study writing, and then returning afterward. Cunningham had punctured what I thought of as the gay glass ceiling, all too visible to me there in that book warehouse. I began to wonder whether his going to Iowa was part of that—and if it was, if it would work for me also.

For years I had mocked the idea of applying to MFA programs, but after that lunch, I became obscurely fascinated by it. I still made snide remarks about how no one was going to force me to write to a formula. I said I didn't want to write fiction that said nothing about the world for knowing nothing about the world (unspoken: Like all those MFA students), and so there I was, out in the world—wasn't that better? I made a point of saying, whenever possible, that I refused to spend two years being made to imitate Raymond Carver.

This wisecrack about Carver was the supposedly damning critique of the biggest criminal of them all, Iowa. If it sounds familiar, that's because the formula for making fun of MFA programs, and Iowa in particular, hasn't changed much in the past twenty years. The fantasy is of a machine that strips away all originality, of people who enter looking like themselves and emerge like the writerly version of Barbie dolls, plastic and smooth and saleable, an army of American minimalists.

I was writing fiction without my MFA then, and getting along—I'd written a story I was pretty sure was my best yet. I was also pretty sure it would never get published, for being a mix of too many strange things, some of them gay. I did not feel like a New York writer, and worse, I had to work a lot to afford New York. My bookstore salary was so low I sometimes had to choose between taking subways and eating. A subway token cost as much as a bagel or a slice of cheese pizza, and so it was always a question which would win. Some of my friends from college, whom I would see periodically, proceeded with a self-assurance that I didn't feel into careers that seemed beyond my reach. I didn't have the connections they had, to get jobs at *The New Yorker*, *The Paris Review*, *Grand Street*, the various publishing houses—and I didn't realize that, if I knew them, I had connections too. Wesleyan had been my entrée into this world, but it was a world they had entered eighteen years before, here in New York or somewhere nearby. I was from Maine, the state where they had all gone to camp together, but I did not go to that camp. "You're not really from there though, are you?" they would ask, incredulous, as if I'd told them I cut a canoe out of the woods and rode it down the Connecticut River to school.

What I did have were my looks, a sharp eye, a sharper tongue, and a penchant for making a spectacle of myself, which I would then use to observe people's reactions. I could do this and be amusing enough that most people didn't mind. Also, all the schools where all the people who knew each other went had at least a few men and women like me around—which is to say, we didn't necessarily have an alma mater in common, but we did have being gay. This was sort of like when I used to meet people outside parties because we both smoked. When these connections led to an offer of a job as assistant editor at a startup called *Out* magazine, I took it on the spot.

Maybe I wouldn't need an MFA, I told myself—which was odd, because I'd never really admitted to myself that I might need one, or that I'd been considering it.

It was around this time that I went to my boyfriend's apartment in the East Village to find he had ordered a slew of catalogs for MFA programs.

My boyfriend was the one I'd moved to New York for just six months earlier, after six months long distance. We'd met at a Queer Nation meeting in San Francisco, and begun an intense correspondence that turned out to be our way of falling in love. He was a writer also, and I thought of us as two young, talented gay writers going it alone outside the system. Everything was possible. But my talented boyfriend was working temp jobs he hated, and while he made more money than I did, he didn't feel as talented as I thought he was, and he felt his education had gaps—he'd been a communications major, not an English major as I had, and he wanted to know more about novels, poems, and stories. He'd never taken a writing class. He thought a program might help. And so, one night after I finished a shift at the bar beneath his apartment, where I worked to be able to afford to ride the train to my own apartment and still eat, I came upstairs to find him on his bed, covered in MFA brochures.

"What are these?" I asked. I felt betrayed but didn't want to say so—I knew what they were.

He replied defensively—he'd heard me crap all over MFA programs—and our short conversation made me understand how differently we saw ourselves and each other. In his eyes, I had a future without an MFA degree and he wasn't sure he did. Me, I was afraid this was his way of saying he was leaving me, a sign of some secret dissatisfaction.

I picked through the brochures and looked at the faculty bios. I chose three schools to apply to, based on which schools, at the time, had produced the most faculty appearing in the brochures—the schools whose students were hired the most after graduation. These were the University of Arizona, the University of Iowa, and the University of Massachusetts–Amherst.

I applied as a cynic, submitting a story that included explicit gay sex, psychic powers, and the occult. "If they're going to have me," I said, "they need to know what kind of freak I am." In the story, a young clairvoyant Korean adoptee helps the police find lost children and is the only actually psychic member of an ad hoc coven. He has penetrative sex with his high school boyfriend, who's also in the coven, and is possessed by a ghost during an informal exorcism ritual. The idea was that a program devoted to the creation of minimalist realism would have to reject me and I could go on my way, my beliefs about everything confirmed. But that's not what happened.

My first letter of acceptance, to UMass-Amherst, came with an offer of a fellowship and a note from John Edgar Wideman. A day later I got a phone call at work from a woman whose voice I didn't recognize. "It's Connie Brothers, from the Iowa Writers' Workshop," she said. "A letter is on the way, but I'm calling to offer you a place in the fall class and a fellowship." She named a sum of money.

I was stunned.

"This is great," I said, remembering to speak, and then blurted out, "UMass-Amherst is offering the same amount."

"Did you say anything yet?"

"No," I said, appalled at my indiscretion.

"Give me a day," she said, and hung up. I hadn't intended to begin a negotiation—I wasn't even aware that negotiation was possible. I was only meaning to be literal: how could I decide between fellowships of equal amounts? I wanted to call back and apologize, but the next day she phoned and offered twice as much, and seemed entirely unconcerned.

"Thank you," I said into the phone. "I'll speak to you soon." I hung up and gave the news, and my coworkers cheered and shook my hand.

Before I gave notice at *Out*, I spent a night walking the East Village, thinking about my decision. I ended up at Life Café, where I ordered an almond-milk latte and a veggie burrito, and I had some copy to edit—an asparagus recipe, in fact. I was still not sure I would leave New York. If I moved to Iowa, I thought, I would vanish forever. I would become unrecognizable to myself and others. And the amount of money in the fellowship, even after they'd doubled it, was that really enough to live on? I wasn't rich here in New York, but if I stayed at the magazine, I knew I could get by and more—I could afford, for example, this meal I was having. I could make my way up the New York magazine-world ladder.

At the next table a conversation about the new Versace leather skirts broke out, if a conversation is people all saying the same thing to each other. They were so heavy, they kept saying. So heavy.

I wanted out, I realized then. I wanted cheap rent and a fellowship and people who were talking and thinking about fiction. A time would come again when I would kill to hear people talk about Versace, but it was not then. Anything you did that was not your writing was not your writing, and New York provided a lot of opportunities to write, but also a lot of opportunities not to write, or to write the wrong things. There were things I wanted, like being a contributing editor instead of assistant or managing editor, and you didn't get there by working your way up. Contributing editors swoop down from above, made fabulous by the books they've finished, which they didn't write while chasing after other people's copy.

## My Parade

My boyfriend didn't get accepted to Iowa, which disappointed him greatly—it was his first-choice school. But he was offered a fellowship to the University of Arizona, which was my first choice, the school where Joy Williams taught, and where I'd really envisioned myself, until it rejected me. We'd both been accepted to UMass-Amherst, but my boyfriend's offer was without aid. We thought about it—we drove up to Amherst and had lunch with John Edgar Wideman, who was, well, John Edgar Wideman—a profoundly intelligent, decent man, but we knew, by the time we left, what we would do.

We had been long-distance before, and were prepared to be so again. We packed up our little apartments and had a last dinner where our friends sang "Green Acres" to us over a cake at Mary's in the West Village, and we made our way onto I-80 West, to drop me off first.

That year, I lived alone in an apartment that was once ROTC housing for married officers at the edge of town, up by the graveyard and the Hilltop Bar. It lent the whole project the air of a failed military mission. The floors were linoleum, and a couch, desk, and table were part of the deal.

The Iowa I found was a gentler place than the one my editor friend had described. Under Frank Conroy, the director when I arrived, the list in the student lounge ranking students from no. 1 to no. 50 had disappeared, and with it, the fierce feuds the list engendered.

Conroy was said to reread the stories rejected first because he believed that real genius is often rejected at first. This rumor endeared him to me when I eventually heard it, but in those days he was only the legend, sitting in his peculiar way—he could double-cross his legs—in a room full of the incoming class, giving the speech he always gave.

"Only a few of you will get to publish," he said. "Maybe two or three."

I remember looking around the room and thinking *I bet not*. I had no way of knowing, but I was right: of the twenty-five students in my class, over half have published a novel or collection of stories. But the talk was not meant to discourage us. If anything, it was a bravura dare, or a whack on the head, like the one the Buddhist teacher gives as he walks around the room.

I never studied with Conroy, but he taught me one lesson I still remember. I was featured in *Interview* magazine that year as an emerging poet, and I showed him the page, with my face, huge, and my poem, tiny, almost hidden in my short hair. He smiled, congratulated me, and then said, "You succeed, you celebrate, you stop writing. You don't succeed, you despair, you stop writing. Just keep writing. Don't let your success or failure stop you. Just keep writing."

I now knew the truck stop was not the town; the town was a pretty university town populated with Victorian houses that had been built from plans sent from San Francisco, the result being that I would experience occasional uncanny moments, passing houses I knew from another place. Not only did no one try to make me write like Ray Carver, no one tried to make me write like anyone. No one even tried to make me write.

The only thing I really had to do was figure out whether my ideas were interesting to me, and then, in workshop, if those ideas were interesting to other people. But attendance was, mysteriously, also not mandatory. It's an occasionally controversial part of the Workshop. But the policy acknowledges a deeper truth: if you don't want to be a writer, no one can make you one. If you need an attendance policy to get you through, then just go—don't just skip class, go and don't come back.

That year, the Workshop accepted 25 students from a field of 727—now the workshop regularly receives 1,100. In the fall of 2001, the numbers leaped upward—as did applications to MFA programs nationwide—and they've never really dropped. This fascinates me still, the idea that the September 11 attacks drove people toward the institutional study of fiction.

The lore around your admission becomes irresistibly interesting once you get in because it seems the odds are so shockingly against you. You either suspect you do not deserve to be there, or you suspect the others in your class do not deserve to be there. Whatever you think at first, it doesn't matter—at some point the projection, for that is what it is, flips. You go from being suspicious of everyone else's talent to suspicious of your own, or vice versa, until finally you get over it. Or don't.

Soon I was walking around town with people I barely knew as if I'd known them forever. The conversations were long and passionate and exhausting, punctuated by strong coffee and the huge, strangely fluffy midwestern bagels, reading and writing, and a fair amount of drinking, for the alcohol was very cheap, and we were writers. The bars of Iowa City we frequented had been frequented by writers for decades. Something was happening to us all, and we were all a part of it, even the ones who wouldn't speak to each other. It was a family.

My first professor was Deborah Eisenberg. I still remember her walking across campus, dressed usually in head-to-toe black, in the seemingly impossibly high heels she favored, an ocean of flip-flop-wearing undergraduates around her. She was the kind of woman I would have idolized in New York, and I'd found her here. She was a walking memory of the life I'd left behind, and a vision of the life I wanted, all at once, and I fell head over heels in love with her. I volunteered to drive her home from workshop, and this became a somewhat regular routine for us, one that thrilled me. I read her two (now four) collections of short stories, and I took her seminar, and read anything she suggested, from Elfriede Jelinek to James Baldwin to Mavis Gallant.

I didn't want to become her, exactly, though it was close—here was a living embodiment of one of my ideals, a writer making serious literary work of the highest order that embodied political and aesthetic criteria I had set for myself. And she was a delight to study with, even when the results were humbling.

My first workshop with her was a revelation. I'd put up my application story—most of us did at some point—with the idea that it was the best I had. She saw straight through it, the way it was a mix of the autobiographical (I really had been in a coven in high school, with my high school boyfriend) and the fantastical (I did not ever help the police find lost children with clairvoyant dreams). I had tried, crudely, to make something out of a Dungeons & Dragons group I'd been in back in high school, but I hadn't done the work of inventing a narrator who was whole and independent of me. Deborah drew lines around what was invented, and what was not, with a delicate pencil, and patiently explained to me how what we invent, we control, and how what we don't, we don't—and that it shows. That what we borrow from life tends to be the most problematic, and that the problem stems from the way we've already invented so much of what we think we know about ourselves, without admitting it.

One common way of trashing workshops is to say that the people who take them are all in some way alike, and that they enforce this alikeness on one another's writing. This makes me think of a great line from one of Deborah's stories: "You meet people in your family you'd never run into otherwise." It's true of families, and equally true of workshops: you meet people there you'd never meet otherwise, much less show your work to, and you listen to them talk about your story or your novel. These are not your ideal readers—they are the readers you happen to have. Listening to their critiques forces you past the limits of your imagination and also your sympathies, and in doing so takes you past the limits of what you can reach for in your work on your own. A fiction writer's work is limited by his sense of reality, and workshop after workshop blows that open by injecting the fact of other people's realities.

I often remember how one classmate said to me, "Why should I care about the lives of these bitchy queens?" It angered me, but I had to consider it, and defend my choices, and live them, and ask myself if I had failed my characters if my story hadn't made them matter even to someone disinclined to like or listen to them. And if this sounds too harsh, well, this was as nice as it was going to get—the real world, the rest of it, is truly harsh.

I think of an MFA as taking twenty years of wondering whether or not your work could reach people and funneling it into two years of finding out. But it's also, still, the real world. One in which my good fortune continued, after Deborah's courses, in the form of study with Marilynne Robinson, James Alan McPherson, Margot Livesey, Elizabeth Benedict, and Denis Johnson. I had taken risks to come here, I reminded myself—I'd left a job, and a man who loved me, whom I loved. That's as real as anything.

We broke up finally in 1994, the year I finished at Iowa. But we'd made a go of it that whole time. He'd reapplied to the Workshop again during our first year apart, and when he was rejected a second time, it ate at him. He said, "You're going to be the famous one, the one everyone remembers," and cancelled our plans to spend the summer together. I tried to give him room for his disappointment, but it felt like he was punishing me for getting in there. He's since had a lot of success as a writer, so in that sense he was wrong. But then I think disappointment, and the desire to revenge oneself on that disappointment, can be an enormous motivator. Being rejected from an MFA can push you as much as getting in can.

The first thing my MFA meant to me, when I finished, was that I seemed to have become unfit for other work, though this proved an illusion.

I was fit for writing—and for teaching. That I knew. I also knew I wanted to teach only in the sort of job you could get if you had published a book. I had by now broken up with the boyfriend who set out on this adventure with me, and as New York seemed like a good place to be single and gay and a young writer, I moved back, the words of that editor ("After we graduated, we all moved back to New York") echoing as I did so. Sometimes it seems we know everything that's going to happen to us before it happens.

That first summer I went on interviews for jobs in publishing, but everyone who interviewed me, on seeing that I'd just come from Iowa, assured me I didn't want to work there. "Writers shouldn't hear the way publishers talk about them," one publishing friend said by way of advice. "Also the pay is crap." I've since known several successful writers who had publishing careers, but I think it takes a canniness that I couldn't fake to go into publishing and act as if one has no interest in being an author.

## My Parade

Deborah Eisenberg had been a waitress, I told myself. I could do that. And a few months after taking my first waiting job, I set plates down between an editor and a newly hired editorial assistant, and nearly gasped at the low figure quoted to said assistant. I stayed at that job for six years, writing my first book, and when it finally sold, I began to get the teaching jobs I wanted.

During those years, I was not above bragging about Iowa in moments of insecurity, but I always reproached myself afterward. And I bore it all because it didn't really matter. The white shirt and black bowtie and apron served as a cocoon for the novel underneath.

I wrote that novel on the subway going back and forth to work. I wrote it sometimes at work—I still have a waiter check with an outline for my novel on it that came to me while I waited for my section to be sat. I wrote it, it was all that mattered. And I made good money. One story Deborah Eisenberg has told of her time as a waitress is about how Joe Papp at the Public Theater approached her to commission a play and was surprised to find her reluctant to leave her job. She didn't want to lose valuable shifts. He asked her what she made on those shifts, and that was part of how the price of the commission was set.

Waiting tables was also a good education in people. I saw things I never would have imagined, and this was only for the best. Your imagination needs to be broken in, you see, to become anywhere near as weird as the world.

After my novel *Edinburgh* was published in 2001, I became a teacher, and have been a teacher ever since. First I was invited to teach at Wesleyan, my undergraduate alma mater, because the creative writing director admired the Q&A I did with students after a reading there. I moved on to Goddard College, then Amherst College, then my other alma mater, Iowa. Then to Columbia, the University of Leipzig, and now, Sarah Lawrence College, with the University of Texas–Austin on deck. It's a strange thing to teach at the schools one once attended, like a stereoscopic narrative, the same story told twice from two or more points of view. The past is always around.

Since attending Iowa, I've learned to talk about Raymond Carver, because he often comes up if I mention the place. He had been part of the lore there, but not the way everyone seemed to imagine. He had not been particularly celebrated while a student at the Workshop, we learned. Neither was Joy Williams, a writer I'd have been more inclined to imitate. And as a professor, Carver was known for being drunk much of the time, at least in the stories I've heard.

If we are to fault Carver for anything, it may be the model of writerly misbehavior, and the resulting blanket reputation—*all writers are like this!*—that has insistently followed writers into academia. Though Carver, of course, had a great deal of company. And we are now told to believe that even our sins are on the decline—more and more there come complaints that we are too well-behaved, we writers. We have become domesticated creatures, apparently—and the MFA is also blamed for this.

The boom in the MFA, whatever you might think of it, didn't come about because young writers wanted to imitate Carver's work, it came about because too many of them imitated the late Carver's life, too much—and administrators everywhere began to demand some sort of proof that the writer knows how to behave. There was a demand for writers with the skill and the will to teach, and to be a colleague, participating in the work of the department. You can sniff all you like that a book is the only credential that matters, but chances are you haven't met a provost. In the aftermath of these unaccredited greats, the rest of us are required to present our degrees.

It may be that you, like many, think writing fiction does not require study. And not only that—that it is not improved by study. That talent is preeminent, the only thing required to become a writer. I was told I was talented: I don't know that it did much except make me lazy when I should have worked harder. I know many talented people who never became writers, perhaps because they became lazy when they were told they were talented—maybe it is even a way to take people out of the game. I know untalented people who did become writers—and who write well. What I mean is that you can have talent, but if you cannot endure, if you cannot learn to work, and to work against your own worst tendencies and prejudices, and you cannot take the criticism of strangers, or the uncertainty, then you will not become a writer. PhD, MFA, self-taught—the only things you must have to become a writer are the stamina to continue and a wily, cagey heart in the face of extremity, failure, and success.

"I am taking this parade down the middle of the road," I wrote in a letter to one friend from San Francisco, soon after arriving at Iowa. A parade is a test of a community—the streets stop for a moment, and one part of that community, typically a minority, has a moment and then moves on. I'd been accepted to Iowa, but I still didn't know if Iowa was going to accept me, a gay Korean American writer. There weren't any such people for me to look up to—Chang-rae Lee's first book didn't appear until a year after I'd graduated, and he was the first contemporary Korean American writer, gay or straight, I'd ever seen. When I said what I said about the parade, I meant: I refuse to be marginalized, I have been invited inside an American tradition, and I'm going to make the best of it.

A favorite photo from this time is of me at a Halloween party, dressed in short-shorts, fishnets, a black motorcycle jacket, a yard-long blond wig on my head, applying lipstick in front of a bull's-eye—studiously not looking at the camera, aware that it was on me. To this day friends stare at the photo in disbelief—I seem to have been completely transformed. I was eventually crowned the Queen of the Iowa Writers' Workshop Prom, an event that saw me appear at the Veterans of Foreign Wars Hall in a red leather coatdress slit up the sides, that same blond wig, Kabuki makeup, and heels. This was me throwing a parade—this was me testing Iowa. I remember the hush as I stepped into the bar area where the veterans sat, the saloon doors swinging, to go and use the restroom, and the pause as I realized I had to decide which one to use.

In writing this, I am trying to see myself as I might a character—I'm trying to do that difficult thing that Deborah Eisenberg began to teach me. I am still, I think, that prom queen, thinking I'm not radical enough, thinking I need to be even more intense, and thus failing to see other aspects of what I was or am.

I know I have taken what seems like a preposterous amount of time to write two novels, but then again I am the former student of teachers who took years to write stories, a decade or more to write a book. I am fortunate to have been the first published gay Korean American author, and am still the only one who has published fiction about a character with those characteristics. My first novel, *Edinburgh*, the one written on the train back and forth to that restaurant, took two years to sell to an independent publisher. Eventually, it was picked up by a major publisher and relaunched with a national tour, the book sold out front on the main table as if it were any other book by a mainstream author. My parade went right down the middle of the street.

If the myth about the Workshop was that it tried to make us all the same, my experience was that it encouraged me to be a writer like none before. Whether I did that was up to me. Going to Iowa was one of the best things I ever did for my writing life. I went because I got in, and because I was afraid. I feared losing the love I lost anyway, and I feared oblivion, because the writers and artists I knew and admired were being ignored by the culture or were dying. I still fear those things, and I'm still here. +

N  Y  C

Right before beginning at Arizona I spent a summer in New York. I was living on Avenue C between Third and Fourth and it was this awesome apartment. The other people who were living there—one was a fashion designer and one was like an in-line skater, but more of the skateboard variety. And so it was this super-cool apartment, everything was so cool and I felt so cool, and I remember leaving and thinking, *This is the only place in the world. I can't believe I'm leaving the only place in the world.*

Eli S. Evans

I don't think New York publishing has changed much. When he was running Vintage, Marty Asher used to muse about how funny it was that the same people who went around declaring the death of the printed-and-bound word, the people who wanted to get creative or get famous in another realm—what's the first thing they want once they succeed in said realm? To write a book. I understand the desire to claim things are done in a vastly different manner, to separate out the motivation behind writing and how the world then digests that writing. Because then it's less scary. Then we can either avoid the problem or lean into it if it's the new way books are being sold and read. But e-readers and tumblrs and Twitter and apps don't fundamentally alter the DNA of a culture like ours. They really don't. They are big deals. But they are earthquakes, not the earth. That's part of what makes book publishing so blessed and so cursed at the same time. You walk down the halls at a major publishing house or into a book launch meeting and it sounds the same as it did fifteen years ago, minus a few ringing phones, since it's mostly email now. Also minus an open bar at the parties, I suppose.

# How to Be Popular

## Melissa Flashman

I am not ashamed to say that I have an abiding interest in popularity. Not my own so much—though I'm as eager to be liked as anyone—but popularity as a process and a phenomenon. Why are certain people, ideas, or stories popular at any given moment? Are there ways to make ideas or works of art that are currently unfashionable, fashionable?

Given this fixation, it is probably no accident that I came to work as a literary agent, in what is essentially the R&D wing of the publishing industry. My path, though it makes sense when viewed with hindsight, was not direct. For me, there was no advanced degree in publishing, no internships at esteemed small presses or literary agencies.

After college I beat a quick path back to academia. My English PhD program proved to be a pleasant reversal of the undergraduate experience. I was paid—enough to live modestly but comfortably in Baltimore—to read books. I chose this program with the hope of becoming an expert on popularity: the popularity of books, mostly novels, though genre hardly mattered. I had the somewhat half-baked idea that I might uncover the secret of why certain books and certain formal concerns are in vogue at a particular moment, from anxieties about signification and point of view in early twentieth-century modernist fiction to vampires in early twenty-first-century popular novels.

I was relieved to learn that my ambition could be slotted into a fancy ism: New Historicism. At the time, New Historicism was the Fight Club of the humanities: no one would admit to being a member. This didn't present much of a problem for me, though, because my program happened to house one of the founders (antifounders?) of the secret academic guild. I assumed I would spend a few years studying and writing about the concerns of my chosen corner of the library—early twentieth-century serial novels or contemporary American fiction; I wasn't sure yet. I'd emerge on the green side of thirty, with a tenure-track job somewhere along the Northeast Corridor, and I would teach the next generation about popular books and what made them popular.

As it turned out, the turn of the century was an excellent moment to be a less than remarkable graduate student—provided you were willing to drop out. The academic job market in the humanities had vanished, like wine at the reception after a visiting professor's presentation. Meanwhile the ascendance of the internet brought a surfeit of new companies, companies seemingly named after robots, companies that would hire almost anyone, including graduate students. I received a job offer from a company called Luminant. The signing bonus was the size of my graduate school stipend. My then boyfriend lived in Williamsburg, Brooklyn. It was an easy decision to pack up my novels, renounce my library privileges, and move to New York.

Luminant was the love child of the legendary advertising agency Young & Rubicam, where I worked the summer before grad school as a copywriter, and some McKinsey consultants from Texas. Job descriptions were vague and ever shifting. There was a lot of jargon. There were flowcharts and endless meetings about "The Methodology." One of our big accounts was Enron. By the time Luminant was poised to become yet another casualty of the dot-com bubble, it had been immortalized in a notorious *New Yorker* piece titled "My Fake Job." But while the rumors of layoffs and worthless stock options swirled around me, I wasn't too concerned. I had been making the most of my hours, Aeron chair nestled close to my pod station, secretly working a second job.

I hadn't given up on popularity. In fact I was taking a more direct approach, moonlighting as a freelance trend spotter. (The technical term, embarrassingly enough, was "coolhunter.") I worked for a company profiled by Malcolm Gladwell in yet another *New Yorker* piece ("The Coolhunt"), which was later included in *The Tipping Point*, his first bestseller. Coolhunting was an exciting new gig for a certain type of young woman fresh from her hip liberal arts college or her cutting-edge grad program. I figured I still had "it," that special female hubris for telling people what they should be wearing, or what their living room walls should be wearing, or what their Vietnamese chicken salad should be wearing.

In my year or so as a coolhunter I reliably filed reports on the habits and affectations and cultural trends that were just beginning to bubble up on the streets of Williamsburg: double-layered slash-ripped T-shirts; ironic graffiti; the color gray. I gave myself license to report on things that I thought *should* be trends. (Tretorns: Bring them back! Bubble wrap: Ideal interior design textile!) I attached the sleeve of a cardigan to its hem with a long strand of thick wool yarn and took a photo of my boyfriend wearing it. Trends, as Gladwell pointed out, were started by a certain type of person. Coolhunters were pretty much by definition this type of person: if you knew enough to recognize trends at their very onset, you could also initiate them. I can't take all the credit, but I did notice that Tretorns were back on the streets within a few short seasons. Didn't you?

But hunting the cool, like the cool itself, has an expiration date. I was nearing mine when my boyfriend sent word that a literary agent in the New York–based book division of ICM, the Hollywood talent agency, was hiring. His college friend was an assistant there—she would tell me what I needed to know. I used the last of my internet cash to buy a slim Katayone Adeli pantsuit from Bergdorf Goodman (fifth floor, but still) and headed to HR. I took a typing test. I met with the agent, a pretty young woman with a broad smile and an even broader laugh. She sent me home with two manuscripts and told me to write reader's reports for each. Perhaps it would be a short trip from New Historicism to the next cool thing in American publishing? I reported for work the following week.

Over the next three years I would work for ICM and then another agent, who was in the process of merging her eponymous firm with a large boutique agency. Both of my bosses were quite discerning, both were well respected among editors for their taste, and both represented authors who wrote what I would quickly learn to call "literary fiction." Literary fiction is a commercial designation, not an academic one. I'd never heard any of my professors use this term, not even in the intimate seminars that were held on the parlor floor of the old English department house, where my fellow grad students and I gathered for our initiation into the jargon of what was still known as lit-crit.

## How to Be Popular

Before joining the publishing world, I'd divided the novels on my shelf that weren't beach reads into three broad and overlapping categories: "classics" (Flaubert, Dostoevsky, Woolf); "modern classics" (James Baldwin, Mary McCarthy, Nabokov); and novels assigned by my professors because they explicitly dealt with the concerns of the course at hand. Given that it was the 1990s, these concerns invariably had to do with cultural identity (Maxine Hong Kingston, Chinua Achebe, Audre Lorde).

The defining characteristic of this last category—by far the best-represented on my bookshelves—was the drama of the struggle to find a comfortable and authentic home between the world of the past, usually defined as the world of the protagonist's parents' culture, and the freedom of self-fashioning permitted by the world of the present. The parents' culture, whether European, African, Caribbean, Asian, or American, was rife with limited, limiting, and often patriarchal assumptions about what it meant to be an adult in good standing. But the culture of parents (and grandparents, aunts, uncles, cousins) was also a place of custom and comfort, often dramatized in tantalizing scenes involving familiar foods prepared by matriarchs. In these novels the modern city, and the modern workplace, were places of both intoxicating freedom and painful alienation.

Cultural identity was everywhere, and while post-1960s writers seemed the most explicit in their focus, my professors often took an expansive view. Books assigned in courses about cultural identity might include pillars of high modernism like *Mrs. Dalloway*; midcentury American fiction such as *Invisible Man*; stories of postcolonial despair (everything by Jean Rhys); novels by or about immigrants (Anzia Yezierska, Willa Cather, Sui Sin Far, Pietro di Donato, Bharati

Mukherjee). Of course, many cultural identity novels also belonged to the category of "modern classics." Maxine Hong Kingston's *The Woman Warrior*, then the most widely assigned novel on American campuses, is entrenched in the contemporary canon. Toni Morrison's *Beloved*, named the best novel of the past twenty-five years by *The New York Times*, was assigned in more than one of my courses.

As an agent's assistant, much of the fiction I read for work—mostly in the evening and on weekends—was written by graduates of MFA programs, and many of these short stories and novels, with their heightened attention to the details of cultural identity, would have been at home on my syllabi: the story of a recent college graduate trying to reconcile her differences with immigrant parents who run a corner restaurant; a sprawling saga set in an extended family in the legacy of Jim Crow; a postmodern pastiche featuring a middle-aged refugee who escaped genocide in his home country only to struggle amid America's network of faceless institutions. Of course, there were plenty of white male protagonists in these manuscripts—but even many of those made pilgrimages to their ancestral homelands, where they searched for clues to their identity. There were also a lot of well-wrought passages about barns.

The query letters that accompanied these manuscripts were standard-issue. A carefully honed paragraph about the novel, more or less in the style you find on book jackets, followed by a paragraph that noted the writer's MFA program, an established author or two with whom she had studied, and a list of awards won and journals published in. I had the sense that we had taken the same literature classes. Given that we were of the same generation, even microgeneration, we probably had. We were all protagonists searching for our authentic selves and our true homes. Regardless of my thoughts about any particular manuscript (they ranged in style from quiet and restrained to blazing Technicolor mash-up; most were competent and many were remarkably assured), it seemed clear that there was still an audience for stories about cultural identity. Many of these MFA novels were sold to publishers, some for well into the six figures.

I began to wonder if our professors, and our professors' professors, had created something like an endlessly renewable audience. Or did the hunger for these novels of identity have less to do with humanities departments and more to do with the culture at large?

It was hard to say for sure, but it was also hard to believe that universities were not at least partly responsible. Many recent graduates cycle back into MFA and PhD programs, and many of them teach undergraduates who, in turn, become the next generation of readers. It made sense that these novels would sell to editors who, if not graduates of MFA programs or PhD programs themselves, were at least graduates of American universities. And these novels would, in turn, be read and reviewed by other college graduates with similar concerns.

Then there was fiction that didn't come from MFA-land but shared its themes. *The Kite Runner*, as I was quick to point out when it came in on submission in those frazzled post–September 11 days, featured quite a lot of wrestling with identity. I thought I was particularly clever to notice that the story also bore the markings of a classic gothic novel (people are not who they seem to be, friends turn out to be brothers, et cetera . . . my reader's report, no doubt, was insufferable). In the draft I read, the local bully, the son of a Pashtun father and a German mother, was hinted to have a certain affection for Hitler. The protagonist fails to prevent his kite-running friend from being raped by the bully. The friend becomes an adult and is killed by the Taliban. The bully grows up to be a Taliban official who then rapes the son of the friend. The protagonist returns to discover his old friend was actually his half brother and then adopts his son. I may not have completely shed my graduate-student sensibility at this point, but I was turning the pages. Rapidly. The audience for this novel would also be college-educated and identity-savvy, like that of the MFA novels, but it would be different, and bigger: book clubs. This novel was going to be popular in book clubs. I was not alone in my thinking. The manuscript was snapped up by another agency, purchased by a division of Penguin, and has sold 7 million copies in the United States alone.

After my apprenticeship had run its course and it was decided that I would be granted my own office and eventually my own assistant, I continued to wonder about popular books. This was, after all, my job. I found myself representing, on balance, more journalists, long-form essayists, and academics than novelists, and so I broadened my inquiry to nonfiction. Why is it nearly impossible to open a newspaper or popular magazine these days without seeing a review or an excerpt of a book on the neuroscience of gender, attraction, or success? What is so attractive about so-called "lens histories" of salt, trout, or whale oil? Why are we so keen to read books that "explain us to ourselves," as one editor helpfully put it over lunch? And just who gets to write these books? I also wondered: What about a topic? Could I help make a topic or an argument popular? I rubbed my hands together in my mind.

In 2005 I kept reading the headlines, persistent but muted, about Americans' negative savings rate. I remember walking through Madison Square Park, outside my office, worried for us all. How would we afford children? How would we afford to send them to college? How would we afford to be old? I went back to my desk and did an exploratory Google search. Had anyone written a good long-form piece on debt? Who owned this subject? After an hour or so of research, I put my quest on the back burner, pulled away by a contract or a manuscript already out on submission, or the publicity efforts for an impending book launch. One afternoon, not many weeks later, I received a query letter from a young filmmaker. He had a proposal for a story-driven book on debt: credit card debt, mortgage debt, the national debt. He had directed a documentary on the subject that would premiere at South by Southwest. The film and the proposed book, as described in the query letter, proceeded from a strong point of view. He'd entered the fast-food franchise business while still an undergraduate at Wharton and had personal experience with debt. I couldn't find any writing credits, but if his proposal was as well executed as his query letter it probably wouldn't matter. His "platform"—the industry term used to describe a writer's combination of expertise and media reach—would be the documentary and his finance background.

I asked to read the proposal, which was everything I'd hoped for. In addition to its strong point of view, it contained a great cast of characters including a famous radio show host, a Vegas real estate agent, debt buyers, collection agents, and a Harvard law professor and bankruptcy expert named Elizabeth Warren. More amazingly, he was a talented reporter. The debt buyers and collection agents said vivid and outrageous things on the record. Elizabeth Warren offered a colorful and scathing inside account of a meeting she'd had with Citigroup.

I called the editors I thought would be most interested, sent out the proposal, and set up meetings with almost a dozen publishers. In nearly every meeting, someone from the publishing house shared his or her own story of secret credit card debt, mortgage confusion, or bankruptcy. It was like an old-fashioned revival circuit. One editor testified that he'd repoed cars in the Deep South. Publishers from the most esteemed literary house to the most commercial participated in what became a robust auction. The manuscript was delivered ahead of deadline and the editorial turnaround was quick. As publication day approached, the publicity department reached out to their media contacts and I to mine with enthusiasm.

Publishing may be an industry, but it is also a cultural ecosystem; it both reflects and shapes the interests of readers. Agents take the pulse of publishing houses, which in turn monitor the appetites of various constituencies: readers of thrillers and suspense, readers of business and think books, fiction readers (who are, mostly, college-educated women), young adults. Agents and publishing houses, via their publicity and marketing departments, also monitor the interests of radio and TV producers and print and web reviewers, critics, and bloggers. No non-Oprah person could be said to move the needle of culture, but a few choice decisions by an agent and editor, coupled with a few lucky breaks in the media, and suddenly we're all reading about dopamine receptors, serotonin, and HeLa cells. Often this process is driven by what the industry thinks the public wants—namely, more of what it already has. But agents and publishers also take risks to promote books they love, and a book that promised to unmask the systemic evils of our economy and anticipate a reckoning seemed like a good risk and an honorable one.

In the case of this book, which was praised for the clarity and strength of its argument, and for its storytelling verve, the praise was not enough to cut though the fizz and champagne that characterized the late stages of an asset bubble. No one wanted to hear bad news—or at least they didn't want to use their second mortgages to pay twenty-four dollars for it in hardcover. Had it been published a year and a half later, as the major banks were asking for bailouts and Iceland and Ireland were having a serious rethink about finance capitalism, the book would have been on the must-read list of every media outlet and drive-by radio listener in the country. Sometimes the books we desperately *want* to be popular aren't. The needle of culture and popular opinion isn't ready to move. It doesn't want to move. It is invested in not moving.

Summer 2009. An editor at *Harper's* put me in touch with a writer he had edited. This writer, an academic well known in certain circles, with whom I had been very keen to work, had been approached by an independent literary press to do a very short book—an extended essay, really—on the same subject: debt. Like most people in publishing, independent presses work hard to publish, and publish well, the books on their list. They play a key role in the intellectual and cultural development of writers, especially for projects that may have a specialized or niche audience. That goes almost double for independent booksellers who champion the books they stock, hand-selling them to readers. Independent publishers and booksellers are, in different ways than agents, also in the R&D wing of the publishing world. We wouldn't have many of our most cherished writers without their undying passion. They can, in ways that complement the efforts of the agent, help make a certain type of writer popular.

And yet many of the writers I represent cannot afford to spend a year or three working on a book for almost no advance. This author

Melissa Flashman

was no exception. He famously does not have tenure, although he has won distinction for his scholarship and is widely considered one of the best and brightest in his field. Outside the field he is known for his activism. By the time this independent press approached him, every major publisher had already signed up its "financial crisis book." Most of these books were acquired within a month or two of Lehman Brothers' fall, and most were being written by well-known journalists at major newspapers—the people who had covered the crisis. Most were on a crash schedule. A few of these books went on to do very well. Many did not. This surprised exactly nobody in publishing.

In 2009 publishers found themselves in real trouble, in part because of the weakened economy and in part because of the near collapse of the two big chains, Borders and Barnes & Noble. We were told it would be a miracle if either survived the downturn. The costs to publishers of shifting their business strategy in an increasingly digital environment would be great. Expensive existing structures, such as warehouses and a national sales force, would take time to unwind and, I suppose, "right-size." Consolidations at several of the major houses forced entire imprints and divisions to shutter. Jobs were lost. The editors who remained were much less eager to take chances. A short book on debt by an untenured anthropologist whose job stationed him a continent away would have seemed iffy at best in late 2008. By summer 2009 it was considered fringe. Very fringe.

We did the deal with the small literary publisher, and the book ballooned to over 100,000 words. The publisher was okay with this. It was a great book, which ranged over millennia and told a story of money and debt that had gone largely ignored. More radically, it raised the possibility of debt forgiveness. By the time it was published in summer 2011, Congress had decided to debate something called a debt ceiling. In the months that followed hardcover publication, the financial world, and then the rest of the world, started to take note of the ways debt was clogging the superhighways of commerce and growth. Various forms of debt had clouded the future of the euro. Talk of debt jubilees started to circulate through the Occupy movement, of which the author, now back in the States on sabbatical, was a planner and participant. Many forces were converging, and they were converging to make this author popular.

The book won awards, and the author was asked to talk to every sort of group imaginable: major European political institutions and think tanks, finance types, students, even libertarians. The book was a heavy hardcover and priced accordingly. It sold a lot of copies, including many at the independent bookstores that championed it. Reprints and special export editions were ordered. Foreign rights were sold. I scrambled to sell the proposal for the author's next book. Though he still didn't have tenure, he could breathe a bit easier financially for the first time.

Many of the ideas in the book and from the author's activism have seeped into the popular imagination. We now all belong to something called the 99 percent. We no longer assume we'll all someday be rich. Neoliberal policies and the financialization of the economy are no longer left unquestioned. *The New Republic* was observed being slightly bullish on anarchism. An old-fashioned debt jubilee made the front page of *The New York Times* website. Ideas, it turns out, can be made popular. And books remain one of the best vehicles for doing so.

I still don't have a unified theory of popularity, though there are leading indicators. Once you cast aside timing, which, of course, no one can control, the most important factor is people. There are people with bullhorns and there are ecosystems of people with bullhorns. There are institutions and networks, formal and otherwise, in which we all live and dream, tell stories and finger our worry beads. The ecosystems in which books are developed, written, published, publicized, and enjoyed are no different.

And when you write your brilliant, book-club-friendly novel about ~~cultural identity~~ / ~~finance~~ / ??????, call me. +

# Into the Woods

## Emily Gould

It's hard to write about being broke because brokeness is so relative; "broke" people run the gamut from the trust-funded jerk whose drinks you buy because she's "so broke right now" to the people who sleep outside the bar where she's whining. But by summer 2012 I was broke, and in debt, and it was no one's fault but mine. Besides a couple of freelance writing assignments, my only source of income for more than a year had come from teaching yoga, for which I got paid $40 a class. In 2011 I made $7,000.

During that $7,000 year I also routinely read from my work in front of crowds of people, spoke on panels and at colleges, and got hit up for advice by young people who were interested in emulating my career path, whose coffee I usually ended up buying after they made a halfhearted feint toward their tote bag–purses. I felt some weird obligation to them and to anyone else who might be paying attention to pretend that I wasn't poor. Keeping up appearances, of course, only made me poorer. I'm not sure what the point of admitting all this might be, because I know that anyone who experiences a career peak in his midtwenties will likely make the same mistakes I did, and it's not even clear to me that they were all mistakes, unless writing a book is always a mistake, which in some sense it must be.

In 2008 I sold a book-in-progress for $200,000 ($170,000 after commission, to be paid in four installments), which still seems to me like a lot of money. At the time, though, it seemed infinite. The resulting book—a "paperback original," as they're called—has sold around eight thousand copies, which is about a fifth of what it needed to sell not to be considered a flop. This essentially guarantees that no one will ever pay me that kind of money to write a book again.

It took me a while to realize that my book had failed. No one ever told me point-blank that it had. It was more like the failure occurred in tiny increments over the course of two years, after which it was too late to develop a solid Plan B.

I spent some of the advance on clothes that no longer fit my body/life, but mostly I spent it on taxes—New York even has a city tax, on top of the state and federal kind—and rent. I lived alone for three years in Brooklyn, paying $1,700 a month ($61,200 all told) for a pretty but small one-bedroom within eyeshot of the Brooklyn–Queens Expressway. I also spent $400 a month on health insurance. At one point I thought I would find another full-time job after finishing the book, but then I must have convinced myself that teaching yoga part time would better enable my writing. I also thought that I would immediately start another book, which I would sell, like the first, before I'd written half of it. In order to believe this I had to cut myself off from all kinds of practical realities; considering these realities seemed like planning for failure. In retrospect it seems clear that I should never have bought health insurance, nor lived by myself.

For many years I have been spending a lot of time on the internet. In fact, I can't really remember anything else I did in 2010. I tumblrd, I tweeted, and I scrolled. This didn't earn me any money but it felt like work. I justified my habits to myself in various ways. I was building my brand. Blogging was a creative act—even "curating" by reblogging someone else's post was a creative act, if you squinted.

It was also the only creative thing I was doing. While some people, mostly young women, embraced my book the way I'd dreamed they might, much of the reaction had been vehemently negative—not just critically, but among my family and friends. In the fall that followed the summer of my book's publication, my entire immediate family briefly stopped speaking to me. No one would acknowledge that this was because of the book—officially, the last straw was a stupid fight that happened during the two-day car ride home from a family vacation. I'd spent the whole vacation whining about my bad reviews and jonesing for the internet. Whenever I took out my computer, trying to write something, anything, to prove to myself that I still could, my mom suspected—as she later confessed—that I was blogging about how miserable our vacation was, and specifically about her. I wasn't, and I felt her suspicions were irrational, but they weren't.

She'd hated the way I'd portrayed her in the book, and I owed her an apology but couldn't muster one that would satisfy her. No one wants to hear you say, "I'm sorry but I might do it, or something like it, again."

But in the months that followed I discovered that, even when I wanted to, I couldn't write well in the first person anymore. I tried, but what came out read as self-conscious, self-censored, chastened—and worst of all, insincere. Then I tried to write straightforward critical essays, but without that dose of "I" I'd reliably been able to inject before, they were dry and boring, and suddenly my lack of real expertise or research skills was glaring—I'd always been able to fudge it before, compensating with feelings and observations when facts weren't at my fingertips. I started to feel like I'd been fired from the only job I'd ever been good at. In a way, I had. I knew I needed to train for another line of work, but I had no idea what it might be, or what form that training might take. Instead I deadened my anxiety and sadness with an unending litany of jokes and observations and news briefs and petty complaints: the real-time collective unconscious that's reliably unspooling on Twitter, even as I type (with my computer's internet access disabled) these words.

Eventually I started writing in the third person as an exercise. *Maybe I'm writing a novel*, I thought at times, but this seemed farfetched. How could someone who had been so mistaken about the narrative structure of her own life hope to write a novel?

By summer 2012 I'd been working on the third-person exercise for two years, and it had become a novel, or part of one, but it somehow wasn't getting longer or better. With the exception of yoga earnings and freelance assignments, I mostly lived on money I borrowed from my boyfriend, Keith. (We'd moved in together in fall 2010, in part because we liked each other and in larger part because I couldn't afford to pay rent.) We kept track of what I owed him at first, but at some point we stopped writing down the amounts; it was clear the total was greater than I could hope to repay anytime soon. He paid off one credit card so that I wouldn't have to keep paying the monthly penalty. When I wanted to cancel my health insurance he insisted I keep it, and paid for it. He was patient when my attempts to get a job more remunerative than teaching yoga failed; he didn't call me out on how much harder I could have tried. Without questioning my choices, he supported me, emotionally, creatively, and financially. I hated that he had to. At times he was stretched thin financially himself, and I knew that our precarious money situation weighed heavily on his mind, even though he never complained. "You'll sell your book for a million dollars," he said, over and over again.

But there was one thing he wouldn't tolerate, and that was all the time I spent clicking and scrolling. He didn't buy the line about it being a form of creativity. He called it an addiction. I said, "It soothes me." He said, "It agitates you." Being a blogger was a part of my identity I couldn't relinquish, but I knew I would have to quit dispersing my energies if I hoped to finish my book and pay him back.

I hatched a plan. Keith was going to the Arctic to report for an article, and before he left we made a deal: if I did the work of cleaning our apartment, finding a subletter for August, and finding a cheaper housing arrangement, I could keep the money we saved. I ended up renting a cottage upstate from an easygoing touring musician named Heather. Heather sent two blurry photos and I said yes, even though all I could tell from the photos was that the house had wood floors and a piano. I don't play piano but it seemed like a nice thing to have. Keith wouldn't be back till mid-August, so I would have two weeks there completely alone; my friend Bennett agreed to help me move in. I planned to stay off the internet, except email. This seemed terrifying but perfect, the exact kind of bored loneliness that could force me to finish a draft of the book.

The house was located, as Bennett and I discovered, on a campground whose—owner? manager?—Heather had warned me about. She said he watched TV all day and night and was "a real character." This detail came back to me as he waved a flashlight at us and glowered, his long, scraggly white beard flashing in the moonlight.

Emily Gould

He looked like a very specific character, the one who appears fifteen minutes into every horror movie about dumb city kids who drive into the country to party in an isolated cabin.

"Who ARE YOU?" he shouted.

"We're . . . I'm staying in Heather's house?" I said. "For August?"

"It's over there," the bad omen said, pointing to a saggy, vinyl-sided structure about twenty feet from the parking lot, facing the road. He shrugged and went back inside, trailing his stale-cig aroma. In my memory it was raining but it may not actually have been raining. We dragged what we needed for the night toward the door of what was apparently Heather's house, and then I fumbled with the lock and we were inside.

When I look at my bank and credit card statements from 2010 it's easy to see what happened, but at the time it was so hard to know which decisions were good and which were stupid. And even had I known, when I received the last quarter of my book advance, that it would be my last substantial paycheck for the next few years, I don't think I would have spent it more slowly. I wouldn't have been able to. So much of the money we spend—or I spend, anyway—is predicated on decisions made once and then forgotten, payments that are automated or habits so ingrained they may as well be automated. You think you'll tackle the habits first—"I'll stop buying bottled water and fancy cups of coffee"—but actually the habits are the last to go. I only stopped buying bottled water when I literally did not have any cash in my wallet at any time. In the meantime, I canceled my recurring charitable donations (all two of them), my cable, my Netflix, all my subscriptions. I moved in with Keith. I stopped seeing my doesn't-take-anybody's-insurance therapist, but only after I owed her $1,760. I regret the bottled water, I

126

regret the cappuccinos, but mostly I regret not realizing that I needed to stop therapy sooner. I think about the money I owe AmEx a lot, but I think about the ruined relationship with Dr. Susan (who was a great therapist) and the money I owe Keith every day.

I don't regret spending thousands of dollars on my cat Raffles, though he has been a pricey liability for years now. He has been threatening to die on a regular basis since the summer of my twenty-second year, when my parents brought him to New York because he'd been getting beaten up all over their neighborhood by cats, dogs, and maybe raccoons, coming home with infected wounds, which became abscesses, which required surgery. It was clear how he got into these situations: he approaches everyone and everything with an openhearted friendliness, head-butting legs and outstretched palms and furniture in ecstasies of delirious affection. It's easy to imagine this not going over well with raccoons.

Raffles contracted feline immunodeficiency virus from the fights, but that latent condition would turn out to be the least of his woes. In 2007 he became diabetic, requiring insulin shots at precise twelve-hour intervals and expensive, foul-smelling prescription cat food. He recovered from the diabetes, but soon developed a host of other expensive conditions: dental problems to rival Martin Amis's, thyroid and gastric disorders, mysterious and terrible fits of projectile vomiting. He became so finicky that after trying all the healthy cat food brands with their cutesy flavor names ("Thanksgiving Dinner") I gave up and started feeding him Fancy Feast, feeling the way I imagine parents feel when they give in to their toddlers' desires to eat mac and cheese for every meal—guilty and slightly relieved, because at least it's cheap.

The most costly of Raff's medical misfortunes wasn't related to any of these chronic conditions. I'd been babysitting my friend's dog, an elderly Lab-mix mutt who took daily doses of arthritis medication, when I noticed Raffles wasn't his usual needy, sociable self. Instead, he was sitting stock-still and open-eyed with pinned pupils. The vet confirmed my suspicion. "He's stoned out of his little cat mind," she said. "Could he have accidentally eaten any medication that was lying around?"

The dog must have spat out her dose. Raffles had his stomach pumped and stayed overnight in the veterinary ER, to the tune of $1,500 or so. They'd given me an estimate along these lines before they pumped his stomach, and I wondered if anyone ever said no. "Let my cat die. I can't afford this." Probably a lot of people did. Possibly I should have. Of course, I didn't. This was when I was still living alone and paying $1,700 in rent every month, still thinking that because I had been once been able to use writing to make the kind of money you can live on in New York, I would inevitably do so again.

Right before we went upstate, Raffles got an abdominal ultrasound ($380, charged to a nearly maxed-out credit card) that revealed he has lymphoma. I thought he wouldn't survive the trip, but a year later it seems to be killing him very slowly; he's thin but not in obvious pain, holding steady on $40-a-month steroid pills.

"I'm afraid to leave you here," Bennett told me Sunday night. He'd stayed for the weekend, settling me in, chauffeuring me to neighboring towns to stockpile food and supplies. Another friend would arrive on Friday, and Keith the Friday after that, so I wouldn't be completely alone. But I would be alone a lot. I don't know how to drive. There was a clunky old bike in the basement that could take me to Rosendale's main street, but not the ten miles to Kingston or New Paltz. I would mostly be trapped in Heather's small, slightly decrepit house, with no one around for miles but the campground-guarding troll and whatever vacationing serial killers were attracted to his campground.

For a certain kind of highly disciplined, possibly Swedish person, the day comes naturally segmented into task-length periods of productivity the way citrus fruit comes segmented into slices: waking, making breakfast, eating, working, exercising, making lunch, eating, working, reading, making dinner, eating, sleeping, all these activities taking place at their assigned times, for their allotted increments. I decided to become this kind of person. I would rise at eight, eat, work for two hours, practice yoga, eat lunch, check email or work for another hour (okay, check email), go outside, eat dinner, go to bed. And mostly that is what I did. "I've been drinking a lot, but I think that's actually okay," I wrote in my notebook. I also wrote that I had been spending a lot of time petting Raffles, crying, and quietly saying "Don't die," and that it was nice to be able to do this unobserved.

When I first sat down to write this essay, I thought I would spend a lot of time describing the scenic beauty of Shawangunk and the sense of deep stillness and isolation that surrounded me there, as contrasted with my everyday life, which mostly takes place in my apartment above a bar. But everyone has been to the country, everyone knows what that's about. Trees, screaming cicadas, sweet-smelling air, routine doses of astonishing ordinary loveliness that exhilarate and revive you like a drug. The white spot that resolves into a bald eagle as you focus your binoculars. The precious sense of being just deliciously exhausted enough that your brain can't create its usual whirl of thoughts. Et cetera.

A week and a half into my Rosendale month, I returned to the city to see the musical *Into the Woods* in Central Park. (I left my friend Sari with instructions about how to feed Raffles his steroid pills.) I hadn't been off the bus long when I realized how much ten days away had affected me. The subway contained too many people, too much information: I looked around constantly, trying to figure out everyone's deal. I stopped at the Strand to buy the fourth *Game of Thrones* book. Two girls around my age were hovering by the bestsellers table, leafing through *Fifty Shades of Grey.* "I hear it's incredibly bad," one of them said.

"It is. You can't even imagine how bad. Worse, it's boring. Bad and boring," I said, though neither of them had even glanced in my direction. They exchanged bitch-is-crazy looks, but for some reason I continued. "Look, I'm reading these *Game of Thrones* books—I'm not a snob! But there's trash and then there's crap, and that's crap." The one who'd spoken said, not really to me, "Well, I want to find out for myself what all the fuss is about," and picked it up and got in line. "Okay, but don't say no one warned you!" I called brightly after them. They walked away fast.

I didn't feel good about how this went down, which might be why, on exiting the Strand, I made eye contact with a sunburned gentleman who was begging for change. "Please, Miss, help me get something to eat," he said, an entreaty I've heard thousands of times and never once responded to. "Okay," I told him, "But I have to buy it for you so I know you're getting food." He eagerly accepted, and we walked to a kebab cart, where he placed a finicky, exacting order. After I'd paid for the kebab and waved away his thanks, he launched into a more complicated sob story, but I was already halfway down the steps into the Union Square subway station.

*What*, I thought, as I waited for the uptown 6, *was that?* I began to worry about being normal for my friend who'd landed us the highly coveted tickets. I liked this friend a lot but didn't know her terribly well, despite which I had sort of invited myself to spend the night at her house. I didn't want to alienate her by crying or acting strange or giving money to homeless people.

*Into the Woods* is a clever, appealing show—appealing to me, anyway—because it's not afraid to be completely obvious. "Going into the woods" is the beginning of everyone's story, and "the woods" are wherever your story begins. While you're there, you encounter monsters and beautiful maidens and princes. Then you get what you want, and find out it's nothing like what you imagined. The monsters turn out to be cool, the maidens to be weird losers, the princes to be dicks. You lose everything you have that can be lost, and find out who you are when you have to live without it.

In the first act, the characters—standard storybook types like Little Red Riding Hood, Cinderella, and Jack of beanstalk fame—go through the motions of the stories we know, overcoming obstacles we know they'll encounter and accomplishing goals they'd announced at the show's outset. But in act 2, which reviewers tend to think is a mess, the curtain rises on a post–"ever after" world that no one, especially not the characters, has ever imagined. There's betrayal and poverty and failure. There's also plenty of death, because that's the foremost thing no one imagines will be part of his story.

When the closing song ("No One Is Alone") came I teared up, as I'd feared, but didn't humiliate myself by sobbing. We made our way back to my friend's apartment without incident, and I surprised myself by falling asleep almost instantly. We woke up early and rode the subway together to Forty-second and Eighth. My friend headed toward her impressive glass office building and I went down into the bowels of Port Authority, where I boarded a bus for my temporary home.

—

My first clue that my book would not be a bestseller came in a marketing meeting about six months prior to publication. Actually there were several clues in that meeting. The first came when a marketing assistant suggested that I start a blog, and I had to explain that her bosses had acquired my book in part because I was a well-known blogger. The second came when my publicist asked how I thought they should position my book. She rattled off a short list of commercially successful essay collections by funny, quirky female writers like Sloane Crosley, Laurie Notaro, and Julie Klam. Books with "Cake" and "Girls" in the title and jokey subtitles.

Having worked at a publishing house, I know that it's not possible for everyone who works at a publishing house to read all the books coming out that season, or even parts of them, or even the descriptions of them in the catalog or in-house "tip sheets." But I also know that if a book is supposed to be a "big" book, everyone in the office will read it. I was a young woman, so of course they had lumped me in with the cake-girl books. But my book was not cakey. I had no idea how to explain this to people. I clearly still don't. Knowing how obnoxious it would sound, but feeling I had to say it anyway, if only to have said it, I told them that they had to "go all out." "Say that I'm the voice of my generation," I told them. They looked at me like I'd emitted a long, loud, smelly fart. And so—swear to god—I amended what I'd said: "Okay, say I'm *a* voice of my generation."

Imagine me three years later, watching the premiere of *Girls* for free on YouTube and reaching the scene in which Lena Dunham, whose character is writing a book of autobiographical essays and trying to convince her parents that she needs to stay on the teat to finish it. "I think that I may be the voice of my generation," Dunham says, bravely and unconvincingly, and then amends herself: "or at least *a* voice of *a* generation." It's a great scene, the elevator pitch for the whole groundbreaking show. She turned her life into art—award-winning, apartment-buying, wildly popular art—which is something I'm still trying to do. Watching her do it has been excruciating. That could have been me, I catch myself thinking, but of course it couldn't have been, or at least it isn't.

Dunham isn't the only person living the life I'd once felt entitled to. Or maybe the problem—well, *a* problem—was that I felt entitled to several different lives. In one of these lives, my book has made me famous as a pundit and wit, the kind of person who's constantly consulted on everything from what feminists should be enraged about to what jeans to buy. This person writes a great book every few years and travels and whips up impressionistic little essays for classy magazines when she feels like it, not because she has to. She's single, or maybe she has a glamorous artist boyfriend. She is beautiful, but not professionally beautiful—beautiful like a French person. Like Charlotte Gainsbourg.

In another of these lives, my writing has given me the wherewithal to live within a bourgeois coziness I've fantasized about for years (my feminist, socialist education making me feel guilty all the while). In this fantasy I'm married to my true love Keith, we own a brownstone and my books pay the mortgage, we have children, and I write novels while they're at school and cook delicious meals every night and the importance of the world's approval recedes into insignificance because I have the much more solid and gratifying love of my family. But I still have it—the approval. Of course. Like Jennifer Egan (though I don't know if she cooks). Like Laurie Colwin, but not dead.

The ridiculousness of wanting to have a baby when you're struggling to afford to feed your cat (and yourself) notwithstanding, I nevertheless felt terrible about turning thirty without having had a baby. Unfortunately this feeling was becoming increasingly unignorable at around the exact same time that Keith admitted to me that he'd donated sperm to his lesbian sister's partner, and she was now pregnant.

I knew I had no right to be as livid as I was, but I was livid and could think of nothing else for days that became weeks. I caught myself wishing everyone involved into nonexistence, especially myself.

"Just write your way out of it," someone once told me. This is terrible advice, as I confirmed when I tried to write my way out of my brokeness and toxic feelings about Keith's gestating biological son/nephew by agreeing to describe the situation, under a pseudonym, for a women's magazine. This meant trying to shape my irrational, evil feelings into an essay featuring a "me" character who is sane, likeable, and relatable, and to make events that were still happening into a story with a satisfying beginning, middle, and end. It soon became apparent that the only way to do this was to pretend Keith's revelation about the baby had forced a painful but necessary reckoning that would lead, I implied, to increased trust, closeness, and understanding in our relationship. The editors at the women's magazine wouldn't let the story alone until it suggested that, as a result of Keith's weird quasi-betrayal, we had sorted through our issues and were now on the verge of getting married and having our own children.

This couldn't have been further from the truth, and while I didn't *exactly* want it to be true at that particular moment, it was still painful to borrow those feelings in order to try to write as though they were mine. I worked on the essay for six months, which included several all-day email volleys from the editor, who seemed constantly ready to kill the piece. I couldn't let that happen; I needed the money so badly.

## Into the Woods

I was incredibly relieved when the issue finally closed. Around the same time, the baby was born. I tortured myself by looking at photos of him on Facebook. He was beautiful and healthy, and even as a tiny infant he smiled constantly. He looked a lot like Keith. The money, meanwhile, disappeared into the maw of my debt without making a discernible dent in it, or any palpable difference in my everyday life.

Two weeks into my Rosendale trip I'd discovered a secret I wished I could share with the world, but it was hard to share it without sounding like the worst kind of judgmental asshole. It was miraculous, I wanted to shout into the wind, how much space opened up in your brain when you stopped filling it with a steady stream of other people's thoughts! Twitter and Tumblr and even email—anything that rewards constant vigilance and creates repetitive cycles of need based on intermittent reinforcement—were the bitterest foes of the sustained concentration that's necessary to making worthwhile art! DUH! How had I been so blind?! How had I lived such a debased life for so long? How would I ever go back to New York? I was determined to preserve my monastic habits when I left Rosendale, for as long as I lived.

When Keith joined me at the cabin I was happy to see him, but I also worried that he would jeopardize my weird solitude and the blithe, happy creativity I'd begun to cultivate. Just having to talk to another person on a regular basis could enable a worm of self-doubt to slither into my Edenic lifestyle. In other words: having him around could lead me to realize everything I'd been writing was terrible. (When I got back to New York, I did realize a lot of it was terrible, but that didn't matter: the draft existed, and so could be revised into not-terribleness.) Anyway, I greeted him by being a huge territorial bitch. Luckily Keith is so oblivious when he's writing an article that he barely noticed. He buried himself in a pile of books about the Arctic and generally made himself inconspicuous. Soon we were back to the patterns of happy coworking we've been cultivating for years, sharing time in Heather's orange-painted office in the mornings and going for hikes in the afternoons. Also it was nice to have regular access to a car.

Then one afternoon he told me that his sister and her partner and all their children, plus his young half-brothers, would be coming through New York State on the last leg of a cross-country road trip. Could they crash with us for a night?

I said no. I was rude about it, too. I accused Keith of "always putting her needs before mine," which in fact he has only ever done once (the baby). He pretended to agree with me and gently brought me around by reminding me how much I love his sister's older kids and his half-brothers, and how rare it is for us to see them, and how special it would be for the kids to camp out on our floor. I finally gave in, then spent the day before their arrival dreading the moment when I'd first see the baby. What if I burst out crying or otherwise embarrassed myself? What if they wanted me to hold him? I didn't think I could handle it.

That afternoon Raffles pooped outside his litter box, then dragged his butt across the bathroom and living room, smearing poop everywhere. The vet had warned me that the cancer was affecting his intestines, but this was the first evidence I'd seen. The cleanup was disgusting, and the worst part was that I had to pick Raffles up and wash his butt. He whined, clearly hating this affront to his dignity, but he didn't try to escape. Either he saw the necessity of what I was doing or he lacked the energy to fight. Either way it seemed like a bad sign. When it's time, I hope he dies in his sleep, both for his own sake and because I can't afford the final few hundred dollars that euthanization costs.

The next day, I held my breath as the car arrived. The kids piled out, rambunctious from being cooped up, and I was too busy greeting them to worry about what seeing the baby would be like, and soon it had happened without my really noticing. We went into the little house and busied ourselves making sleeping-bag beds on the floor. The baby passed around from kid to kid, and then I was holding him.

I registered his adorableness and shocking docility. I didn't feel a gut-punch or an ovary-twinge or a heartbreaking tightness in my chest. No part of my torso or spirit ached. I felt nothing, but that "nothing" wasn't numbness, it was just . . . nothing. Seeing this child with his parents—and those two women, not Keith, were unquestionably his parents—undid my possessive, paranoid fantasies in an instant. I didn't even look for his resemblance to Keith. The problem with the dumb article I'd written, besides being full of made-up feelings and lies, was that I was wrong to think I was that story's protagonist. I am *this* story's protagonist, but I was also wrong to assume, three years ago, that my story would move predictably toward its perfect happy ending.

I don't know if I will ever have any of the things I once considered necessary and automatic parts of a complete adult life. I might never get married, or have children, or own a home. I will pay back the money I owe Keith, though, and my novel will be published—I sold it that December, for $30,000. In January I began a full-time job that, while it leaves me no time to write, is helping me slowly repay the debts I incurred by imagining that writing was my livelihood. Act 1 is over—it's been over for a while—and I'm headed back into the woods. +

# The Next Book

I'd written a number of magazine pieces after which editors would call and say, Why don't you write a book? But I didn't want to write a book that felt like a glorified magazine piece. The columns that led to *The Long Goodbye*, though, felt different—some editors approached me, including Megan Lynch at Riverhead. I wrote a proposal based on the columns, and the book was sold based on that. I had thirty-five pages of the book, probably.

At the time I felt very self-conscious about having sold the book before it was written, and I couldn't write for a while. It made me think a lot about the virtues of writing secretly versus writing publicly with a contract. I see all these people, all these students, in a rush to publish. I think there's a real virtue to that secret period when you're developing your work and no one has read it. To me that's the best time. It's the worst time too, because you're alone with your doubts! But it's the best time, because you're in your own little world. No one is commenting on it, or misunderstanding it, or praising it. You are making this little baby, and nobody comes in to say, Why does it have blue eyes, I think it should have green eyes.

Although you would never write a new book if you weren't horrified by the last book. Writing a book is so hard, so there's this moment when you're like, I've done it, ta-dah! Then that curdles into self-loathing and disgust and hatred, and if anyone brings up the name of your book you just feel ill. So you start a new book.

**Meghan O'Rourke**

# The Disappointment Business
## Jim Rutman

The second time I tried to quit my first full-time job, my boss shook his head, confused: "I don't understand. What do you think you'll find that's more interesting? We read books. For a living."

The question gave me pause. It had taken most of my first post-college year and a generous recommendation from an editor at my unpaid internship to find this job: assistant to a well-known literary agent. I'd moved to New York with an inapplicable degree from an unrecognizable Ohio college and no plan. I wanted to work in *Publishing*, but the word exuded an alien, leathery, haute-bourgeois knowingness that intimidated me greatly. My prior experience consisted of a minimum-wage job at the last large independent bookstore in Cleveland, where the assistant manager once told me her brother worked for either Cambridge or Oxford University Press. She added that his salary was unjustly small, and tried to share other cautionary details. But all I could hear was the glamorous name of the institution. Cambridge! Or Oxford! I was an immigrant from Ukraine who lived in Cleveland. I was impressed.

There were other names that impressed me. During my first weeks in the city I temped in the windowless depths of Carnegie Hall. (Do you know why signatures on donation-seeking letters from large institutions look so genuine? I do.) A rejection postcard from Miramax promised to "keep my name on file." And the fact that I failed to make conversation with the elusive "editorial" assistants (some from Yale!) at the Japanese publishing house where I answered the phones simply proved how impressive they were.

Thus the literary agency assistantship, when I got it, represented a glorious advance in responsibility, wealth, and privilege. Here, it was explained by the two other members of the staff, I would field calls for our boss—from book and magazine editors, from the writers our agency represented, and from unseen but surely important media figures. I would make lunch reservations at storied-sounding restaurants. Most magically, I would read and assess the manuscripts that floated daily into this basement home-office hub. (Our boss, the agent, spent his time upstairs, in the office attached to his beautiful Gramercy apartment—an apartment earned by reading books.) People's fates rested in my sweaty hands.

The city was a field of wonders. On my first day of work, I glanced in the window of my boss's neighbors'—a woman was serving her kids breakfast, and the woman was unmistakably Paulina Porizkova, who'd graced the cover of my first *Sports Illustrated* Swimsuit Issue. That doesn't happen in Cleveland. On an evening jog in Central Park, I passed Ben Stiller. And when I borrowed the boss's coveted key so I could eat my lunch in manicured Gramercy Park (the city's only private park), I made sure to aim my gaze north toward the mouth of Lexington Avenue, which led directly to the Chrysler Building. I hadn't yet learned that these icons, and my yearning toward them, were clichés.

The Disappointment Business

The two assistants with whom I shared the basement were my first real colleagues (and the people who took me out for my first cocktail). Our tasks were divided with what I would later learn was unusual specificity. The most senior oversaw various subsidiary rights—magazine excerpts, foreign rights, audio. She understood the procedural elements, after three years on the job, but also had special insight into our boss's priorities and inclinations. She knew our author list and understood these people's needs with effortless assurance. She seemed to have countless friends who were notable editors. My other colleague handled the mechanics of submissions, back when manuscripts were fit into tasteful boxes to be messengered to editors. She was something like a managing editor and kept close, confident track of the material going out. Soon she would depart to do a PhD in history.

As the occupant of the third, most frequently turned-over chair, I handled our boss's calls and typed up the dozen or two dozen letters he hand-drafted daily to editors, our authors, and the would-be authors he solicited after reading their stories in his sprawling assortment of literary magazines. We did not have email.

The three of us also shared the job of manuscript reading—a job that, as I quickly learned, was not to be done on the premises. Rather it was to be done in the evenings and on weekends, and it would never be finished. This seemed both dispiriting and romantic, somehow: I would have no life . . . literature, the discovery of literature, would be my life!

My interest in books had developed late; my degree was in "Communications," and I'd tacked on a minor in twentieth-century English lit for dignity's sake. Thus my mental library consisted of no more than seventy or eighty novels and poetry collections, most of them read quickly, under threat of a crappy grade. I'd enjoyed most of those books, and when I hadn't enjoyed them, I'd been able to rest assured that it was my fault: they were classics, assigned by people with PhDs, supported by Penguin or Vintage or Norton Critical Edition spines.

These manuscripts, by contrast, arrived as vulnerable as newborns. And I was equally vulnerable. My brain would have to engage these ink-jetted pages without benefit of a syllabus, lecture, or introduction—without any orientation at all. An unknown writer (sometimes at the behest of my boss; more often not) wrapped up the result of an incomprehensible labor and sent it to us, in New York, to render expert judgment on its aesthetic and commercial possibilities—in short, on the author's worth. How do you treat a stack of pages that wears, in Malcolm Lowry's phrase, "the dumb pleading disparate and desperate look of the unpublished manuscript"? The personal significance tied up in each package was nearly overwhelming, as I tried to reconcile my wonder at the sustained commitment and discipline that produced each tower of loose pages, with the quickly blooming realization that the result was, with vanishingly few exceptions, awful.

Like many civilians, I had never read anything terrible. I had been confounded or bored into resentment in high school by, say, James Fenimore Cooper, Pearl Buck, or a Melville novella. I was wholly unprepared to appreciate these books, and so found ways around finishing them. But now, day after day, manuscript after manuscript, I was disliking and dismissing everything I read, and I didn't know how to absorb so much displeasure. Did every published book begin in such tatters, only to be remade by the brilliant guidance of an all-seeing agent and editor? Was the magic somehow added in the publishing process? Or was the magic of reading itself a sham, deviously manufactured by cover designers, publicists, and some kind of collective delusion? Had the covers encasing the classics I'd admired just cleverly obscured the badness of all lengthy texts?

As the books that lined our office shelves attested, my boss could divine which manuscripts warranted the loving attention of professionals. But I couldn't find a glimmer of possibility in anything I read. Each day's outgoing mailbag was stuffed with our rejections. Presumably there were manuscripts that stayed behind, but they weren't the ones I read. Meanwhile my part in filling those mailbags was taking a toll on my psyche.

Many of the envelopes traveled a very short distance to our Gramercy office. (For instance, a predictably high percentage of boring, Bukowski-like novels about manly dissipation came from within a few blocks of nearby Tompkins Square Park.) But so many more came from unassuming, distant addresses, from people with no publishing pedigree to speak of. Every single manuscript tugged on my sympathies, even as collectively they chipped away at my fragile interest in narrative prose.

Which manuscripts did we accept? Over time a shifty set of criteria, gleaned from imprecise exchanges with my boss, started to come into view. They were different from the criteria my professors had used. You couldn't have too much narrative intrigue or pull. You needed depth of character. Competent sentence-making was quickly elevated to "beautiful writing" if the setting was pastoral, effortfully manicured, and/or historically accurate. All literature was the literature of transformation, about convincing personal growth and lyrical crisis management.

Because my boss had sold so many manuscripts to major publishers over the course of his career, the fact that we agreed on nothing led me to suspect that I was in the wrong business. The first book party he hosted during my brief employment was for a debut novel soon to be published by the most esteemed house in the city. Hungry for esprit de corps, I read the still warm advance edition that arrived a few weeks prior to the party and felt immediately, intractably confused.

So this book, with its neon-frosted, heartland sentimentality, its square, high spirits, was the source of our office's—and the industry's—highest hopes and expectations? Huh. Was my boss just lucky enough to share the public's dull tastes? Or was I, being a young person, just deeply committed to not liking stuff? My boss and I had more than once disagreed about material we were both reading; he would exhort me to dial down my critical pride, or, more succinctly, to stop trying to impress him. But those were mere differences of opinion about hypothetical not-yet-books. While *this*, this was a material object, soon to be unleashed upon the world, adamantly supported by booksellers in several countries, accompanied by advertisements in all the right magazines. This was business. And the book was no good. I couldn't get over it.

First I flirted with a New Media design company (they were ubiquitous then), and thus secured a $1,000 raise at the agency. After another month, I concluded that I lacked the discipline—and the courage required to deepen my loan debt—for grad school. I found an unpromising job outside of publishing that would pay $7,000 more a year and told my boss about this decision in his sunny, top-floor office.


"So what, you, like, read all day? *That* must be nice." This benign or envious or dismissive question, always with a little curl around "that," has been asked of me often. I explain that, while I feel lucky to have my job (or any job), there's no time to read manuscripts during the workday, so that's how I spend my evenings and weekends. Thus I have little time for "outside" reading, at my desk or anywhere else, and content myself with a half dozen or so published books a year, devoured during holidays. But I do read a lot of book reviews, I add. I like book reviews.

I write this having recently passed the fifteen-year mark at my current agency. I have my own nice view now, from inside a handsome, architecturally significant building where my senior colleagues found a way to install us in the mid-1990s. At the Frankfurt Book Fair a couple of years ago, I bumped into my former boss, whose booth was just across the way; he sweetly pretended to recall my short time in his employ, and was curious what I was doing at the Fair.

After quitting that first job, I moved to a lame but better-paying one in the membership office of the Lotos Club, a "literary club" on the Upper East Side, where I shared a large, silent office with three others, including the president of the place. I eventually grew tired of rotating between my ties (jackets and ties required at all times), despite breakfast being served on honest-to-goodness silver trays, and quit that job too.

I moved back to Cleveland. I slept in my old bedroom, attended high school classmates' weddings, worked very odd jobs: sub–file clerk at an East Cleveland bank; bill collector (by telephone) for a slippery-seeming and thriving computer outfit started by family friends; gutter cleaner and lawnmower for anyone who asked. I saved enough money ($1,500) to spend a cold month backpacking in Europe, then returned to sleep on my sister and brother-in-law-to-be's living room floor in the East Village. A friend alerted me to an ad in *Publishers Weekly*, and soon I was back to assisting a literary agent—this time, the president of the large agency where I still work.

After a few years as an assistant, I was given an unforeseen opportunity to become an agent myself. A young agent at our firm decided to leave the industry, and I, nervously, but with the tentative confidence that comes with your own office, assumed responsibility for about two dozen orphaned authors.

During those years I read thousands of predictably hopeless manuscripts—some of them solicited, most of them slush—and slowly refined my own ideas of what I liked and wanted to represent. I was also reading the books-to-be from my boss's frequently superb authors, and observing the methods and habits that allowed him to earn the trust that was everywhere evident. Also during those years I was learning to go to lunch—three or four times a week, week after week after week, in the company of bookish strangers, some of whom became bookish friends, as we politely introduced each other to our reading preferences and biases in the hope of someday finding a project we could share.

In a typical week, my assistant Dwight and I receive ten to twenty unsolicited manuscripts and queries by post. Another twenty to thirty arrive over email, though many of these lack even a personal salutation, suggesting that they're indiscriminate blasts to a throng of recipients. Around 80 percent of all these submissions are instantly recognizable as unsuitable, either because they inhabit a genre I don't work with or, more likely, because the first lines of the cover letter (not to mention the book itself) suggest an uninspired writer. And most of the remaining 20 percent are clearly not right for us either.

But then there are the competent ones, the commendable ones, the publishable ones. Now that I've been an agent for many years, I receive many inquiries from writers whose credentials, circa 2001, would have led me to high-five the nearest colleague. This is nice, but also bewildering. Most of these writers have extensive publication histories, whether because they are placing post-MFA stories in reputable journals or because they have published books that attracted enough critical commendation to fill an author website. The latter may be seeking some kind of career revitalization, and parting ways with their current agent; the former are all promise and expectation, unburdened by a sales history and thus a potential target of exuberant optimism from a captivated publisher.

Right now, for instance, Dwight and I are actively considering at least a dozen manuscripts. No fewer than four are first novels by literary-magazine editors, each of which possesses considerable wit and charm. Another is a smart and competent historical crime novel by a former book editor—I can't yet tell whether it's smart and competent or much more. There's also a fearsomely brainy academic satire with perhaps an excess of farcical energy. And a lyrical present-tense novel, ten years in the making, by the former MFA classmate of one of my authors. Another author's former MFA classmate (same program, different year) sent me the first hundred pages, thoughtfully revised, of a manuscript I read six months ago. A former client's friend just reminded me that I still have not responded to the *other* novel he sent me, eight months after I passed on his first. Last weekend I finished not one but two novels that ably tweaked, but maybe didn't entirely rejuvenate, the conventions of the superhero narrative. A Nigerian writer's joltingly earnest bildungsroman needs to be finished now, as other agents have reportedly offered eager praise. And—crap!—I forgot to respond to a relative by marriage of an editor I admire, who wrote a lachrymose, largely autobiographical account of her youthful wanderings in Eastern Europe. I don't think I will be the agent for any of these fine books.

This confusing wilderness of technical, imaginative, and observational competence, a region that grows at roughly the rate of MFA program expansion, is where Dwight and I spend most of our reading lives. I currently represent about seventy-five authors, some substantial percentage of which, at any given moment, are angry at me for neglecting them. I have no business taking on new writers unless to read them is to be thrilled. Unless I love their work.

But what is love, in this context? That's a messy question. There's love-love: the elusive, transfixing devotion you feel for your favorite books, regardless of when they were written or by whom. But love-love is so rare that work-love necessarily comes into play, and work-love is a slippery, contingent thing.

My intuitions have, I'm sure, shifted over the years to absorb the pragmatic imperatives of the job. My personal affection for writing is now indivisible from a reasoned expectation that the editors I trust—at least one or two of them—will think the same. These editors live inside my head; or maybe they *are* my head. This is my job. My clients hire me to sell their books, not to like them. But I need to like them in order to sell them; and I need to think I can sell them in order to like them. My own taste is, in many ways, not my own: it's an amalgam of that of every reader and publishing professional I've interacted with over fifteen years. It is made from a tense and ever-changing web of projections, suspicions, compromises, and hopes.

This taste, such as it is, took a while to develop. Whether it was better or purer when I hated all those manuscripts in the basement of my first boss's Gramercy home, I don't know. In a sense, I was right: none of those writers was as good as Samuel Beckett. But in a deeper and frequently reaffirmed sense, I was wrong: only by publishing the very best of the not-as-good-as-Becketts will we, eventually, come up with someone nearly as good.

Even for the lucky books that do make it to publication, disappointment awaits. A robust majority of all published books will not justify the advance paid by the publisher, even if that advance was a pittance, as it likely was. The book was not reviewed widely or well enough. The cover was wrong, and the publicist was negligent. The stores barely took any copies. The stores that took copies barely displayed them. There are no stores. The agent did not find the right publisher, after all. The writer was transformed into an author, but the author's life, unlike the lives of authors they know or read about on the internet, was not transformed, or not transformed enough. A different, deeper order of disappointment and regret takes over.

So we live in hope of being, or representing, the celebrated exception. Two years ago, I started working with a young author on the basis of a warped but skillful story collection published by a tiny press. She was embarking on a novel. I was thrilled to be on board. But when she showed me the first fifty pages, I felt she was on the wrong track and reluctantly tried to explain why, worried that our relationship would end before it had truly begun. She absorbed my words with excessive grace. After a few more conversations, she decided to take a stab at something altogether different. Less than a year later she sent me a novel that trampled whatever boundaries I had previously respected between literature and provocation. The book dug its claws into a tabloid staple—the illicit sexual relations between a beautiful twenty-six-year-old teacher and her eighth-grade male student—and invited us to question the nature of our fascination. The novel introduced, and didn't condemn, a scheming narrator who is all hyperbolic libido; free of the soft hope for emotional connection, she is left only with a taste for a very specific and very illegal satisfaction. A female antagonist was allowed to hold the center of a brave and dangerous book without apology. I shook my head in approving disbelief, seeing very little room for improvement.

Weeks later, after alerting a trusted handful of editors, I sent the book to twenty-five publishing houses: a large submission. I impatiently awaited a set of reactions I had less idea than ever how to predict. I was sure my author had written, with skill, a fearless book: poignantly overripe, oozing with a satirical force that was matched only by its exuberant descriptive power (descriptions, as it happens, of illegal sexual acts). Whether anyone but me would like it, whether anyone would find it commercially viable, was another story.

I didn't have to wait long. By 11:00 p.m. on the day I submitted the manuscript, one justly renowned editor called to tell me that the book was a "a big mistake," for a variety of reasons he went on to detail: it gives away too much too soon; it's not sexy, somehow; it gives us nothing, no one to care for, no one to love. This was not how I'd wanted to start. The next day brought several bemused "Well, well . . ." emails, indicating people had read far enough (past the first paragraph, in this case) to encounter the book's more lurid attractions, but this did nothing to diminish my cluelessness. I know better than to expect conclusive responses so soon after submitting, but I do start my anxious monitoring the moment I set the manuscript free. After two evenings, more robust reactions started rolling in. Everyone was appalled, some much more happily so than others. Admiration and repulsion were running even. I began making calculated assumptions about the early interest: Whose appreciation seemed likeliest to survive their house's internal debates? Which editor, and which house, seemed like the book's best advocate, based on reputation, precedent, and the elusive notion of "fit"? At these moments I tell the author as much or as little about what's happening as she wishes to hear; I prefer to err on the side of understatement.

After another few days, I'd registered enough legitimate interest to begin figuring out how best to arrange an auction: good news. But even as interested editors were seeking support at their publishing houses and requesting meetings with my pleased and flustered author, the *nos* continued to mount. Each hallelujah conversation about the novel's ruthless courage and scorching wit was interrupted by another email arguing that readers could never make peace with a protagonist so devious and unreformed. I barely stifled the impulse to spend my time indignantly correcting the *no* editors' misreadings in long emails that would serve little purpose.

As we moved toward a closing date for the auction, the number of participants was still in flux, as it always seems to be. (Last-second disappearances are infuriatingly common.) But among that crowd was an editor whose appreciation of the book's filthy virtues was edging ahead. She decided to float the idea of a preemptive bid. After talking through potential scenarios with my now hyperventilating author and vaguely warning the other interested parties that things might come to an early conclusion, I saw no reason to discourage that tack. After a few rounds of practiced but anxious volleying, we arrived at an offer the author could happily accept. I called the other editors to relay the news. In just over a week, we had cycled through the stages of uncertainty about as concisely and gratifyingly as can be.

Most of the people who participated in this process were, in the eyes of most of the others, wrong. The twenty-five editors who received the book reached a motley range of conclusions, as they should. Some were lucky enough to be unmoved enough not to have to trouble themselves with the pursuit. The ones who wished to pursue set off to recruit colleagues and check-writing superiors to their way of thinking. Most of these encountered fatal resistance and were forced to concede. Others marshaled enough support to move toward an auction, but either they or their house thought the eventual victor's enthusiasm was too much. In the end, the author found her book a home and a guiding editor who intends to try to make the book a happening. As I (like all agents everywhere) like to remind my authors: It only takes one. And it does. Now we'll see how many readers are prepared to agree with us. +

# People Wear Khakis

## Lorin Stein
## with Astri von Arbin Ahlander

A: When you were in college, what career did you foresee
for yourself?

S: You know, I remember thinking I'd probably end up being a
lawyer. I wanted to study philosophy at first. Lucky for me, my best
friend was a really talented philosophy student—she is now a don
at Oxford and works on Plato—so it was pretty clear because of her
that I didn't have much talent for philosophy.

Then I thought that I would do a PhD in English and become an
Americanist, and that I would specialize in the nineteenth century,
in particular the 1840s and 1890s. I was working on my senior thesis
and staying up very late. I was living on the ground floor of this res-
idential hotel, so there was never any light in my room. The phone
rang at one-thirty in the afternoon, and it was the department head
at NYU. He said, "Just to review the terms, we will fund you for X
amount for five years . . ." And I suddenly thought, "Five years?!" I
hung up the phone and thought, "I can't do that."

So I had no idea what to do with myself. It was the end of senior year. I was walking down the street and I bumped into my college adviser. I said I didn't have any idea what to do and I'd already missed the entrance exams for law school. He encouraged me to apply to the poetry program at Johns Hopkins. I said, "I'm not a poet!" and he said, "Oh, I know you're not a poet. But if you go, you can study with these interesting people in other subjects, and if you get a teaching fellowship you can see if you're a good teacher. And it's an MA so you could potentially go on and get a PhD . . ." That was very good advice. It was a one-year program and I was able to try teaching and take a few upper-level academic courses. I was such a terrible teacher that it really made it obvious that that was a miserable attempt at a career.

**Why were you such a terrible teacher?**

I guess it was hard for me to know what the point was of teaching stuff that the students weren't interested in.

**Why weren't they interested? Was it a mandatory class?**

It was the easiest class to take to fulfill the English requirement. I thought this stuff was naturally engaging. And as soon as I met students who were very intelligent and driven and good students in other things, but didn't have any interest in this stuff, even in the shallowest introduction to it, I was stumped. I couldn't think what to do. I was a terrible cheerleader for it. I sympathized with them sleeping through class because they had stayed up studying organic chemistry. One kid didn't like "Ode on a Grecian Urn," and I just didn't know what to do! I had no move. I had no game.

I remember going in desperation to one of the professors in the program, a poet named Mark Strand, and saying, "I don't know what to do with my kids, they just hate all the shit that I give them." He said, "Give them Keats. Everyone loves Keats." I remember one kid laughing at the line, "More happy love / More happy, happy love." It made him think of that cartoon. With the Chihuahua . . . ?

**[*Laughs*] And yet there you were in the poetry program.**

The first day of Mark Strand's workshop, everyone but me came in with a poem. And Strand was very hard on the poems. I found myself not disagreeing inwardly with some of his criticism. And when I went home that day to my new grad-student apartment, for the first and last time in my life I had an inspiration. I wrote something that I kind of liked. The next week I brought it in. He didn't praise it to the skies, but I got off easier than the others had. After that, nobody spoke to me for the rest of the semester.

**No! Come on!**

It felt that way, at least. And I never wrote another thing that I liked. It was so hard. You had to write a certain number of pages to make up a thesis and I was using the title pages—each poem had a one-page title page, even if it was just a one-page poem—to try to make up for page count. It was humiliating. I learned that I wasn't a teacher and I found the writing of verse very, very hard.

I also found that I didn't much like the workshop atmosphere. It wasn't a matter of fault. I didn't like it as a way of seeing poems be taught. We spent some time studying a long poem by Seamus Heaney called "Station Island." And I remember thinking that the poem was very impressive, but the workshop naturally took the poem and turned it into something to emulate. I didn't think there was much room for these young Americans—we were all Americans—to imitate a poet from a small country. I thought the problems we had in coming up with something worth saying were *so* different from the problems Heaney had that it would have made more sense to study that poem outside a grown-up craft class.

**So there you are thinking,** *Teaching is not for me. Writing poetry is not for me.* **What were you thinking** *was* **for you?**

I wanted to write a novel. I really wanted to write a novel. And in some sense, that was always part of the plan. I always wanted to write a novel. So I went to New York—I didn't even stick around for the graduation ceremony at Johns Hopkins. My friend came by in a pickup truck, we put all my stuff in the back, and then we drove to New York. I crashed on a friend's floor and then I got a cheap room and I tried to write this novel. And I never even finished a page, but it went on for months.

**Were you only writing during this time?**

It's all I was supposed to be doing. I would turn on the computer every morning and I would sit in front of it and at a certain point I would go out and get a drink! [*Laughs*] And this went on forever.

I remember, I was having dinner with a friend of a friend, a very nice guy, who lived in the Village. He took me to dinner and he leaned across the table and he pinched my middle finger, between the knuckles, and he said, "I can tell that you're not eating your vegetables and you're drinking too much and it seems to me that you're not getting any writing done. I have some advice for you. You should go to Barnes & Noble and try to get a job." I was going to do that. But I noticed the next day that St. Mark's Bookshop had a HELP WANTED sign. I went in and started filling out the form. The guy told me to go home and really study it. When I came home, the phone was ringing and it was a friend who'd heard about a secretarial job at *Publishers Weekly*. So I did that.

I should say that while I was trying to write a novel, I was also hoping that someone would give me a job at a magazine. I was reviewing restaurants for *Time Out New York*. It was a very small gig. I would do the little restaurant reviews. They would give you something like a fifteen-dollar allowance for a meal that wouldn't possibly be less than fifty dollars. So you would have to call the restaurant and say that you were coming from *Time Out*, but *Time Out* would disclaim any knowledge of you if the restaurant called to check. So it was very humiliating. And I didn't have any nice clothes, so I looked like a kid who was trying to scam the place.

**Perhaps what you are giving us is a tip for how to get a good free meal in New York.**

Actually, a friend of mine who is a reporter taught me how to pitch. He said, "When you go into a restaurant, say you are from such-and-such a magazine even though you haven't gotten the assignment yet, and always introduce yourself by first and last name. And when you pitch, always send three pitches." I mention this guy, his name is Mark Gimein, because he was teaching me everything I know today about how to get into a magazine.

Lorin Stein

He and I had a drink one day in Little Italy. He said he had some news for me. He had been assigned to the Washington bureau of the magazine he was writing for. And as a going-away present, he gave me a beat-up copy of a big book I had never heard of that had come out the year before. It was *Infinite Jest*. I asked what it was about and he said, "It's kind of about Hamlet. But don't let that bother you." That was the best going-away present. I read it in that bar, during the afternoons. I stopped bothering with my writing and just read the book. And I felt absolutely let off the hook. I just thought it was the novel I would have dreamed of, and the fact that someone had captured the world this way meant that no one needed me to beat my head against a wall that was never going to give way. I just felt hugely relaxed. I can't tell you, it was such a relief.

**That is interesting. Because your reaction could also have been: Here is the novel I wish I had written. Damnit!**

I must have known I didn't have enough talent! I hadn't been able to make up the first scene. To this day, when I try to tell my godson a bedtime story I can't get past "Once upon a time . . ."

**And yet you wanted to be a writer.**

Yeah. I don't think I knew what was involved. I think I kind of wanted to be an editor. I think what I wanted was to see books come out that I had some involvement in. The actually writing part . . . I never enjoyed making stuff up.

**So you apply for the job at *Publishers Weekly*. And you get it. What was that like?**

158

Well, it was a part-time secretarial job. The guy who hired me has become a good friend, his name is Jon Bing. When he called I asked, "Do you want to interview me?" And he said, "No, that's not necessary." And I said, "What do people wear?" He said, "People wear khakis." So I put on some khakis and showed up for work the next day.

And pretty soon—and I think this happens in magazines—sooner or later someone needs copy and there is no one around to produce it. So, if you're sitting there and you can do it . . . They needed some copy edited and I did it. I got a crash course in how to edit these little reviews—I remember because they were harsh lessons. But you are under deadline, so people will teach you quickly. And I ended up being very fast at it. I ended up editing and writing or rewriting a couple thousand of those reviews in a year and a half.

**Wow.**

Yeah. It was a very good education. We reviewed everything. Of all different kinds. For a little while I felt very expert in urban women's fiction.

**What was life like for you at that time? Where was this cheap room you had?**

It was on Elizabeth and Prince.

**Nowadays that's quite a nice address.**

New York has changed a lot. It was fun, but it was pretty lonely too. I remember that I would feel . . . It's hard to walk into a party full of people you don't know. And when you first move to New York, if you get invited to a party, you won't know anyone. The parties that I was getting invited to, usually by my friend Jon Bing, were often—like many parties in New York—partly professional. And if you don't have a title that means something to people, they may not know what to do with you. They don't know quite how to include you. I remember feeling very daunted, very shy, very lonely.

I remember going to a *Paris Review* party, actually. Jon hoped it might be a place where I might meet someone who would give me a real job. I was getting worried because I didn't have any benefits, and I had realized by then that I wanted to work for a publishing house. I remember feeling very discouraged; I felt like I'd been letting him down because I was so shy. I just talked to the first person I met in line for drinks. She introduced herself as the mistress of a writer whose book I had just read. And I had never met someone who introduced themselves as somebody's mistress before, so I was perfectly happy to go stand in a corner with this nice middle-aged German lady.

**That scene is like out of a book about coming to New York.**

It's true. The other thing I remember from that night is meeting George Plimpton and Bishop Paul Moore, who was a liberal hero. He was wearing his cassock, with his pectoral cross and stuff. I remember running home—I couldn't wait to call my mother the next day to tell her I had been to a *Paris Review* party.

**Then as now, the world of publishing in New York was very close-knit. Did you enter this community pretty early on?**

I was lucky. The people I was hanging out with at *Publishers Weekly* were great and smart and interesting. I am not sure that we thought of ourselves as being in the publishing world—I guess we were on the edge of the publishing world. But my colleagues were very literary. They were probably not so much in the publishing world as they were involved in literature.

And eventually, when I got a job at Farrar, Straus and Giroux—the publishing house that I had my heart set on—I found myself surrounded by young editors and editorial assistants who were my ideal of what it would be like to be in the office of a publisher. The two assistants I came to know first were Natasha Wimmer and Elaine Blair, whose translations and criticism now mean so much to me. So, we three were having beer after work every day. That felt very lucky, even at the time.

**Tell me about the job.**

I worked very long hours. The first three months I felt sick to my stomach all the time. My boss was Jonathan Galassi, I was his secretary. He doesn't like it when I use that word. I used it at the time and he scolded me for it, but I *was* his secretary. And this was before email really caught on at FSG, so there was a lot of drafting of letters, and writing up of letters, and correcting typos and stuff. And a lot of using reference books. You'd have to have, like, a reference book when you were writing copy. There wasn't Google yet. So the job of an assistant definitely took more hours of the day than it does now. An assistant before me had gotten in trouble for camping out secretly on Roger Straus's chaise lounge. I remember thinking it was so unfair that you would get in trouble for that.

Lorin Stein

**True! All you're trying to do is work longer.**

I remember leaving the office very late. I've just been watching *Mad Men*, and every time Peggy is alone working on silly copy, I am reminded of that office. It was probably the last office where you would hear the clickety-clack of a typewriter, because Roger Straus's secretary always used a typewriter.

**And how did you distinguish yourself?**

I don't think I distinguished myself. I just happened to be the secretary of the most powerful editor in the building. And I managed not to get fired for things like screwing up restaurant reservations. I remember running down to the Union Square Café—where he would always go for lunch—the moment they opened their doors because I couldn't get them on the phone and *begging* them, begging them to give me his normal table because I had forgotten to put in a reservation. You could just see them at the reservation desk looking at me, a kid in his shirtsleeves, thinking, "Oh, get this fucker out of my restaurant." You do whatever it takes.

**Do you recall your first editing project?**

I do. Did you see the movie *Wonder Boys*?

**No.**

Well, the movie and the book revolve around a professor of creative writing, played by Michael Douglas, who has this two-thousand-page novel he's been working on for many years. In the last scene of the movie, the wind picks it up and blows it away. But in real life, that novel was sent to FSG. And I ended up editing it. It's called *The Honeymooners*, by Chuck Kinder.

Chuck was very gentle with me, but in general if I could go back and do it again, not specifically Chuck's book but all of them from the early time, I would be less sure of my judgments. Not judgments of what I like, not that I would edit less. But I realized later on that every strong editorial feeling I've ever had, every fight I've ever had over an editorial question, after enough time I didn't think I was really right. That has been true, always. Once you begin arguing about an editorial question, there will come a time when you look back and think that you weren't right. I wish for the sake of some of the books and some of the people I worked with, that I had known that.

**Do you think the way you work changed over time?**

Yes, I know it did. Nowadays, if I find myself in disagreement with a writer, I partly know that given enough time, I will end up agreeing with the writer.

**And does that guide how you edit now?**

I hope so. Of course, in the heat of the moment, you still get bossy and wrong.

**Looking back, can you think of the best advice you were ever given?**

I am thinking of a few different ones. There was a teacher, Mr. Thomason, who, at the end of our senior year in high school, told us to read *Remembrance of Things Past*. That was good advice.

There is the advice of a newspaper editor who is a family friend. He said, "Be brilliant if you can, but what is safer and more likely is to file things on time." That was good advice.

There is Liebling's advice for interviewers. Clearly you don't need it. But it is: to not talk. To not be afraid of silence.

And I would say, for people who want to go into book publishing or any kind of publishing, it is good to have experience writing really short stuff for really conventional magazines. Because once you learn how to spit out boilerplate, whether it's for *Elle*, or *Publishers Weekly*, or *Bon Appétit*, that skill translates into all kinds of memo writing and copywriting and back-of-the-book stuff and letters that you need to write. I think training in the world of schlock journalism can really give you skills that are useful in other areas.

**I wanted to ask you, finally, if you were to look back at your twentysomething self and tell yourself something that you think would have benefited you at the time, what would it be?**

[*Long silence*] If you had to do it, what would you say?

**Well, I still am in my twentysomethings.**

I know you are. But what about yourself five years ago?

**Oh . . . I would say: Perk up, you are worth more than you think.**

That's good. It's funny, it makes me think of the first lines of this poem we just worked on: "I've had the courage to look back / at the dead bodies of my days / they litter the roads I have taken / and I miss them."

I think I wish . . . I don't know how to put it, but I think I would just say: Be nicer.

**To yourself, or to others?**

A little of both, a little of both. +

# Publicity

When my book came out, Norton didn't really send me on a tour, but I wanted to do one, so I put a lot of things together myself, and paid for my travel myself. I'm glad I did all that—it helped. Not so much because people buy books when you read to them at the bookstore, but when you go to different cities—for instance, my sister lives in Seattle, so I went there—you end up with a review or an article in *The Seattle Times*, which might not have happened if you didn't come to town. A radio interview here, a review there—these things add up, and bring the book more attention.

**Ellen Litman**

What are the two things that will kill an author during the publicity process? One, their peers. You see .05 percent of books take off, get endless amounts of press and money and placement, and despite being an otherwise rational human, you assume this is normal and that if you don't get the same treatment you're abnormal. You assume there's a code you can crack—or, worse, that your publicist, who had zero part in acquiring or editing the book, can crack. Two, the writer not knowing what he or she wrote. It's amazing to watch the same journalists who told you there was no way in hell any of your angles would work for their magazine now see every angle when it comes to their own book. It's as if they poured memory-erasing acid on their own professions and dissolved years of hindrances. When I was a publicist, there were definitely times an author could "really imagine a *New York* magazine feature" on their novel because it featured one character with a Brooklyn accent. I'd think: You're either not reading *New York* magazine or you sincerely do not have a sense of what you wrote. Or maybe you wrote it too long ago and you remember the intent instead of the finished product. Or maybe you're letting ego or pride or financial desperation speak for you. Or, with a more established author, there can be a misplaced faith in the traction of past successes—successes that have little to do with the current book. Either way, this is not going to end well for anyone.

**Sloane Crosley**

# Nine Lives
## Jynne Martin

In my early days as a publicist at St. Martin's Press and Simon & Schuster, I approached the media in a manner not dissimilar to how my cat approaches visitors to our apartment: first, postponing the encounter as long as possible; then lunging forward in an aggressive and inappropriate way; then retreating in horror and embarrassment. I called editors and journalists on the West Coast in the early hours of the morning, and put off phone calls to East Coast producers until evening, so as to ensure voice mail on the maximum number of occasions. When Sue Solomon, the tough-nosed producer of *The View*, actually picked up her phone, I panicked and hung up, then burst into tears. I was twenty-two years old, knew nobody in the media, had a rusted desk in a supply-room closet of Rockefeller Center, and kept having dreadful flashbacks to my high school telemarketing job. I lay awake at night wishing I'd waited for a job opening in editorial, instead of jumping at the first publishing job offer that came my way in hopes of paying off my credit cards. (Tip: no one should ever go into publishing to pay off credit cards.)

My epiphany came when a very successful literary publicist a decade older than me invited me to her birthday party. There in the flesh, holding Powell's tote bags and glasses of sauvignon blanc, were the people I'd been terrified to call: It's John Freeman! Kera Bolonik! Peter Terzian! They were her friends! It blew my mind at the time. Not only that, they weren't scary at all. They were kindly book nerds, just like me. Peter and I bonded over our shared love of the unsung writer Julie Hecht and Andy Kaufman films; John advised me about relationship problems; Kera had not one but *two* cats. For the first time I understood that my job could be about great conversations about literature and life and cats and the books I was working on, instead of panicked attempts to push products onto antagonistic recipients.

Everything changed from that day forward: I wrote much more personal letters and press releases, and I began the process of getting to know editors and writers as friends. I channeled my high school punk rock zine-making and collage skills into making press kits, and I handwrote cards to hundreds of editors. When I read articles or reviews that I found particularly provocative or exciting, on any arts topic whatsoever, I emailed the journalist so that she would know I was paying attention. I kept *Rain Man*–like lists of which book critics shared my passion for cult fiction writers like Mark Danielewski or Kelly Link or Jess Row. I started sleeping again at night, to the relief of everyone except my cat.

Around this time, I fell in love with the manuscript of a book called *Prep* that was under the radar at Random House. The publicity and marketing budgets were virtually nonexistent; the novel was given one page in the catalog and scant attention at weekly sales meetings. Even worse was the initial slapdash jacket treatment: dark, heavy ivy hanging over the word PREP carved into a stone buttress.

Curtis Sittenfeld and I joked it would be mistaken for a John Grisham ripoff, mass-market legal thriller called *PERP*. The editor and I begged for a better jacket design, and Curtis herself suggested J. Crew–style belts. The resulting design, a white cover crossed by a green and pink belt, was perfect.

With the hugely improved jacket as inspiration, I, and a team of publicity assistants who also loved the book, crafted a green and pink prep school–themed gift box, and a letter that included Xeroxes of our high school yearbook photos to go out with the galleys to women's magazine editors and their twenty-one-year-old assistants. It quickly became clear that the twenty-one-year-old assistants were doing the screening, and that they loved both our cheap preppy gift boxes and Sittenfeld's novel. We ultimately secured a lineup of nearly twenty magazines, a *New York Times* feature, and a *Washington Post* feature. The eight-thousand-copy print run sold out the first week. It was an intoxicating experience: even with most other elements stripped away—no advertising, no front-of-bookstore placement, no selection by indie bookstores as an "Indie Next" pick, no broad sales rep support—a publicist's passion could make a difference in the life of an outstanding book.

Since then I've experimented with a wild and weird variety of ways to get the right media and booksellers excited about the writers I work with. I've snatched up an auction lot of vintage Vegas post-cards on eBay, had moonshine smuggled up from North Carolina, and bulk-ordered boxes of flapper-era black wigs. "Etsy that shit out" is gospel among my current team at Riverhead Books, and we constantly try to innovate with the types of packages we create, the events we host, the media we work with, the social media campaigns we create, and the partnerships we've built with everyone from *Granta* to the Brooklyn Brewery to MakerBot. Of course, these efforts don't always lead to the blockbuster sales we hope for—some books just don't catch on the way we think they will. But the publicity team never stops trying.

Another essential quality of a good publicist is the ability to be brutally honest. Some people think of book publicists as insincere shills; they see our work as one step removed from that of a used-car salesmen, a screechy NBA cheerleader, or Tom O'Dell on the Home Shopping Network shouting about ninjas. But only a bad book publicist is dishonest or shrill; for the rest of us, our work requires a trusting and frank relationship both with our writers and the media.

And so when one of my writers shows me an early draft of her op-ed, guest blog post, letter to the editor, *O Magazine* "Aha! Moment" essay, or even her next novel, I give an honest response. I strive to be just as frank with the media: when editors call to ask what the big debut fiction of the year will be, or what to put in their holiday gift guide, I tell them the truth, even if the truth involves a book from a different publisher. This may seem a missed opportunity, or even a fireable offense. But when I call the next month, or next year, to say there's an amazing writer they've never heard of, named David Mitchell or Téa Obreht or Helen Oyeyemi, who has written one of the biggest books of the year, and that they must read the galley I'm sending over immediately, they know I mean it. Most book review editors receive hundreds of galleys and books a week; getting them to even open your crumpled jiffy package—much less read the first few pages, much much less read the entire book, much much much less cover it in their publication—is an enormous challenge. Their trust is essential to securing coverage, particularly when working with newer or lesser-known writers.

What's required, though, is more nuanced than mere honesty: it's about knowing the tastes of individual editors and writers, so I can pitch them books they'll want to read. It's knowing who majored in Russian history, who danced ballet, who read all 1,164 pages of *The Letters of Kingsley Amis*, who loathes Richard Powers, who lived in Berlin, who owns a cat. Getting to know these preferences and histories takes years and years of lunches, drinks, and weekends reading reviews and features in dozens of magazines and newspapers. The task is Sisyphean: editors get laid off, new writers emerge, cats die. But I love this part of my job.

It's a job that's never done—no matter how much or how little has happened for a book, there's always one more angle to pitch, one more producer or journalist to try. Sometimes it's finding every obscure blog and freelancer who has some connection to the subject matter; or messaging every fan directly on Instagram, Tumblr, and reddit; or pitching the same major outlet I've already pitched, but a different editor; or the same editor, but with a new angle; or same angle, same editor, but coupled with books from other publishers so now it's a "trend"—books with "tiger" in the title! Memoirs about gay dads! The possibilities are infinite. It's a point of pride that under my watch Gary Shteyngart was interviewed in every *New York Times* section save Sports, and that—ultimate publicist career triumph—the *Times* ombudsman chastised the paper for too much coverage of my author Jon-Jon Goulian.

Of course, it's never enough. A Greek chorus of authors, agents, and editors echoes each day:

"Any word from *Fresh Air*?" (As though I might be keeping it a secret.)

"Have you tried telling *Colbert* about my [famous parent / MFA degree / weird hobby / film rights being optioned / pet fish]?"

"I heard *Morning Edition* today discussing [topic tangentially related to my book] with Warren Buffett. Do they want to have me on, too?"

Jynne Martin

"Any word from Oprah? Does she know my novel contains a [minority character / aha moment / sexual assault]?"

"Hey, just checking one more time about *Fresh Air*?"

The anxiety is understandable. Each and every published book represents years of someone's life, and the process of releasing a book into the world is freighted with hope, expectation, and profound existential fear. This emotional cocktail reaches peak strength during the publicity process, and being a good publicist also means being a good friend to the writer through these dark, psychologically tormenting hours.

Authors aren't merely anxious about what media coverage they are or aren't getting—they phone me to brood about an early bad review, or a positive review that still somehow missed the point of their book; about low event attendance, a scathing tweet, or a drunken tour hookup; about a one-star customer comment on Amazon, a poorly worded answer to the Rumpus reporter, their sister's wrath over the plotline loosely based upon her divorce. And those are just the run-of-the-mill phone calls that come in during office hours. My writers call me after midnight, too—when a brutal Michiko Kakutani review gets posted online in the dead of night (to run in the *Times* print edition the next day), when they're stuck at Midway in a blizzard, or when there's no hot water in the hotel room ("Did you try calling the front desk?" "Oh! No, I just thought I'd try you first.").

Yet I find there's something to love in each and every author, no matter how crazy, and I've been fortunate to work primarily with writers who are phenomenally kind and generous and sane. Even the more "difficult" personalities have been laboring for years over a project they believe in deeply, and they are entrusting me with the task of easing its birth into the world. I have compassion for all the neuroses and bad behavior that the publication process can awaken. It's truly terrifying to have a project you've poured yourself into doggedly, alone, suddenly become public, subject to critical evaluation, poorly worded Amazon reviews, blogger backlash—or, worse than all that, ignored. It's why I come to work excited each day to find every way I can to give each book a fighting chance to find its readership, why I feel fiercely protective of my writers, and why my publicity campaigns are never, ever over. +

# Money (2006)
## Keith Gessen

How much money does a writer need? In New York, a young writer can get by on $25,000, give or take $5,000, depending on thriftiness. A slightly older young writer—a thirty-year-old—will need another $10,000 to keep up appearances. But that's New York. There are parts of this country where a person can live on twelve or thirteen thousand a year—figures so small they can be written out. Of course it depends.

My wife and I moved to New York after college, at twenty-two. We lived in Queens and paid $714 for a one-bedroom apartment (inherited, complete with artist's installation, from my friend, the poet and founder of Ugly Duckling Presse, Matvei Yankelevich). That year, the two of us combined made $24,000. But we had a car, and on weekends we visited my father on Cape Cod. I wrote stories; she organized an art exhibition. We were young.

We moved to Boston. Our rent rose to $900, but it was 1999, even a doorpost could create "content," and I was more than a doorpost. I wrote long book reviews for an online magazine that paid 50 cents

Keith Gessen

a word. Our combined income rose to $34,000. I failed to write stories, though; journalism took all my time.

The magazine collapsed with the NASDAQ. We moved to Syracuse and broke up. I stayed on at the MFA program, from which I received $15,000, then $12,000, then $15,000. I wrote stories again. My rent for a two-bedroom apartment was $435.

But I hated Syracuse. I moved back to New York; another friend, a novelist, sublet me his apartment. My rent was $550! That year, with what was left on my graduate stipend, plus some journalism and a book translation ($1,500), I made $20,000. I put $2,000 of it into *n+1*.

I turned thirty. Things had to change. I moved to Brooklyn and signed a one-year contract for $40,000 to review books for *New York* magazine. This seemed like so much money that I immediately sent some to my ex-wife, who was back in Boston, with those high rents.


There are four ways to survive as a writer in the United States in 2006: the university; journalism; odd jobs; and independent wealth. I have tried the first three. Each has its costs.

Practically no writer exists now who does not intersect at some point with the university system—this is unquestionably the chief sociological fact of modern American literature. Writers began moving into the university around 1940, at the tail end of the Federal Writers' Project, which paid them to produce tour guides of the United States. The first university-sustained writers mostly taught English and composition; in the 1960s and especially the 1970s, however, universities began to grant graduate degrees in creative writing. Now vast regiments of accredited writers are dispatched in waves to the universities of Tucson and Houston, Iowa City and Irvine. George Saunders, the great short-story writer and my adviser at Syracuse, told me he knew only two nonteaching writers in his generation (born around 1960): Donald Antrim was one and I forgot the other.*

The literary historian Richard Ohmann has argued that the rise of English departments in the 1890s, and their immediate bifurcation into Literature on the one hand and Composition on the other, emerged from a new economy's demand for educated managers. Our own age—born around 1960, and variously called postindustrial, informational, service/consumer—demanded copywriters and "knowledge workers" and, with the breakdown of traditional social arrangements, behavior manualists (*He's Just Not Texting You*). With the rise of Communications came the rise of Creative Writing, and the new split of English departments into Literature, Creative Writing, and (still) Composition. It's pretty clear by now where this is tending, and which hundred-year-old discipline will become less and less relevant from here on out. We do not have a reading crisis in this country, but we do have a reading comprehension crisis, and with the collapse of literary studies it will get much worse.

For now, the university buys the writer off with patronage, even as it destroys the fundamental preconditions for his being. A full-time tenure-track position will start at something like $40,000, increasing to full professorial salary—between $60,000 and $100,000—if the writer receives tenure. That's good money, plus campuses have lawns and workout facilities and health insurance, and there are summer vacations during which the writer can earn extra as a counselor at one of those writing camps for adults.

On the minus side, he must attend departmental meetings and fight off departmental intrigues. Worse, he must teach workshop,

---

* Antrim now teaches at Columbia University.

which means responding intelligently and at length to manuscripts. A writer who ignores his teaching duties in favor of his own writing will spend an inordinate amount of time feeling guilty; one who scrupulously reads and comments on student manuscripts will have a clearer conscience. But he will be spending all his time with children.

Journalism's pitfalls are well known. Bad magazines vulgarize your ideas and literally spray your pages with cologne. Good magazines are even worse: they do style editing, copyediting, query editing, bullet-proofing—and as you emerge from the subway with your trash bag of books (a burnt offering to the fact-checker), you suddenly realize that you have landed a $6-an-hour job, featuring heavy lifting.

Yet the biggest pitfall of journalism is not penury but vanity. Your name is in print; it is even, perhaps, in print in the most august possible venue. But you are still serving someone else's idea of their readership—and their idea of you. You are still just doing journalism—or, worse, book reviewing. "What lice will do, when they have no more blood to suck," as the nineteenth century put it.

Odd jobs—usually copyediting, tutoring, PowerPoint, graphic design; I don't know any writers who wait tables but probably some exist—seem like a better idea in terms of one's intellectual independence. But these can lead to a kind of desperation. What if your writing doesn't make it? How long can you keep this up? You have no social position outside the artistic community; you have limited funds; you call yourself a writer but your name does not appear anywhere in print. Worst of all, for every one of you, there are five or ten or fifteen others, also working on novels, who are just total fakers—they have to be, statistically speaking. Journalism at least binds you to the world of publishing in some palpable way; the odd jobs leave you indefinitely in exile. It would take a great deal of strength not to grow bitter under these circumstances, and demoralized. Your success, if it comes, might still come too late.

And then, of course, a writer can make money by publishing a book. But if it is depressing to lack social status and copyedit *Us Weekly*, it is even more depressing to talk about publishing—because *this* in fact is what you've worked for your entire life. Except now you will learn about the way of things. That book you wrote has sales figures to shoot for; it has a sales force to help it. And you are in debt. Publishers have always used anemic sales to bully their writers—Malcolm Cowley speaks of their claim that only after ten thousand copies sold could they break even; of course, says the good-natured Cowley, "they may have been displaying a human weakness for exaggeration." Now publishers come to lunch armed with Nielsen BookScan—to the same effect. The comical thing about this up-to-the-minute point-of-sale technology is how inaccurate everyone agrees it to be—"522 copies trade cloth" sold might mean 800 or 1,000 or 1,200 because so many bookstores don't participate. The less comical thing is that, as a measure of short-term popularity, it is all too accurate—*Everything Is Illuminated*, a work of Jewish kitsch, has sold, according to BookScan, 271,433 copies since it came out in 2002; meanwhile, Sam Lipsyte's *Home Land*, a scabrous work of Jewish humor, has sold 13,503 copies; Michael Walzer's *Arguing about War*, a work of political philosophy in the skeptical Jewish tradition, has sold 3,136. Of course one knew this; of course, one was not a fool; yet it's still hard to believe.

The very precision of the numbers numbs the publishers into a false sense of their finality. They cannot imagine a book good enough to have its sales in the future. Publishers wish things were otherwise, they will tell you; they would rather publish better books; *but the numbers don't lie.* The chief impression one gets of publishers these days is not of greed or corporatism but demoralization and confusion. They have acquired a manuscript; they know how they feel about it; they probably even know how reviewers will feel about it; but what about the public? Those people are animals. Over lunch the publisher tells his writer what it's like out there—"You have no idea." In fact the writer does have an idea: he lives "out there." But the publisher can't hear him; he is like an online poker player, always checking the computer. Nielsen BookScan rules.

"That equivocal figure," Pierre Bourdieu calls the publisher, "through whom the logic of the economy is brought to the heart of the sub-field of production." Yes, but he's all the writer's got. Is he looking tired? Poor publisher—last week he became so discombobulated by the "realities of the publishing industry" that he paid $400,000 for the first novel of a blogger. "He'll be promoting the book on his blog!" the publisher tells his writer over seared ahi tuna. "Which, you see, is read by *other bloggers!*" He is like Major McLaughlin, the cursed, hapless owner of the Chicago Blackhawks who once became so frustrated with his team's play, and successive coaches' failure to mend it, that he hired a man who'd sent him a letter about the team in the mail.

Once the book is published it only gets worse: the writer proceeds to the Calvary of publicity. Advances on first books vary—about $20,000 to $60,000 for a book of stories, though sometimes higher; between $50,000 and $250,000 for a "literary" novel, though also, sometimes, higher. Even the top figure—$250,000—which seems like so much, and *is* so much, still represents on both sides of the writing and rewriting, the prepublication and postpublication, about four years of work—$60,000 a year, the same as a hack lifestyle journalist in New York. But the costs! The humiliations! No one will ever forgive a writer for getting so much money in one lump—not the press, not other writers, and his publisher least of all. He will make certain the phrase "advance against royalties" is not forgotten, and insist the writer bleed and mortify himself to make it back.

Our forefathers the Puritans used to have, in addition to days of thanksgiving, "days of humiliation," when they prostrated themselves before God and begged for an end to their afflictions. "Before long," the intellectual historian Perry Miller wrote, "it became apparent that there were more causes for humiliation than for rejoicing." And so it is for the published author. The recent dressdown of James Frey and his publisher by Oprah was an event that people at publishing houses gathered to watch on their office televisions as if it were the *Challenger* disaster. But this was just karmic revenge on publishers and their authors, who spend every day prostituting themselves: with photographs, interviews, readings with accordions, live blogs on Amazon.com ("In the desert, it probably doesn't matter if the groundhog sees his shadow," went a recent entry by the novelist Rick Moody, a man who for all his sins is still the author of *The Ice Storm*, and deserves better than this. "Oh, by the way, the film *Groundhog Day* is one of my favorites!") Henry James complained about writers being dragooned into "the periodical prattle about the future of fiction." If only that were the worst of it. Consider the blurb: how humiliating that younger writers should spend so much time soliciting endorsements from more established writers, and how absurd that established writers should have to apologize for not providing them. If they'd wanted to be ad

Keith Gessen

copywriters, they'd have done that, and been paid for it. But they once asked for those blurbs, too.

In the age of BookScan, only an unpublished writer is allowed to keep his dignity.

—

Most writers lived as before, on crumbs from a dozen different tables. Meanwhile a few dozen or even a hundred of the most popular writers were earning money about at the rate of war contractors.
   —Malcolm Cowley on the book-of-the-month-club era, 1946

Not long ago I found a very interesting letter, a letter of advice, folded into one of my mother's old books. It was from the Russian émigré writer Sergei Dovlatov, to another writer, apparently newly arrived. My mother was a literary critic, but I don't know how that letter got into that book; in any case, it describes literary life here in the States—the two clashing editors of the émigré journals, in particular, one of whom is pleasant and never pays, while the other is unpleasant and does. And so on.

Dovlatov had done his Soviet army service as a guard in a labor camp and wrote dark, funny stories about camp life—"Solzhenitsyn believes that the camps are hell," he wrote, explaining the difference between himself and the master. "Whereas I believe that hell is us." In 1979, he emigrated to Forest Hills, Queens, and began writing about the Russians there. He published some stories in *The New Yorker*, met often with his good friend Joseph Brodsky, and died, mostly of alcoholism, at the age of forty-eight. He had liked it here. "America's an interesting place," Dovlatov concluded the letter that was folded,

182

for some reason, into one of my mother's books. "Eventually you find someone to publish you. And you earn some money. You even find a wife. Things work out."

It's true. It's mostly true. And when you think of the long-standing idea of art in opposition to the dominant culture, if only by keeping its autonomy from the pursuit of money—the only common value great writers from right to left have acknowledged—you begin to sense what we have lost. Capitalism as a system for the equitable distribution of goods is troublesome enough; as a way of measuring success it is useless. When you begin to think the advances doled out to writers by major corporations possess anything but an accidental correlation to artistic worth, you are finished. Everything becomes publicity. How many writers now refuse to be photographed? How many refuse to sit for idiotic "lifestyle" pieces? Or to write supplemental reading group "guides" for their paperbacks? Everyone along the chain of production compromises a tiny bit and suddenly Jay McInerney is a guest judge on *Iron Chef*.

Publicity is not everything; money, also. Émile Zola was so concerned that he would lose his position in French artistic circles because of his incredible popularity that he formulated an aesthetic theory to explain his art. As recently as 2001, Jonathan Franzen, worried lest *The Corrections* might seem to have fallen outside the main development of the American art novel, justified his work in aesthetic terms. (For doing so, for letting his guard down in public in tortured meditations on aesthetic value, Franzen has been made to pay, and pay again, by inferiors whose idea of good literature is German film.) Now writers simply point to their sales figures and accuse other writers of jealousy. Well, it's true. Everyone wants money, and needs it ("a woman must have money and a room of her own"). The only relevant question is what you are willing to do for it.

As for me and my $40,000, I recently went off contract at *New York* so I could finish a book of stories. My last article for the magazine, written as a freelancer, was about the New York Rangers. I received $7,000—a lot. Two weeks later I hurt my finger playing football on a muddy field in Prospect Park.

Sitting in New York Methodist, my finger worrisomely bent and swollen, I watched a man in scrubs yell into his cell phone: "One-point-two million! Yeah! We put down four hundred!" The doctor had bought a condo.

This was the hand surgeon. After glancing briefly at my X-rays, the hand surgeon declared I needed surgery.

"How about a splint?" I said.

"No way."

I decided to negotiate. "I can afford three thousand dollars," I said.

"I'm not a financial adviser."

"Well, how much will it be?"

"Seven thousand."

Ha ha. It was like an O. Henry story: I wrote the article, they fixed my finger.

Except it wasn't like that, because I declined the surgery and kept the money. At my current rate of spending, it will last me three months. That should be enough. I hope that's enough. +

T H E

T E A C H I N G

G A M E

# Teachers

Richard Yates, who wrote *Revolutionary Road*, was my teacher for my first year. He was pretty straitlaced, aside from his drinking problem; pretty old-fashioned in his values. He was very, very generous with writers whom he liked, and he was very adept at pointing out what was good. We would have these individual conferences, and I remember bringing him three stories. He said, "This one is crap and this one is crap, but this one—this is what you should be doing." The first two were pretentious and full of too much graduate school, which can be deadly for a writer. The third one was just a little modest story about Brooklyn when I was a kid and making model airplanes. I thought it was almost too easy to do that. But he convinced me that that was good writing, because the people were real and it wasn't about ideas, it was about people.

**Mark Dintenfass**

My first semester, [redacted] was doing a one-semester guest professorship. I was in her workshop and she and I did not get along. I mean, I wanted her to like me—she was rich and famous. But from the moment we met I really touched a nerve in her, so she was just killing everything I wrote and humiliating me in an angry way. And I was like, what is the deal? She responded by saying, "Well, you have to be able to take it because if you have millions of readers and sell millions of books and people are writing about you, newspapers and stuff . . ." and I was like, "Well that's you, you have to be able to take it because you're rich and famous. You're supposed to be my teacher!" So then she said I needed to write more about what I know.

**Eli S. Evans**

# Money (2014)
## Keith Gessen

And then I sold my book. I finished it, I sent it to my agent, and she sent it to publishers. It was fall 2006; the weather was nice. I was dating a Columbia grad student and spending a lot of time uptown. I remember, about a week after the book went out, sitting on the steps of the Cathedral of St. John the Divine, across the street from the Hungarian Pastry Shop, talking on my cell phone with my agent, Sarah Chalfant, as she ran through the offers. There were two good ones and a few bad ones. We decided to go with a good one, from Viking. At that point I had $1,000 in the bank, and was grateful for the free coffee refills at the Pastry Shop. The book sold for $160,000, and Sarah proceeded to sell translation rights for about as much again to European publishers. After discussing Viking's offer with her that day, I closed my phone, looked up at the Cathedral of St. John the Divine, then crossed the street and went back into the Pastry Shop, a rich man.

What was it like to be rich? It was fun. I paid for dinner a few times. I went to my college roommate's wedding in Brazil without worrying about it. It was as if a great stone—*economy*—that had lain

Keith Gessen

on my mind, dictating what I could and could not do, what stores or cafés I could or could not enter, had suddenly been removed. I remember leaving the *n+1* office late one night with my roommate and coeditor, Chad, and Anne, the grad student. We were in production, and Chad had been spending entire days proofreading. The office was on Chrystie Street, on the Lower East Side, and to get to our apartment in Brooklyn we'd have to take two trains, neither of which ran very often so late at night. It would take about an hour. Or we could take a cab, which would take ten minutes. But a cab would cost $15. We discussed it. "Chad is very, very tired," Anne summed up the arguments. "And Keith is rich!" We took the cab.

Almost exactly six years later, in fall 2012, I was again sitting outside, talking on my phone about a moneymaking proposition. Anne and I had broken up. I had been together with Emily, a writer, for nearly five years, and we'd been living together in Brooklyn for a year. We were broke. In fact a few weeks earlier we'd received a perplexed phone call from our Jamaican landlord saying that our rent check had bounced and his bank had charged him $50. It was a screw-up—we did, barely, have enough money for that month's rent, and had written the check from the wrong account. But it wasn't like the right account held $100,000: it held $3,000, minus that month's rent, now minus $50, and there was no money coming in. I sat talking on my phone on a bench next to the parking lot of a ShopRite off I-84 in Connecticut while Emily tried to keep her cat, Raffles, from running under a car.

How had I managed to squander all that money? Sometimes it seems unbelievable to me, something out of Dostoevsky; other times

188

Money (2014)

I can see pretty clearly how it happened. In the past five years I've translated two books and edited two others; the payments I received totaled
$8,250. It's certainly easier to translate or edit a book than to write
one—I could never have *written* four books in that many years—but it
still takes time. In those years I also wrote articles and book reviews for
several magazines, but not that many—about two or three a year. All
in all I made $100,000 from my journalism in the period between the
two phone calls. That, plus my book advances, minus commissions,
amounted to about $330,000 of pretax income over six years. This is
pretty good money for a thrifty male with no children, and going into
2011 I had a $60,000 nest egg in my checking account. I liked keeping
it there, where I could see it. Then two close friends got into financial
trouble and asked me to bail them out. I was liquid and I didn't really
think twice about it. Suddenly I was down to $10,000. And then $7,000.
And then $3,000. Then we bounced that rent check.

The person calling me with a financial proposition was an old
friend; years before, he had sublet his apartment to me for very little
money, allowing me to move to New York while I was still in graduate school. He was also one of my first editors, at *Dissent*. Now he was
the head of the creative writing department at a college near the city.
They had just learned that more students had enrolled in creative
writing classes than expected. The college could turn back some students but not this many; they wanted to hire an extra teacher to do
a fiction workshop. Today was Friday; the semester started Monday.
Would I be willing to teach a fiction workshop? They would pay me.
I had to create a syllabus; I had to meet every student for conference
every other week; I had to read and comment on their work. But I did
not have to attend departmental meetings, or any meetings. That
was the deal.

I had never wanted to teach. Part of it was that I'd been unhappy in college, and in grad school, and was glad to be out of reach of the university. Part of it was me teaching: I'm not friendly enough. And part of it was teaching writing: it seemed fraudulent, more fraudulent than other kinds of teaching, and bound up in a more fraught dynamic. Students don't take French or history classes because they want to become French or history professors; they take them because they want to learn about French and history. Whereas writing students take writing classes because they want to become writers—at least, I always did. In fact what I most wanted was to be told, by a writer, that I was myself a writer, that I had it. And so by teaching such a class, weren't you taking part in that deception, in the deception that all these students might become writers? And weren't you also forced, all the time, to lie to them, in effect, whether mildly or baldly, about their work?

In short, I had hoped to avoid it. But I looked now at our car parked in the ShopRite parking lot. It was a 1995 Honda Civic with more than 180,000 miles on it, and for the last hundred miles it had been making a funny noise. I looked at Emily, who was still working on her novel, the completion of which might or might not get us out of our financial rut. I had just completed a reporting trip for a magazine, during which I'd grown a dramatic beard, but it would be months before the article was finished and I got paid. I looked at our cat, Raffles, whose recent illnesses had drained the last of our resources. In the past six months I had written an introduction and given several paid lectures—on translation, long-form journalism, and the writing life—at universities. But it was barely enough, and I *still* didn't have health insurance. I said I'd be happy to teach a fiction workshop.

## Money (2014)

Later that day, as we were pulling into Emily's parents' driveway, the back left wheel collapsed. That's what the funny noise had been. About fifty miles after that, as we headed up 95 to New York, the hood of the car popped up, smashing the windshield and blocking my view as we pulled into the breakdown lane. I sold the car to the auto body shop we got towed to, and used the money to rent a car to drive us home to New York.

The college was small and bucolic, a thirty-minute train ride from the city through leafy Westchester County. It was a fifteen-minute walk through town to campus; on my first day and on subsequent days, I bought a bagel with veggie cream cheese for $2.99 at Bagel Town. The campus was on a hill, just like in *White Noise*, and so I tended to arrive at my office a little out of breath. The office was tiny, one desk and two chairs, and I split it with another creative writing teacher: she had it on Mondays and Tuesdays, I had it on Thursdays and Fridays. Still, it was nice to have an office. I checked my email there and prepared for class.

I had fifteen students, ranging from first-years to seniors. Some had taken workshops before, others had not. There would be, according to my reading of the class list, eleven girls and three boys, with one wild card (Mackenzie). But then it turned out that Logan and Sameer and Mackenzie were all girls, which made fourteen. At least Tyler was a boy. He was rail-thin and had green hair, but at least he was a boy. Not that it mattered. I could teach writing to anyone.

The first class did not go as well as I had hoped. My plan was to begin at the beginning. After briefly introducing myself and scheduling everyone's workshops for the semester, I asked the students to list their favorite authors. I wrote them on the board.

Aimee Bender
Michael Ondaatje
Carl Hiaasen
George R. R. Martin
Orson Scott Card (this was Tyler)

OK. Well, OK. I then asked the students to name some *old* writers they liked. Jane Austen, they said, and Tolstoy. That was more like it. My next question was this: Why write? Why—when there is so much writing in the world, so much great writing, some of it listed now on the board, and so much of it unread—would we continue to produce more?

I was hoping, I think, that someone would say, "You're right. There is no reason. This is hopeless." And then slowly, together, we would feel our way toward some arguments for why—maybe—a person could justify attempting to write. I figured it would take up most of the two hours.

In fact, no one even blinked. "Values have changed," said one student. "There is new technology," said another. "That's right. Cell phones. The internet." "We have a different vocabulary, new words." "You want to intervene in contemporary political debates," Tyler put in.

These were all correct answers. I just hadn't expected to get to them so quickly. I was reeling. I bought myself time by writing the answers on the board. But I didn't know what to say.

"It's a profound question," I concluded, lamely. "We'll keep thinking about it as the semester goes on."

Money (2014)

We moved to my next profound question: What do you know that no one else knows? My premise was that good writing depends on a kind of specialized knowledge—whether of some process, or some relationship, or some situation or event. If people would just tell us what actually happened! We would know so much; we would learn so much. Of Kafka's commitment to telling the whole truth about himself and his life, Elias Canetti wrote: "A human being who offers himself to knowledge so completely is, under any circumstances, an incomparable stroke of luck." We do not have to be Kafka—but we can at least tell one truth, or two, about our lives. As the editor of a literary magazine, I had read so many "stories"—fiction or nonfiction, it didn't matter. They were made-up, and the more made-up they were, the more conventional. Where truth was left out or kept general, cliché filled the void. The mistake made over and over was to search for the "universal," when (this is itself a cliché, maybe, but still) it was the specific stuff that readers wanted to know. But of course it's not so easy to figure out what the specific stuff is. One's life contains so many things; how are you to know which of these things is distinctive?

In some form, I put this question to the class, and the answers were again disappointing, though in a different way. The answers to the first question had come too quickly, like the class had been asked the question before. The answers to this question came too slowly, like the question made no sense to them, like they were hostile to it. "Experiences of culture," someone said. "Your childhood," someone else said. Eventually someone said: "Your family." (An answer that can be right or wrong. "My crazy Jewish family"—bad, because conventional. "My repressed Jewish family"—interesting.) But no one said something so simple as "What I did last weekend." Or "How I lost my virginity." Or: "Why I no longer speak to my former best friend."

"It's something we're going to keep thinking about as we go through the semester," I said again, hopefully. "It's okay to use your experiences in your fiction. Your life is interesting and contains drama. The trick is figuring out where the drama is and what it means." The stories I liked best, I said, were ones that made you think they were true, even though they might not be.

The first student I lost was a first-year who'd never been in a workshop before. She emailed me the day after class to ask if I would let her out. I wrote to her adviser and said that of course she could drop the class if she wanted, but she was also welcome to stay. "Thank you for being so understanding," the adviser replied. The student, he said, had been intimidated by the pace of the first class; she felt like she'd been air-dropped onto an alien planet.

Maybe I had plunged into things too quickly. But more experienced students were also thinking of leaving. One student dropped the class without explanation. Two others, a self-identified "magical realist" and an "experimenter with language," came to discuss with me the question of whether my approach—too realist, they said—was right for their particular unique styles of writing. "I've had a happy and normal life," one of them claimed. She didn't think she would have anything too interesting to write about if she had to write from her own experience.

I assured both the magical realist and the language experimenter that we could work together. I wasn't *prejudiced* against their styles of writing. All styles are great. Kafka was a magical realist! I said. Joyce was an experimenter with language! We could read those writers and learn from them together. And surely I had things to learn about their approaches. We could learn from each other, I said.

## Money (2014)

I was lying. In fact I had no idea what to say to these students. I had read their first exercises and they were not for me. They were obscure; rather than being less self-involved than traditional first-person writing, they were *more* self-involved. I should have said: "You are not ready to do this sort of work. You need first to figure out what you are trying to say to the world, and only then go about finding the means adequate to the saying. I can help you figure out the first thing. If you're not interested in that, this class will not be useful." But I didn't say that.* I didn't want to put my friend, who'd hired me, in a bad spot. He had brought me in because too many students were being rejected from the classes, but now students were rejecting me. What kind of teacher loses 25 percent of his students *after one class*?

The second class went better than the first. We discussed a terrific short story by Chris Kraus called "Trick," about a young woman who moves to New York to become an artist and ends up working as a stripper, and Philip Roth's "Goodbye, Columbus," which struck me as less interesting than I'd remembered it: certainly a very good long story, but formulaic. You wouldn't have known, necessarily, that this guy was going to write *Sabbath's Theater*. Maybe Roth didn't know, either. During the discussion, one of the students, Charlotte, made a brilliant observation about Brenda Patimkin: she has very bad vision, and yet in the first scene she jumps off the diving board,

---

* "And furthermore," I should have said, "Joyce and Kafka were realists, obviously. They were not fleeing experience—they were trying to describe it. And they especially did not do this because they had happy, uneventful lives—though Joyce at least was a happy person, through it all." Anyway, I didn't say this.

Keith Gessen

despite the fact that she might not be able to see the pool—that's how confident Brenda is that the pool will be there.

That second Friday, before class, I held my first conferences. Conferences last thirty minutes. That may not sound like much, but you'd be surprised. What is there to talk about? The students had written short exercises, but these were slim reeds on which to sustain a half-hour discussion. My first conference was with Mackenzie, a first-year from Wisconsin. She hadn't done much writing before. For the assignment—which was to describe something that only you knew about—she'd written about a visit from a boy to her house in the middle of the night. This was her secret, and not a very interesting one. But during conference it emerged that she'd grown up in a town of four thousand people. That her high school had three hundred students. That she'd worked at the Dairy Queen, which was owned by a scary Norwegian guy named Otto. In fact there were a lot of Norwegians in town. They had celebrations and Mackenzie, not herself a Norwegian, was left out. As she described all this, a whole social world appeared before our eyes in that small office. "Is this interesting to you?" I said. "Usually I think it's boring," she said. "But it's interesting to talk to someone who finds it interesting." I was feeling pretty good—a person who was not entirely a fraud—as Mackenzie left.

Then came Julie, the magical realist. I had been unable to make head or tail of her writing exercise. It appeared to be a ghost story of some kind, with the ghost possessing erotic potential. Did the narrator have sex with the ghost? This is what I wanted to know. But Julie wouldn't say. Magical realism was her thing. In fact, continued Julie, she had written a novel. Would I be willing to read it and discuss it with her in conference?

Well, I said. What about workshopping it in class?

"I want to workshop other things in class," said Julie.

196

Money (2014)

I was stumped. I hadn't expected this. The tuition at this college was very high—it regularly ranked as the most expensive college in America. So these students should get good service. On the other hand, I was just one person. A person who did not want to read Julie's novel. Not only did I not want to read it, I didn't *believe* in reading it. Who would benefit from this? Already she had read it with her previous semester's writing teacher. And now she was going to read it with me? She was going to drag this novel from class to class, from teacher to teacher—in hope of what? The whole point of a workshop was to put your work in front of your peers, to see what it feels like to have a readership, to see how they react. I said we'd see about the novel. In the meantime, I wanted Julie to consider that there is realism in magical realism. But I knew that a more experienced teacher would have handled all this better.

It was time for class. After class, I returned to my office for the next set of conferences, and there again was Julie. Had she forgotten something? No; she was holding an Add/Drop form. I signed the form. The conferences rolled on.

I met with Vanessa, my chattiest student—her chattiness was bad for class, but it was good for conference. The half hour flew by. Next up was Charlotte, who had made the penetrating remark about Brenda in "Goodbye, Columbus." Charlotte was working in the fantasy genre. This seemed to mark her as yet another student who had nothing to learn from me. And maybe that was true. But unlike the magical realist Julie and the language experimenter Leslie (who also dropped the class), Charlotte didn't think I was an idiot. She explained the ways in which her deployment of orcs and elves in her work differed from and even subverted the tropes of ordinary fantasy fiction. I didn't mind discussing all this, even as I found it surreal. These were the times we were living in. I was on a college campus. I was a visiting professor. And I was sitting in my office, bearded and wise-looking and, in all seriousness, discussing orcs.

We settled into the semester. There were, it soon emerged, three types of student in the workshop. There were three upperclassmen who had taken several workshops already. They were not necessarily the best writers in the class—not at all—but they were used to classroom discussion of literature, and brought to it some maturity and poise. There were some first-years who had done a lot of writing in high school and were genuinely talented. In fact one of them, Allison, was so talented I didn't know what to say to her. And then there was the rest of the class, music and theater majors for the most part, who had never done much writing. These turned out to be the students to whom I had the most to say, and who were the most eager to listen.

The question of criticism, and of lying to students about their work, continued to trouble me. I am by nature a critical person—but I know that people need positive reinforcement about their writing. I have always needed it, for example, and still need it today. So how critical should one be? The school was so expensive. It seemed to violate some law of capitalism that someone should pay so much to attend a college and then be told that her work is no good.

My first encounter with this, after the departure of the experimental faction, was with Logan. She was a jazz-singing major; she hadn't done much writing before. Her first exercise was an unpromising and brief account of her parents' divorce, told mostly in cliché. Then, nervous about the story she was going to hand in for workshop, Logan sent it to me in advance. It was a highly conventional story about a girl who lives alone in Manhattan (on what money?!), goes to a museum, meets a boy, and then goes home with him. They stay up the whole night talking. They don't even sleep together.

I did not know what to do. I had no suggestions for how to improve the story. And it wasn't the world's worst story. I just knew that I found it boring, and not just because they didn't sleep together.

I told Logan, as gently as I could but probably not gently enough, to try something else. There had been a hint, I thought, in one of her exercises, of a slightly angrier person than the one she was presenting in this story. During conference I suggested that this would be interesting to hear more about; her anger at one of her friends, who treated her badly. With examples. Logan nodded and left conference. Then I didn't hear from her. I spent several days worrying that I'd shut her down entirely, that by rejecting her first story attempt I'd rendered her unable to write. Finally she handed in her story: it was a funny and angry monologue about her Mexican grandmother, a model and a man-eater. It wasn't a masterpiece but it was entertaining and new. The class liked it. I liked it.

The low point of the semester may have been the workshop of Carrie's first story. Carrie was one of my talented first-years. She was also a devout Christian who had missed class—very apologetically—to go on a retreat with fellow students. She wrote several exercises about her Korean family in San Diego—sharp, observant, funny, very sweet. But for her workshopped story she'd decided to write about teenage Japanese prostitutes. Why?! Carrie wasn't even Japanese! I spent the days before class thinking about what to say. Then it came time for workshop. The students, it turned out, loved the story. Charlotte said that she had cried at the end. When they were done praising it I mumbled a few elliptically derogatory remarks. Carrie looked pained—less for herself, I thought, than for me. The students left class thinking that I was not only a fraud, but also an asshole who had no sympathy for Japanese girls who'd decided to sell their bodies for a few extra yen.

Objectively speaking, the classes were getting better. We read and discussed George Saunders's "Sea Oak"; an excerpt from Sheila Heti's *How Should a Person Be?*; several stories by Ludmilla Petrushevskaya; a section of *The Corrections*; and Curtis White's great story "Combat" from *Memories of My Father Watching TV*, to name the most popular pieces. In addition to workshop stories, I assigned exercises to be discussed during conference, and some of these turned out really well. An exercise for which the students simply recorded a conversation they had and transcribed it yielded a series of extraordinary transcripts. (The follow-up exercise, to create a short narrative around the transcript, was less successful.) Still, I could not shake the feeling that the whole thing was a sham. The fact that students had to pay so much to attend school; the entire process of teaching writing; and most of all, me. I was a fake. Tyler, who in his understated, green-haired way had emerged as one of the more thoughtful students in the class—at the end of a discussion he would ask, "Why did you assign this story? Do *you* like it?"—always pulled up his chair to face mine when he came for conference. One day he pulled it up and asked, quietly, what sort of fiction I wrote. I admitted I'd only written one book of fiction—and not very recently, at that. Tyler took this in stride, but what was I doing? What did I know about fiction? I knew more than my students. That didn't seem like enough.

Still, it was a pretty good way to make a living. It took me two full days to prepare for class—and I learned quickly that the more I prepared, the better the class—but that was because I'd never taught before; the syllabus I was developing could be used again, and I'd only get better at discussing those stories and novel excerpts. I wrote years ago, in the predecessor to this essay, that the problem with teaching writing was that the writer spent his time hanging out with children, but it was fun to hang out with these kids. They came from all over the country, and I could see glimpses of what they would, or could, become. And as they began to write more along the lines that I was encouraging, I learned more about them, and it was interesting. It was genuinely interesting.

I'll say another thing for the job: it was nice to have a job. I'd spent fifteen years—too long—as a freelance writer. I was the (unpaid) editor of a magazine few people had heard of, and though I wrote articles for much larger magazines, which people *had* heard of, I did this irregularly. I did not go into an office or draw a salary. Much of the time, when someone asked what I was working on, I didn't have anything substantial to say. I was always working on this or that; I was always working. But it felt precarious. It was precarious.

About halfway through the semester, I had drinks with friends from college. We saw each other about once a year. Two of them had gone into finance; two had gone into law. All of them earned a fair amount of money and owned their homes. I, meanwhile, always had little to show for what I'd done. This time around, however, I was a college professor. I was teaching students. We met on a Friday, and I came straight from Grand Central, in my suit.

I felt like a person. I wasn't making very much money, but I was only teaching one class. A full course load would be four classes; if you multiplied my salary by four, you'd have a decent salary. Plus benefits. Plus you got to hang out with kids all day—and talk about fiction. I never entirely shook the sense of my personal fraudulence as a teacher of fiction, but the enterprise of teaching fiction began to seem a little less ridiculous as the semester went on. It wasn't something "real," something applicable, it wasn't math—but it's not as if I daily apply the math I learned in high school, or even remember it. And learning fiction may not be difficult in the way that, for example, learning critical theory can be difficult—but, looking back on the critical theory I studied in college, what a lot of mumbo jumbo! Very few of my professors were equipped to present it in an accessible way, free of incomprehensible terminology (and ideology). At least my students were studying actual literature. And after we read the opening section of *The Corrections*, and the students didn't seem as familiar as I'd expected with the theory that Chip spouts while standing in the street with his sister Denise—"I'm saying that I personally am losing the battle with a commercialized, medicalized, totalitarian modernity right this instant"—we read Foucault's "What Is an Author?," which was lots of fun.

I even began to feel, in a way I'd never felt as a student, that the old saw about how you can't teach writing was possibly untrue. My attempts to teach grammar failed; no matter how many times I put various examples of speech attribution on the board, showing when to capitalize *He said* and when not to, the next set of stories would feature the same mistakes. Nor was I able to do much for Allison, my most talented student. After reading a few of her exercises, in which the use of figurative language was nothing short of astonishing, I became convinced that there was very little about writing that she could learn from me. Perhaps I could give her some books to read? For conference I suggested we go to the library—where it turned out that she had, in fact, already read everything. Of course she had; you don't just wake up one morning writing like that. But what did happen, as the semester progressed, was that the students began to write more about their own lives, to find the interest, the drama, in their own lives. Not the things that were obviously dramatic—family illness, divorce, death, et cetera—but the little things that made life interesting, and specific, and unlike the lives of others. Whether this holds up as a theory of fiction more generally, I don't know. I do know that it made the stories interesting to *me*.

So what's the problem?

There's no problem. For the most part, I liked my students; I liked going in to talk to them about fiction; I usually felt I could be honest with them. When I could not be honest, I enjoyed meeting up with my friend and supervisor to complain—mostly about the dismissive things students had said about works of fiction I really liked. I loved getting up in the morning, dressing, and catching a train from Grand Central. I loved having access to a decent university library. As I learned when I returned a DVD a week late, faculty don't pay fines.

I did sometimes think of what a publishing executive said to me when I came to the realization that a book editor had to perform two very separate functions—an editorial function and a sales function; the shaping of a manuscript and the convincing of other people to read it—and that an aptitude for both was probably quite rare. Weren't these actually two separate jobs?

"Yes," said the publishing executive. "But it's more convenient when they're combined in one person."

It's more convenient for a writing teacher to be both a writer and a teacher—but these are separate things. I was an okay teacher; I did my best. But someone who had trained to be a teacher would have done a better job. And when you are teaching it is not easy to be a writer. I had written the bulk of the magazine article for which I'd traveled over the summer before the semester began, but the issue it was in closed near the end of the semester. During the final week and a half of closing, you go through fact-checking, which amounts to a full-time job, and also last-minute editing, which adds to that. Usually I just stay on the phone for five or six straight days. But this time around I was busy: I had my students' stories to read and mark up and prepare. I did less for the fact-checkers than I would have liked, and they noticed. One Friday after class I found a rare voice message on my phone; it was from the head of the magazine's fact-checking department, and he was not happy. Meanwhile, I went back to being the lousy teacher I had been at the beginning of the semester. How some people manage to do a lot of writing while also teaching well is, frankly, beyond me.

If the students noticed that I was slacking off, they didn't show any sign. A lot of them were leaving a day early for break, and so would be missing the last class. As a result, there were only six of us at the end. And we had to workshop four stories. We ran through them quickly, too quickly, and then held our final conferences. Mackenzie, from Wisconsin, had been through a lot in her first semester—a love affair, a class in film history that made a deep impression on her—and she was going to be taking the train home to Wisconsin with some of the books we hadn't gotten a chance to read. Logan, the jazz singer, had learned that anger could be a positive element in art. Carrie had forgiven me for my comments on her Japanese teen prostitutes story and written her next story about her family. "Will I ever see you again?" she asked after her last conference. I didn't know! Charlotte did not stop writing about orcs, but she did start trying to inject some real-world details into her fantasy stories. Some of her exercises—nonfantasy—were terrific.

Money (2014)

Allison, my best student, had the last conference of the semester. She asked me, very humbly, the question I had carried around unceasingly my first year of college, and especially during my first writing class. I'd wanted to know if I was a writer. When my first writing teacher said, "Yes, you're definitely a writer," I thought I'd won the lottery. I relaxed. It wasn't my teacher's fault, but it probably cost me a couple of years, years I should have spent working and developing, instead of basking in the fact that someone had acknowledged me.

Allison asked the question more gently: Did I think she could someday be published?

The answer to me was obviously yes. She could probably be published tomorrow. But I tried to be careful. I told Allison she was extraordinarily talented, and that I really looked forward to reading what she wrote. But I also said that whether or not you became a writer, in the end, depended on a lot more than talent. Many talented people I knew in college decided to pursue other things—they became academics, or screenwriters, or rabbis. Being a writer required you to make the decision, over and over and over again, to write. No one would care if you stopped doing it, even if they noticed. So there would be many moments in the future at which to decide to stop; or to decide not to stop, and to keep going.

With that, the semester ended. The students went back, by bus, train, and plane, to Michigan, Wisconsin, Texas, North Carolina, Colorado, and California. I cleaned out my desk; returned my library books; and caught the 8:22 back to Grand Central, and from there to Brooklyn. +

# Teachers

What was really important for me was running into Gordon Lish. He took my head out of theory and put my nose into my sentences, really changed everything. I learned the theory of hydrology from the other courses, and then I got a plumbing degree from Lish—how to fix your pipes. Still, I'm as happy to have gotten away from him as I was to have found him. He's a pill, a problem guy. But he gave me the permission to treat my prose like I was treating my poetry.

Lish's workshop met once a week, and there were maybe 120 people in his class. Instead of being theoretical, it was all, What does this sentence sound like? How to create a voice, and to get authority of voice by "saying it wrong"—what he called "burnt tongue." It's a way of writing as if you were speaking, of making your prose sound raw or strange or off or wrong or weird. Basically of fucking up your syntax.

In Lish's class, you read aloud. You started your piece, and if he didn't like a sentence he stopped you and criticized you and you couldn't read any more. So he would follow your first sentence, how it moved to the second sentence, how it moved to the third sentence, and as soon as any sentence didn't work, you had to shut up and he would criticize you. It was tough going to his class. There was a lot of tension in the room, because of his personality. He had no qualms about making you feel like a fool. "Oh, no, no, that's enough, you're way off line there. Next!"

There were these two women who were very good friends, and for six weeks he would say, "Oh, Mary, Mary, you're really, really great, that's a great story, you're fantastic." And then he'd turn to Mary's friend Joan right next to her and say, "Joan, what's wrong with you? How come you're not writing like Mary?" Then, halfway through the semester, Joan would start reading and he'd say "Oh, Joan, Joan, Joan, fantastic," and, "Mary, you're losing your grip." People wanted to throw themselves out the window. It was just sick, sick shit. So I got myself out of there.

Who knows why he acted that way? There's all kinds of ways that people try to figure Lish out. My feeling is he just wanted that control. Threatening to take away his approval was a way of having a hold on people. You're a writer and coming up in the world, and here's this guy who calls himself Captain Fiction. He was Raymond Carver's editor—everybody wanted to be Raymond Carver at the time—he had been the fiction editor at *Esquire*, he was an editor at Knopf, he had his own literary magazine, *The Quarterly*. And so here was this guy who was, like, It, and you got to meet him. Wow, he's talking to me, he's going to read my stuff. Wow, he's commenting on my stuff, wow, he likes me! Uh oh . . . Now he doesn't like me . . . You know? It's just natural.

He did have a magnetism though, and a lot of power. He told me that he was going to publish my first book, *Faraway Places*. He called me up on the phone, and he knew I was gay, so he made a big deal of himself being in the bathtub. Like, "I am in the bathtub naked, Tom, talking to you, and I am going to buy your book." It was pretty icky. "We're going to publish this fucker, Spanbauer, we're going to publish this fucker. I've really got a hard-on for ya." He's a culprit and a manipulator.

I know it sounds like all I'm doing is dissing Lish. He's a prick for sure, but he did something very particular for me. He gave me the permission to do something that I wouldn't have got from anywhere else, and I have to be thankful for him.

**Tom Spanbauer**

# Seduce the Whole World
## Carla Blumenkranz

Todd Solondz's *Storytelling* famously features an encounter between a
writing instructor and a college student. He has just eviscerated both
her and her boyfriend's work, calling the boyfriend's story "a piece
of shit." When she sees him at a bar, she claims that she agrees with
him, she's "really happy with the class," and she's "a great admirer
of [his] work." He says almost nothing. So she asks, "Do you think I
have potential as a writer?" "No," he says.

In the next scene she follows him, with obvious terror, to his
apartment. In the bathroom she finds an envelope that contains
nude photos of the student he says has talent. He tells her to take
off her clothes and, in the one note of complexity that enters the
story, is able to dominate her partly by exploiting her fear that she
may be latently racist. (She's white and he's black.) His other tool of
domination is the workshop dynamic. Despite having told her she's
hopeless as a writer, here he's willing to be prescriptive.

Predictably (the script itself is self-consciously modeled on a
"workshop story," with carefully articulated motivations and a neatly
turned ending) she reads aloud in class a fictional account of what

she describes as rape. The student whose photos she found says the story is dishonest. "Jane pretends to be horrified by the sexuality she in fact fetishizes." The instructor agrees. "Jane wants more, but isn't honest enough to admit it." Still, he says, this story is better than her last one. "There's now at least a beginning, a middle, and an end."

Solondz has written a workshop story in more than one respect. The first rule of writing about workshop is that there should be some sex. One student should be sleeping with another or with an instructor or ideally both. How could a story get by with characters who only want to write fiction? Some other desire has to intervene to make it interesting.

Theresa Rebeck's play *Seminar* revolves around a famous instructor who, for a substantial price, agrees to lead a workshop for four young writers. The instructor, Leonard, is charismatic, demanding, and not only seduces one of the women but incessantly talks to all of them, men and women, about sex. As soon as the play appeared, in New York in 2011, critics made the connection between the Leonard character and the highly influential, erotically fixated longtime writing teacher Gordon Lish. Like Lish, Leonard evaluates his students' writing after having heard a single sentence, and does so almost entirely in terms of its capacity to seduce. The one story he praises, written by the young woman he goes to bed with, has "a lightness, a touch, a sexual edge to the language which is I got to say, it got me on board. Va voom."

Rebeck doesn't appear to have taken one of Lish's classes (if she had, she could probably recall a more articulate response than "va voom"), but basically she knows the score. Lish—who taught and edited young writers from the 1970s through the '90s, editing fiction at *Esquire* and Knopf and teaching at universities and private apartments—asked students to write to seduce him, and when female students succeeded he often took them to bed. Once he became an

editor at Knopf he often bought his students' work as well, sometimes midsemester and sometimes, or so it seemed, midclass. So in
two ways his workshop extended beyond the established boundaries
of the classroom: if he really liked what you were doing, he might
sleep with you, or he might publish your book.

Lish figured out how he wanted to run his workshop when he started
teaching undergraduates at Yale in the early 1970s. He had just
turned forty and had earned a reputation as a dynamic young fiction
editor. One afternoon a week, he came from the Manhattan *Esquire*
office full of a sense of power. He asked each student to read from
her work but stopped her as soon as he lost interest; usually this was
before she finished the first sentence. Then he took advantage of the
silence to describe, in intensely eloquent monologues that could
last hours, how to write work he would want to hear read aloud.
"Remember, in reaching through your writing to a reader, you are
engaged in nothing so much as an act of seduction," former student
Tetman Callis recalls him saying. "Seduce the whole fucking world
for all time."

Lish's willingness to be bored and show it was one of his strengths
as an instructor. He created a situation in which each student had to
approach him, like a stranger at a party or a bar, to see if she could
catch his attention. Lish shot down these nervous suitors one by
one, not even bothering to hear out the pickup lines they fretted
over. Then he shifted in an instant to a masculine role: talking endlessly, enacting his charisma, awing his listeners into submission.

David Leavitt was one of the Yale undergraduates who took an
early Lish workshop. Around that time Leavitt wrote his great story
"Territory," which appeared in *The New Yorker* and then in many anthol-

ogies, forever marking him as having been a precocious writer. Leavitt later wrote a novel, *Martin Bauman*, about this period of precocity. His descriptions of the Lish character, Flint, show how eros, writerly ambition, and the writing teacher get bound up together:

> I suppose now that I was a little in love with Flint. And why shouldn't I have been? He was a good-looking man, lean and surly, with hands like broken-in leather gloves. Nor did his reputation as a womanizer in any way detract from the effect he had on me. On the contrary, it served only to intensify my idea of him as an avatar of masculine virility. For what I wanted from Flint, I told myself, wasn't so much sex as permission—to write, to think of myself as a writer. Today I recognize the degree to which this need for approbation encoded a desire I had heretofore never admitted: the desire for men—and more specifically, for older, fatherly men who didn't desire me.

Lish, always a troublesome employee, was fired from *Esquire* in the late 1970s; the same thing happened at Yale in 1980. By then he had become an editor at Knopf, where within the next few years he would publish Raymond Carver's *What We Talk About When We Talk About Love*, Barry Hannah's *Airships*, and Mary Robison's *Days*. He became the man who made experimental fiction (only later did it come to be called literary minimalism), and it no longer mattered what anyone thought of him.

After leaving Yale, Lish started teaching a class at Columbia for adult students. He taught in the continuing education program, which meant the class was open to anyone who was accepted and willing to pay for it. These students came to class knowing how he taught and how he wanted them to write, and they wanted to meet his expectations. In this environment, Lish became more than a demanding teacher—he made himself into a guru of fiction. His classes went from three hours, as had been the case at Yale, to five or more. He developed an eccentric outfit he wore to class, composed of a cowboy hat, khaki shirt and pants, and gleaming leather boots. The novelist Lily Tuck, who has written about being his student, thought he bore "more than a passing resemblance to Steve McQueen."

His waxing power at Knopf added a new charge to the classroom. In early 1983, Anderson Ferrell, a former Broadway dancer, "read two paragraphs he had written about a tobacco farm in North Carolina, near the place where he was raised," Lish's longtime student Amy Hempel later wrote in an article for *Vanity Fair*. "Lish found the work so good as to be 'disabling.' The next morning Ferrell had a contract with Knopf." Lish had never signed up a student, and as word spread he wrote to Hempel (who hadn't been in class lately) to ask if she was hurt. She claimed not to be, but at that moment the rules of the workshop had changed.

Lish told his students to seduce the world, but in practice they wrote to seduce him, and he became adept at playing them off one another in order to maximize their interest. From one session to the next, he knocked down students he had praised, always in the strongest terms. Lish himself was an expert seducer: he worked hard to make his students want to please him, and to make their literary and erotic motivations impossible to extricate from each other. Here is how Callis recalled his "show, don't tell" lecture:

> It's just like sex—you don't say, "OK, now I'm going to lean in and kiss you on the mouth, and my mouth is going to be open so I hope yours is too, and I'll touch my tongue lightly to your lips, then kiss your closed

eyes, and, oh, while I'm doing this, I'll reach one arm around you, brushing your nipple and breast as I move to pull you closer, and while I'm doing all this, you'll shift in your seat and reach one hand between my legs . . ." Sounds like great fun, but you don't say it, you just do it.

We are not supposed to want to sleep with our instructors (or our students), but it happens in fiction and in fact, and very often the appearance of erotic desire makes us produce better work. A charismatic instructor suggests that students could seduce him with a great story, and a confident student plays up her own charisma, in class and on the page, to hold his attention. Neither may have any intention of breaking the rules, but the idea of breaking them is attractive, and to really write for someone you have to want to do more for him than turn in ten pages by the end of the day Friday.

So the best instructors learn to cultivate and deflect the interest of their students, and the most attentive students are able to play along, to everyone's satisfaction. Both teachers and students create the possibility of seduction in the workshop, as a way of heightening its potential, but most often an understanding is maintained that nothing may happen between them. The workshop, like the psychoanalytic session, is meant to be a space where seduction is rehearsed but specifically not enacted. Actual sex is forbidden—but the most successful workshops (and classes in general) are the ones most charged with erotic potential.

Some straight male teachers can produce this kind of spark with male students, some gay male teachers with women, and so on, but most often we're best at drawing others out when we feel real erotic potential: not in a situation of sexual solidarity but of sexual tension. A male teacher working with a young female student is the most familiar, most common, and not the least compelling situation. It combines the archetypally masculine narrative of striving to surpass a father figure with the more ambivalent feminine one of obtaining an older lover. The student may surpass her instructor as an artist, and as she does so she may bring him various kinds of pleasure. This makes for a complicated narrative in which coming into power is not necessarily an escape from domination; it can also be a deeper and more rewarding form of complicity with it.

What's particular about a writing workshop is that another kind of desire is omnipresent: the desire to become known, viable, famous, great. In other words, to publish. In most workshops, the expression of this desire is forbidden too: of course you're supposed to want to have sex, and to publish your work, but you're not supposed to weigh down the workshop with the messy specifics of either. In workshop, this second taboo often takes the form of a strict emphasis on "craft" and "art": you are simply there to write, and the less pure world of publishing can be entered later, if at all.

Lish is now best known for the work he did in the late 1970s and early '80s with Raymond Carver. For cutting most of Carver's best-known stories to half their intended length, turning a deeply traditional writer into a groundbreaking minimalist, he is remembered as one of the most controlling editors on record. But the more characteristic story of Lish as an editor and teacher is not a battle of wills, as was his work with Carver. Rather, it's an emotionally fraught collaboration with a most likely female student.

What was it like to begin his workshop? It was, for one thing, to enter an extreme imbalance of power. Each student came to the class willing to remain still and silent for hours on end, to read her work when called upon but be cut off without protest, and eventually in the private classes to pay thousands of dollars for twelve sessions. She agreed to this in return for the privilege of learning to please Lish and getting several chances to please him; because of his extraordinary combination of personal authority and editorial power, most students probably understood "please Lish" as having the same meaning as "produce literature."

At the first class Lish established just how much he would demand of his students. He started at least one term at Columbia by asking them to tell their most shameful secret, "the ineffable, the despicable, the thing you will never live down," as Hempel wrote in *Vanity Fair*. One student admitted to having run someone over; another may have for the first time come out of the closet. When the exercise was over, Lish smiled. "Did I say," he asked, "that this secret doesn't have to be true?"

Hempel said that this exercise set the stakes of the workshop: students would have to give everything they had to even attempt to please him. It also set the terms: Lish wanted students to approach him from a position of complete vulnerability. The effort to satisfy Lish would be about more than literature—it would be personal. Pleasing him would not only affirm their worth as writers but put them back on tolerable footing with him as human beings.

How did Lish tell his students to do this? By using their vulnerability to perform a feminine seduction. Like all writing instructors, Lish told his students they must have authority over their material, Lily Tuck wrote. But authority for a writer "is not just possessing what you speak but being possessed by it." A writer maximized her authority by choosing a subject she knew intimately and that made her feel helpless. "The best writers are those who put themselves at risk—first destabilize yourself, then restore yourself," Lish said. How did they restore themselves? By dramatizing their confessions in a way that commanded attention: that was tense, taut, and confident, that had the feeling of an emotional striptease about it. "Mystery is at the very center of what engages the fictional transaction," Callis recalls Lish saying. "Writing is not about telling; it is about showing, and not showing everything."

There was an archetypal student for whom this approach worked best. She was a woman, and most likely an attractive woman with some confidence, who intuitively understood the tactics Lish described, and was able to translate them from life to the page. She felt some uncertainty about the direction of her life but had real financial security—a young woman from a wealthy family, or a middle-aged one who regretted giving up work for her family—and this combination allowed her to commit totally to the workshop. Like most of us, she possessed a reserve of personal trauma, which she could have explored as easily in therapy as in workshop. But she was in workshop, which meant that she would dramatize her reckoning in tense and enticing sentences. Simply coming to terms with the more difficult facts of her life would not be enough; she would have to come to terms with them in a way that made her vulnerable, attractive, compelling. Within this framework, Lish became, in various combinations, teacher, analyst, correspondent, editor, lover, and publisher.

This method helped to produce any number of books, among them Amy Hempel's *Reasons to Live* (1985), Yannick Murphy's *Stories in Another Language* (1987), Sheila Kohler's *The Perfect Place* (1989), Diane Williams's *This Is About the Body, the Mind, the Soul, the World, Time, and Fate* (1990), Noy Holland's *The Spectacle of the Body* (1994),* Dawn Raffel's *In the Year of Long Division* (1995), and Christine Schutt's *Nightwork* (1996). One difficulty with the method was that it only really worked once.

---

* Holland starred in what may have been the most remarkable Lish workshop. She brought to class an eighty-page novella, "Orbit," that so entranced Lish he allowed her to read it from start to finish.

Most of us have only so many secrets, and after a certain point we lose interest in telling them. The Lish workshops produced many good first stories, and many good first books, but they have been less successful at launching careers. Those who have persisted have made clear in the transformation of their work that they are drawing on different resources.

What does it sound like when many writers are appealing to one person—and that person fundamentally understands writing as seduction? The results are more different than they are alike, but they sometimes have a goofy brazenness that feels like it's aimed at a shared target.

Holland, "Absolution":

> Me and him, we're lovers. Sure, I know he's a crazy motherfucker. And I'm the Banana Queen of Opelousas.

Williams, "My Highest Mental Achievement":

> Baby, I will miss you with your common sense, and with your blindness to psychology. My prediction for you is that you will have a fascinating life and that you will stay eternally young, and that you will never lack for love. I am interested in all aspects of you.

Hempel, "Housewife":

> She would always sleep with her husband and with another man in the course of the same day, and then the rest of the day, for whatever

was left to her of that day, she would exploit by incanting, "French film, French film."

When I read Diane Williams's best stories I feel, as she must have when she completed them, exuberant. One complicated aspect of learning to write to seduce is that for many women it was a form of empowerment. Williams was a suburban Chicago housewife, a former editor, and a dissatisfied amateur writer when she traveled to take one of his classes. She was looking for something to change her life, and this was it: within a few years she had moved to New York, where she became a professional writer and teacher and founded the literary magazine *NOON*.

In an interview with *The Review of Contemporary Fiction*, Williams said, "I studied with Gordon for two semesters in New York because I understood what he was offering—the special chance to become hugely conscious of how language can be manipulated to produce maximum effects." For her, language became a source not only of literary but of real personal authority. "So often, in our naturally powerful speech, we only understand dimly how we are doing it, so that we are deprived of the good fortune of being in charge of it, rather than the other way around."

By the mid-1980s Lish was completely engaged with cultivating new writers, to the point where the actual work of publishing books came to seem a distraction. So he threatened to quit unless he was, like editors at a few other publishing houses, given his own literary magazine to edit. Random House (of which Knopf is a division) assented, and so *The Quarterly: The Magazine of New American Writing* was founded. From the start, it served as the publishing arm of

Carla Blumenkranz

Lish's fiction program, and his career rose and, before long, fell with it.

The first issue of *The Quarterly* opened with a new story by Hempel, "The Harvest," which would become the standout story in her next collection. The rest was filed with the work of Lish students, among them Peter Christopher, Nancy Lemann, Yannick Murphy, and Janet Kauffman, all of whom would eventually publish books at Knopf. Only about half their contributions, however, were presented as finished, titled stories; the rest, usually shorter pieces, were always called "To Q." These were mostly works in progress that a student had brought to class or simply sent to Lish. Lish, of course, was Q.

During this time, Lish was as powerful as he would ever be. Journalists wrote feature stories about New York's most powerful and charismatic fiction editor. *Esquire* printed an elaborate chart of the publishing industry that placed its former editor at the "red hot center." As soon as the great claims were made, however, the backlash started, and was compounded by Lish's having produced compilations of his work in the form of *The Quarterly*. The patterns across his students' work were easy to point out, and what made them seem contemporary when considered separately suddenly came across as a weakness. Critics began to speak about the School of Gordon Lish—meaning both the classes and the work itself—probably most perceptively Sven Birkerts, in his article of that title, which appeared in *The New Republic* soon before the founding of *The Quarterly*. After surveying the works of Ferrell, Hempel, and several others, Birkerts wrote,

> The writers are, as I say, outwardly various enough. But from a
> certain angle, taking a tight noon-hour squint, one can discern a
> common style. It is all very modern, or postmodern. The byte-sized

perceptions, set in an eternal present, are the natural effluence of
an electronically connected, stimulus-saturated culture. In a sense,
they are what we have earned for ourselves: these writers may satisfy
themselves that they have, intentionally or not, mirrored our world
to us, mimicked the sensations of contemporary experience. Still,
in another sense, their work represents an abrogation of literary
responsibility.

Birkerts, as usual, was astute—and as usual, he channeled his critique through his preoccupation with technological change. But there's another way to read this "common style" that's less electronic than erotic. To call a piece of fiction "To Q" is to understand story as seduction, and fiction-writing as love letter to a particular person. Perhaps it is. Or perhaps this can be, at least, an extremely useful way of thinking. If fiction is about possibility, then the best workshop is the one in which anything seems possible, and the best teacher is the one who makes everything seem possible, sex and love and literary fame not excluded.

But to call a hundred stories "To Q" is something different. Instead of possibility, there is only Q—a kind of constant to be solved for. A teacher, an editor, even a lover isn't supposed to become the world, but rather to point the writer toward it. +

# Application

## Diana Wagman

---

**1. Please describe your previous place of employment.**

---

It was lovely. Gray clapboard buildings trimmed in white. Big trees
and crickets chirping. As if a film producer had found the perfect
small-college location for an exclusive low-residency MFA program
in creative writing. You could practically smell the metaphors flow-
ering in the hot summer air.

I arrived from Los Angeles, a new fiction instructor, so nervous I
was sick to my stomach. I had never attended a beautiful school like
this, but here I was teaching at one of the most acclaimed writing
programs in the country. Before this I'd been holding a novel-writ-
ing class in my home for a piano teacher, a Disney accountant, and
two retired government workers. And I'd been teaching part time
at a state university, not a University of California school but a CSU,
the blue-collar brother of the system. Everybody who applied was
accepted, unless currently incarcerated. My classes, CRW 303 and
CRW 403, beginning and intermediate creative writing, each contained twenty-five students, many of whom spoke English as a sec-

ond language. I was tired of being an adjunct, getting stuck with the worst classes, sharing a desk with three other teachers, carrying my materials in a cardboard box in the back of my car, always wondering whether I would have a job next semester. The teachers I worked with hadn't written anything in twenty years. I admit it, I wanted colleagues I could admire and learn from and who could help me get to Bread Loaf, or at least AWP. I wanted, badly, to belong.

I'd missed the email about the shuttle bus, so a $65 cab dropped me at the picturesque stone gates. I dragged my suitcase through campus searching for the WELCOME sign. Already I felt lost and unprepared—a feeling that would only grow over the next ten days. The humidity was making me sweat.

Finally I saw a cluster of what had to be MFA students. All fortyish women, all wearing flowing skirts and those walking sandals. Each carried a tote bag that held, I was sure, a healthy snack, a volume of poetry or short stories, and an artisan-made journal to collect their best thoughts.

"Hi," I said. "Are you here for the MFA?" They nodded yes, eyed me up and down. My jeans were too tight, my shirt cut too low, my heels too high. "Can you tell me where to find the office?"

These women were a far cry from my overweight Latino under-grads in Target jeans. Their sandals looked new and expensive. One was probably a lawyer, another the head of an NGO, another a shrink. These women had money and time to explore their creative sides. I was worrying about my sixty-five bucks. The sweat trickled down my temples, collected between my breasts. I could feel my hair frizzing.

"What's your discipline?" one of them asked.

"I'm a fiction instructor. I'm Diana," I said, then added, "Wagman."

Application

"Oh right," another responded. "You're the screenwriter."

It was the first time *the screenwriter* was said to me in that disparaging tone, but it would not be the last.

Fucking MFA programs. The students were arrogant because they had been accepted by this fancy program. They were also desperate to believe they had done the right thing—that being there would help them, change them, save them in some way. That very first evening, in the introductory meeting, I could smell it: the students' raw desire, overpowering my own.

## 2. What position did you hold?

Bent over, grabbing my ankles. The students paid their money and even if they sucked they could stay. My position was more tenuous. Would the students like me? More importantly—much more importantly—would the faculty?

I was on probation, auditioning for a permanent job. The director told me that being asked back right away was rare. He rotated instructors, he said, serving up a fresh salad of teachers for each residency, but at that first meeting it was obvious most of the faculty had been regurgitated from the time before and the time before that. They hugged and kissed one another and shot furtive glances at me and the other new recruit, a large, hairy man. I smiled. I needed this, not just for my career but to pay the bills.

The low-residency MFA system works like this: For ten days twice a year, usually in January and July, students and faculty gather on campus. There are seminars, lectures, readings, workshops: constant activities. It's meaningful. It's intense. Every day someone is moved to tears. The students stay in the dorms, and since their average age is thirty-six and most are women away from their kids and husbands for the first time, it's not exactly like you remember summer camp—way more alcohol is involved.

During the session, each student is assigned a faculty mentor for the ensuing months. After the session, everybody returns to his or her regular life and career—including the faculty, most of whom also teach in traditional MFA programs—and mentors work one-on-one with their students via email. Low-res is perfect for people who work a full-time job, or have a family, and can't take two years off to go back to college. And communicating one-on-one, even via email, amounts to a private tutorial with an established writer. It's a new model, but it seems medieval, in the best way—the scholar hired to teach one student, the computer acting as the tower room filled with books and a globe and tapestries. The student-teacher combo has the freedom to digress, to wander down an idiosyncratic, unforeseen path—something that can't happen in a class of twenty-five, or even of ten.

This pattern repeats, with different mentors each session, for two years, and then the students graduate. So far, so good: no wonder low-res programs have grown. The first was established in 1976, at Goddard College in Vermont, but by the early 1990s there were still fewer than a handful. Now there are fifty-one.

From the university's perspective, the economics are fantastic—they use facilities like classrooms and dormitories to generate revenue during periods when they'd otherwise sit fallow. And the revenues can be substantial. Students pay a sizable tuition, despite being on campus only twenty days a year. This esteemed program costs about $18,000 annually, plus travel expenses and the cost of taking four weeks off work. State schools (which make up thirteen of the fifty-one programs) tend to be a little cheaper. Standard college financial aid is available, and a few students are on scholarship.

Application

Out of roughly sixty students at my program, only two were minorities. Most everyone seemed much better off financially than me. And better connected. They had letters of recommendation from important people and lofty GPAs from lofty colleges. The acceptance rate was less than 15 percent.

It was the most money I'd ever made teaching. For spending ten days as a camp counselor, and then tutoring three students throughout the term (from my living room, in my pajamas), I earned twice what I did for a class of twenty-five students at CSU. If I made the permanent rotation, and did this twice a year, I could give up all other jobs and stay home and write.

I took deep breaths. I chanted silently the names of my three published novels. I had no reason to be intimidated, but probably my desperation was obvious. Just like in high school, dinners, meetings, and gatherings of any kind were all about who sat where. We watched jealously as the Young Novelist shared a private joke with the National Book Award Winner. I had wanted colleagues to admire. But just like in high school, the cool kids were as insecure as the rest of us. They showed off, doing the equivalent of skateboard tricks in the cafeteria, citing obscure texts, dropping names, and skittering away when too many questions were asked.

3. Describe your education.

I was never a creative writing major, or even an English major. At my state university—the only place that would take me—I majored in drugs, easy virtue, and skiing. Waitressing was a big part of that, too. I've taken exactly one writing workshop in my life. I started another but dropped it because I was having an affair with the instructor. I finished my BA in seven years. Then I went to film school because

I love movies and I hated my job as a picture framer. I now have an MA that I am well aware is not a terminal degree, from a university not known for its film department. I write by ear, from reading and from my gut. Still, I've sold short stories and essays, and those three novels received some good reviews. My second book won a medium-size award, but at this pastoral fucking MFA program all anyone mentioned was my one unsuccessful straight-to-DVD movie. I was "the screenwriter."

That first night in the damp, unair-conditioned faculty women's housing, I puked up my anxiety in the shared bathroom. I was hoping this job would make me a real writer. I would know the right people; I would become part of that rarefied world; I would receive invitations and emails from accomplished novelists and *New Yorker* contributors. We would share ideas and opportunities. We would be friends. My face hurt from smiling so much. My brain hurt from trying to be witty. I washed lots of dishes in the faculty communal kitchen, but the women weren't friendly and I think I made the straight guys nervous. I decided to give up my high heels and wear the flip-flops I had brought for the shower. I wanted to do it right. I wanted to be cool.

### 4. What were your responsibilities?

I was prepared to lead a seminar, give a reading, and respond to the students' writing. Each student sent one story to be read by the entire fiction group—eight faculty members and about thirty students—before the residency began. The fiction faculty would team-teach the workshops, two of us for six to eight students, divvied up and moving around through the five workshops over ten days.

## Application

I had read each story many times. My primary responsibility was to the students, the little chicks straining up at me, beaks stretched wide, chirping, "My story must be told!" I'd enjoyed a couple of the stories, and it was obvious these students knew where to put quotation marks and how to use spell-check. I looked forward to getting to know them better.

Until this job, I had taught successfully. I had excellent evals and students who continued, years later, to send me work and news. I thought teaching would be the easy part. Ha!

First, the other newbie and I were given a bewildering lecture about how to "do workshop." Never mind our years of experience; in this program there was a proper way, and we were about to learn it. We were told there might be long silences in the workshops while we waited for observations from the students: this was natural. We were told we should allow things to rise organically to their appropriate expression. A favorite faculty member had written workshop guidelines under a helpful acronym: COSMO—Clarity, Order, Sense, Meaning, and Originality. It was suggested we memorize this and use it often.

I had to assume this approach worked; the program had been around a long time and the students seemed happy, though often a little *too* wide-eyed and openmouthed, as if they'd been stunned. But I wasn't familiar with the director's phraseology, and I was afraid to reveal my ignorance of this lingo only real writers knew. "Encourage the narrative desire." What? "Remember: intention is elemental." Huh? "Do not instruct, lead, and, at the same time, allow yourself to be led." Um, okay.

"I need a cigarette," my hairy compatriot said. I don't smoke, but I stood up with him.

"Be sure to read stories three and four," the director called after us. "You'll be workshopping them first."

Workshopping. We're writers. Words are our business and still we take this noun, "workshop," and turn it into a verb. We verb it.

Story three—or maybe story four—was a mess. It contained some beautiful language, lovely descriptions of the honey on the table and the light through the kitchen window, but the author stayed aloof from the woman sitting at the table, whose husband had just walked out on her. For class I was paired with a veteran instructor, and I tried to follow his method of leading and not instructing. "Why did you choose to tell the story this way?" I asked, and "What might be this character's emotional journey?" The author's answers were as meandering as her work. I looked at her troubled face and felt responsible. The proper way wasn't working.

"Look," I said. "What if you did something like this?"

I gave her a concrete example: the woman digging the butter knife into her perfect kitchen table. The student smiled broadly. She understood. The other students got it too. I felt pretty smart—a good teaching moment—but my partner frowned.

"I thought the example would make it more clear," I said to him after.

It was clear he did not agree. "That's not how we do it."

"But it worked."

"That's not the point."

## 5. May we contact your previous employer?

Go ahead. He can't say I did anything terrible. In a private conversation he warned me against fraternizing with the students. No hanky-panky. I was still on West Coast time and my plastic-coated mattress had kept me up all night. I told him not to worry, I'd already filled my quota of dorm-room fornication. I asked if any of the students were staying in a real hotel. He didn't laugh.

We left his office and walked over to the big faculty meeting, the one where we would divvy up the students, deciding who would work with whom for the next five months. It seemed like the most important decision of all, this pairing of students with teachers, but no one had explained how it would be made. A couple of students had requested me, but that was shunted aside. First, I was asked to comment on a story. It felt like a pop quiz. I pulled the story out of my bag.

"This seemed rushed," I said. "I can feel the writer hurrying to get to the end." I could practically taste the story's little quick words, and then and then and then.

"You're a screenwriter, aren't you?" one of the other fiction instructors asked. He was tall and very handsome. He taught at an Ivy League school and his last book had been called "luminous." (There's a word you don't see on book jackets often enough.)

"I'm a novelist *and* a screenwriter," I said. "I wasn't looking for car crashes. I wanted more breath."

He smiled as if he had a secret, or had laid a smelly fart no one could pin on him. Turned out this student was a favorite—a scholarship student. Three other faculty members jumped in to disagree with me. "He's come so far," was the refrain. Well, how was I supposed to know that?

In the next discussion, I kept my mouth shut. Sure enough, my exact thoughts were spoken aloud by Mr. Bestseller. When I added, "That's what I thought, too," a woman across the room snickered like a horse.

In retrospect, I can see we were all frightened. Not just me, not just the students, but the entire faculty. I've admitted I thought teaching there would help my writing career. Some better-known author would write "luminous" in a jacket blurb for me. My stock would go up. But everybody wanted the same thing and so everyone got petty and snide. And, like overweight counselors at a fat camp, we competed not only with one another, but with the students. A couple of those students had been published. They received a different kind of attention, both solicitous and dismissive.

Each faculty member gives a lecture open to everyone, poets and fiction writers and faculty alike. Mine was on dialogue. Too late I realized the topic was a mistake; I was already denigrated for being the screenwriter. And the short-story examples I thought so unusual were well known to most of the faculty. Every teacher was there in the little lecture hall, and the triumvirate sat in the back row, their arms crossed against their chests. Mr. Bestseller called out an observation I had planned but hadn't yet made. He continued, telling the students that when he had dinner with the author of the sample, said author told him exactly why he wrote the scene. The students were enthralled. I grew too flustered to look at my notes, and it started to feel like one of my waitress nightmares, a thousand tables and my feet in lead boots. It was a talk I've given successfully many times, and it crashed.

"That was just craft," a faculty member said to me after. "Usually we try to . . . reach farther than that."

She had given her lecture about a hinge on the gate to Hell in an old painting. She had slides. One of the painting, another a close-up of the hinge. I saw a few students sleeping, but who can blame them? It was a big gate with a big hinge. On one side, hell. On the other, life. Whoop-de-do.

Application

## 6. What is your teaching philosophy?

There is no better feeling—and yes, I include sex—than writing a perfect sentence. Finding the right word can set me up for the whole day (and make that night's sex a whole lot better). But someone has to tell the little chicks the truth: Writing Is Hard. You have to practice. You can't sit at the café and smoke cigarettes and wait for the muse. You wouldn't expect Kobe Bryant to make all those tough shots without practicing. You have to write every day, you have to read, you have to think about words and stories and characters and emotions, and you have to do the work.

There are now 214 MFA programs in creative writing in this country—*twice as many as there were eight years ago*. You think being in this program makes you extraordinary? Think again. You think being in this program makes you a writer? Not a chance.

"I don't know how to write about men," a young woman student said. "So all my stories are about women."

"Try it," I said. "Think of it as an exercise. You're here to learn."

"I don't have time for that," she replied. "I'm graduating next semester."

If she writes 180 pages of her women, she will receive her MFA and leap into the growing ocean of people who call themselves writers. She will get that *terminal* degree, and then . . . what? The diploma, one story published online, and a series of metaphorical blow jobs for the appropriate faculty members might get her a chance to be considered for a teaching position somewhere. Two hundred and fourteen programs graduating even just five MFAs every year equals more than a thousand people looking to pay back their student loans. No wonder publishing is exhausted, overfished by every graduate with a thesis on the hook. I can't blame anyone for getting on her knees.

No matter where I'm teaching, I cannot say it to my students enough: Just write. But if they're not up next in workshop, or it's spring break, or they got drunk last night, they don't bother.

I used to be the one with faith. Faith in the power of a story, faith in the students, faith in the future of writing—hell—of the world. But writing has changed and I worry it's because of programs like this. The work is so earnest, so temperature-controlled and perfectly modulated, that it never stops being just words on a page.

"I'm wondering if the narrator couldn't learn something in this story," said a colleague about a piece with an unhappy ending. "If she came to a better place, then we could feel better too."

That kind of leading—don't call it instruction—is exactly the problem. Some stories aren't uplifting. Sometimes endings really are awful. But after being *workshopped* again and again, even the stories of neglect and abuse become appropriate, each word slipping noiselessly into the next. The messy narrator is scorned, coarse or uneven language discouraged, and the disturbing image should always be beautifully rendered.

Toward the end of the residency, a student brought in a tale of rape she had rewritten many times.

"So well written," hummed the workshop. "The rainbow metaphor is lovely."

Then why was I fighting to stay awake? How could the rape of an eleven-year-old girl be so boring?

That night I got drunk. I had a bad cold and I drank too much Jack Daniels—a killer chaser for Theraflu—because being sober hadn't done me any good. Then I asked the assembled faculty if they didn't think MFA programs had ruined the game for the rest of us. I said it reminded me of the occupation of Iraq, a surge of poor, clueless soldiers into places they didn't belong, spending way too much money, and thinking what they were doing would actually mean something a year from now. It was not, admittedly, a perfect analogy.

The only colleague who didn't look shocked was the new guy. I liked him. At that moment, I liked him a lot. He would not be invited back either. I knew it about him before I knew it about myself. He complained too much. He bitched about his mattress and the shower mold, plus the schedule, the workload, and especially the students.

"Who lets them in here?" he asked. "They're idiots. I thought this place was supposed to be prestigious."

"We do a valuable service here," was the response. "We turn out writers."

"We turn out people who write." Possibly I slurred as I said it. "There's a difference."

## 7. What was your reason for leaving?

I had to get off campus. I was depressed. At a final faculty meeting earlier that day, it became clear that I would not be invited back. I felt it emanating from the director and his assistant, a very nice woman—not a writer—who looked at me with that little smile that is more of a frown, like the meter maid who listens to your story and gives you a ticket anyway. As I sat there, I was already updating my résumé and deciding where to try next. I'm discouraged by teaching—I guess that's obvious—but what else can I do? What else is there for most writers?

I have a writer friend who's a lawyer and one who's a chef and one who's a VP at some company. They complain about having to write on the side. I can't write on the side, because the side is all I've got. I missed the good-job bus long ago. I wish I'd made more than fifteen grand on even one of my well-reviewed novels, but the way it's going, next time I'll have to pay the publisher.

I used my cold as an excuse to hitch a ride into town with a student, a soon-to-be MFA who would be taking my job and my publisher and who was probably married to a doctor because she wasn't a doctor herself and she had a really nice rental car for the whole two weeks.

Naturally, she was excited to discuss her work. She'd almost finished her first novel and her first short story was about to be published. She was confident, diligent, and young. I knew she would go far. She would be a professor in some recognized university well before I had published my next novel or found a one-day gig teaching "journaling" to housewives. And because she was beloved by the faculty and I was still holding onto the faintest hope of returning, I told her I too loved her work.

At least she was a good driver and we got to town quickly. Inside the grocery store the light was fluorescent, the air was conditioned, and it smelled of freezer burn and dog food. The real world still existed. Not one of the customers or checkers or baggers or stock clerks had a book under his or her arm.

I threw a big bar of chocolate and some other stuff on the conveyor belt and the young checker smiled at me. She was the blond and blue-eyed best of rural America. Then I noticed she was missing her right hand. The cuff of her grocer's smock flopped limp and empty. She kept smiling and rang up my items with her left.

"That'll be five eighty-nine," she said.

What if I were missing a hand? What if I had lost it to a shark attack or frostbite climbing Everest or the cleaver of a murderer whom I then subdued? I would be one-handed and remarkable and a role model.

Application

Standing there, watching her, I felt absolutely sure that even if my books were terrible, one-handed I would be a famous writer. I would teach wherever I wanted.

Obviously, that was untrue. Obviously, that was my depression talking. I'm sure there are plenty of writers with missing limbs whom no one has ever heard of and who don't teach anywhere. But the desire to distinguish myself from the crowd, to break into the circle, maybe not the inner-inner circle of bestsellers and big-prize winners, but the outer-inner circle of teachers with good steady jobs, can get perverse. Especially with more and more programs producing more and more credentialed writing teachers, if not writers. Especially when my own best efforts, three books and so many years of teaching, hadn't made me all that legit. One-handed, I'd at least stand out, and that's something. The National Book Award Winner might ponder how I manage to type. Mr. Bestseller might be impressed with how I pull up the zipper on those tight jeans.

But that's not what I want either. I've been an oddity all my life, even with both hands and feet attached. I want to fit in. I want to be taken seriously, even though I wrote a screenplay. I want to be remembered, appreciated, my thoughts and opinions valued, just the way I am.

In the exalted world of careful, precise writing instruction, I don't know how to make that happen. I don't have a terminal degree and I never will. I don't know the jargon or the secret handshake. I wasn't special enough for this fucking MFA program and I wanted it a lot. I tried hard. Elective amputation isn't the answer, but what is? I would tell my students to keep writing. I would say the only solution is to work harder and write a better book. But do I believe that, for myself? If I close my eyes and put myself back at that dinner table in the faculty building in that celebrated, extraordinary low-residency

MFA program, I can see my one-handed self getting help opening the mustard, but even with an empty sleeve and a full list of awards under my belt I can't see myself getting asked back. Maybe it's my problem. Or maybe that's the way this program—every program—works. There are those who fit in, and those who don't.

I gave the girl a ten. She made change with her one good hand, smiling all the while. +

# TWO VIEWS ON THE PROGRAM ERA

# Advice

Don't go into debt. Don't go into debt. Don't go into debt.
   **Ellen Litman**

If you want to spend $80,000 on being a creative writer, you should send it to me and I'll give you one-on-one classes for two years. It's not something you should pay for, especially if you don't have the money. You should never go into debt to study creative writing. Because real writing, to be an artist and really write meaningful creative fiction or nonfiction? That doesn't pay anything. I'm publishing my seventh book next year, and I'm living on $30,000 a year. And I think I'm toward the high end of that spectrum—most people are not that fortunate.

People go to MFA programs and they think they're gonna be connected. That's not going to help you publish. It's a myth. Writing's not about connections, writing's about writing. If you work on your writing, everything else will follow. You'll do fine. There's editors at publishing houses all over the place looking for good books. It's hard to get paid, it's hard to make a living, but it's not hard to publish a good book. So you don't need to put yourself into debt to get an MFA. And if it's not going to put you into debt, because you have enough money that you can get an MFA and not really worry about spending $80,000, then I think maybe you should take a hard look at yourself and where you came from and give some of that money back to the people.
   **Stephen Elliot, Stegner Fellow, Stanford University, 2003**

# The Invisible Vocation

## Elif Batuman

*This essay and the following one originally appeared in the* London Review of
Books, *in response to the publication of Mark McGurl's* The Program Era.

The world of letters: does such a thing still exist? Even within the
seemingly homogeneous sphere of the university English department, a schism has opened up between literary scholarship and
creative writing: disciplines that differ in their points of reference
(Samuel Richardson vs Jhumpa Lahiri), the graduate degrees they
award (doctor of philosophy vs master of fine arts) and their perceived objects of study ("literature" vs "fiction"). Mark McGurl's *The
Program Era: Postwar Fiction and the Rise of Creative Writing*, a study of Planet
MFA conducted from Planet PhD, might not strike the casual reader
as an interdisciplinary bombshell, but the fact is that literary histo-
rians don't write about creative writing, and creative writers don't
write literary histories, so any secondary discourse about creative
writing has been confined, as McGurl observes, to "the domain of
literary 'journalism'" and "the question of whether the rise of the

writing program has been *good* or *bad* for American writing": that is, to the domain of a third and completely different group of professionals, with its own set of interests, largely in whether things are good or bad. McGurl's proposal to take the rise of the program "not as an occasion for praise or lamentation but as an established fact in need of historical interpretation" is thus both welcome and overdue.

The central claims of *The Program Era* are beyond dispute: the creative writing program has exercised the single most determining influence on postwar American literary production, and any convincing interpretation of the literary works themselves has to take its role into account. (In a series of inspired readings, McGurl demonstrates that the plantation in *Beloved*, the mental ward in *One Flew Over the Cuckoo's Nest*, and the bus in Robert Olen Butler's *Mr. Spaceman* all function as metaphors for the creative writing workshop.) McGurl also provides a smart and useful typology of "program" fiction (defined as the prose work of MFA graduates and/or instructors), divided into three main groups: "technomodernism" (John Barth, Thomas Pynchon), "high cultural pluralism" (Toni Morrison, Sandra Cisneros) and "lower-middle-class modernism" (Raymond Carver, Joyce Carol Oates), with Venn diagrams illustrating the overlap between these groups, and their polarization by aesthetic subtendencies such as maximalism and minimalism. Despite his professed indifference to the pro-con debate, however, McGurl also sets out to defend the creative writing program from its detractors, assuming the rhetorical burden of proving that (a) postwar American fiction is at least as "creative" as any other literature, and (b) that its most "creative" features are specifically the product of the program.

I should state up front that I am not a fan of program fiction. Basically, I feel about it as toward new fiction from a developing nation with no literary tradition: I recognize that it has anthropological interest, and is compelling to those whose experience it describes, but I probably wouldn't read it for fun. Moreover, if I wanted to read literature from the developing world, I would go ahead and read literature from the developing world. At least that way I'd learn something about some less privileged culture—about a less privileged culture that some people were actually born into, as opposed to one that they opted into by enrolling in an MFA program.

In perhaps McGurl's most ambitious defense of program fiction ("as rich and multifaceted a body of literary writing as has ever been"), he decides to prove that the slogans "write what you know" and "find your voice" were enormously productive for twentieth-century fiction. As it turns out, he views these catchphrases not as interchangeable exhortations to authenticity, but as philosophically opposed dictates. "Write what you know" really does seem to mean "write what you know," but "find your voice" actually means "find *someone else's* voice": thus Styron "found his voice" in *Nat Turner*, reimagining "authorship as a kind of ventriloquism . . . which is an offense against the rule of writing what you know."

McGurl never quite articulates the law that enjoins some writers to write what they know and others to find their voices, but he comes close to it during a discussion of Bharati Mukherjee's essay "Immigrant Writing: Give Us Your Maximalists!" (1988). Mukherjee, an Iowa graduate who writes about Bengali Americans, claims perspectival mobility "as the special property of the immigrant writer," enabled "without difficulty to 'enter' lives, fictionally, that are manifestly not [her] own." "Chameleon-skinned, I discover my material over and across the country, and up and down the social ladder," she writes, striking that note of naïveté mixed with self-congratulation often sounded in the program discourse by "writers on writing." As McGurl astutely observes, the "facts of literary history" belie Mukherjee's claim: it has been largely "white writers like William Styron and Russell Banks and Robert Olen Butler and Neal Stephenson who . . . assert the privilege of other-narration," while "minority writers . . . have typically been asked to slot themselves into a single ethnos."

But McGurl doesn't follow this thought to its logical conclusion. The point is less that Mukherjee has been "asked to slot [herself] into a single ethnos" than that she has never been made to feel that her writing would be "richer" or more "multifaceted" if she wrote from the perspective of an autistic concentration-camp survivor. In the program discourse, "virtuosic" chameleonism is the purview, not of immigrants, but of people like the Iowa graduate and Vietnam vet Robert Olen Butler, whose story "Mid-Autumn" (1992) is narrated, ostensibly in Vietnamese thought-language, by a pregnant woman to her unborn child:

> We are lucky, you and I, to be Vietnamese so that I can speak to you
> even before you are born. This is why I use the Vietnamese language.
> It is our custom for the mother to begin this conversation with the
> child in the womb. . . . It is not the custom among the Americans, so
> perhaps you would not even understand English if I spoke it.

There is no arguing with taste, and there are doubtless people in the world who enjoy "the virtuosity of Butler's performance of narrative mobility." To me, such "performances" are symptomatic of the large-scale replacement of books I would want to read by rich, multifaceted explorations whose "amazing audacity" I'm supposed to admire in order not to be some kind of jerk.

## The Invisible Vocation

The law of "find your voice" and "write what you know" originates in a phenomenon perhaps most clearly documented by the blog and book *Stuff White People Like*: the loss of cultural capital associated with whiteness, and the attempts of White People to compensate for this loss by displaying knowledge of nonwhite cultures. Hence Stuff White People Like #20, "Being an Expert on *Your* Culture," and #116, "Black Music That Black People Don't Listen to Anymore." Nonwhite, non-college-educated or non-middle- or upper-class people may write what they know, but White People have to find the voice of a Vietnamese woman impregnated by a member of the American army that killed her only true love.

The situation is summed up in McGurl's construct of the World Pluribus of Letters (a play on the critic Pascale Casanova's World Republic of Letters):

> While the citizen of the Republic of Letters disaffiliates from the nation in order to affiliate with art, the citizen of the World Pluribus of Letters disaffiliates from . . . the super-nation, in order to re-affiliate with a utopian sub-nation, whether that be African- or Asian- or Mexican- or . . . Native-America. . . . Whether they have been the expression of formerly enslaved, immigrant, or indigenous populations, these subnational cultural interventions . . . forge symbolic links to an international literary space which is not, however, the space of universal literary values but a pluralized space, a space of decolonized global cultural difference.

The World Pluribus of Letters has replaced a primary standard of "universal literary value" with a primary standard of persecutedness, euphemized as "difference." It seems strange to me that McGurl, who sees the situation so clearly, seems not to view it as a problem.

Perhaps his status as a White Person prevents him from objecting to the ideals of the Pluribus. But my hardworking immigrant parents didn't give me a funny name and send me to Harvard for nothing, so I'm going to go ahead and say how damaging I think this all is. Although there is nothing intrinsically wrong with writing about persecution, for either the persecuted or the nonpersecuted, there is a genuine problem when young people are taught to believe that they can be writers only in the presence of real or invented sociopolitical grievances.

This really is the message that some young people take from the program, as we learn in a quotation from the Chicana writer Sandra Cisneros (*The House on Mango Street*, 1984):

> Until Iowa I had never felt my home, family, and neighborhood unique or worthy of writing about. I took for granted . . . the strange speech of my neighbors, the extraordinary lives of my family and relatives which was nothing like the family in "Father Knows Best." . . . What could I write about that my classmates, cultivated in the finest schools in the country like hot house orchids, could not? . . . What did I know that they didn't? . . . What did I know except third-floor flats. . . . That's precisely what I chose to write: about third-floor flats, and fear of rats, and drunk husbands sending rocks through windows, anything as far from the poetic as possible.

There is nothing objectionable in a young writer plumbing her childhood and family for literary material. It isn't even a huge problem that poor people have been a "poetic" subject since at least Romanticism. But I was deeply depressed to learn from McGurl that Cisneros here is making "canny use of an operational paradox involved in . . . the 'wound culture' of the contemporary U.S.: a paradoxically enabling disablement." "Almost all artistically ambitious authors in the postwar period 'self-commodify' in this sense," McGurl continues, inviting us to "think of Tim O'Brien and his lifelong use of nine months in Vietnam." Indeed, think of Tim O'Brien. As a White Person, he couldn't write about most of his life experience, which was probably just like *Father Knows Best*. Instead, in *If I Die in a Combat Zone, Box Me Up and Ship Me Home,* and the several novels that followed, he had to write about the period of his life when he—like the conscripted Native Americans, like the napalmed Vietnamese—was the victim of the murderous policy of the White Man.

Defending Cisneros and O'Brien against charges of cynicism, McGurl suggests that both authors are really concerned not with "market value but aesthetic value: how does one write good fiction? What interesting stories do I have to tell?" To argue that the writers of victimhood aren't out to make a quick buck is beside the point, since what's at stake here is literary, not financial, capital. But how does one calculate the literary value of sociopolitical grievances? If you spend any time living in a ghetto or fighting in a war, might this be objectively the most narrative-worthy period of your life? As Tolstoy put it, "All happy families are alike": isn't literature all about wounds, otherness, trauma, alienation, and persecution? It is. But it's equally true that all unhappy families—not just "formerly enslaved, immigrant, or indigenous" families—are unhappy after their own fashion. Tolstoy wrote equally compellingly about war *and* peace. Literature is best suited for qualitative description, not quantitative accumulation. It isn't an unhappiness contest, or an unhappiness-entitlement contest. The danger of Cisneros's dig at her Iowa classmates, "cultivated in the finest schools in the country like hot house orchids," is the implication that the children of privilege don't have stories to tell; that, because they aren't from the barrio, they all have families like the one on *Father Knows Best*.

This danger is inherent to "high cultural pluralism," which tends to assign novelistic alienation to the domain of "the alienated ethnic outsider." Novelistic alienation—the realization that lived experience doesn't resemble literature—was invented in *Don Quixote*. And, ever since *Don Quixote*, the novel has been concerned with social inequality. Class and religious difference are, after all, two major reasons why certain forms of human experience don't get documented. Hence Cervantes writes not only about windmills mistaken for giants, but also about prostitutes mistaken for noble ladies, and Moriscos who carry ham under their arms as a badge of racial purity. But, in *Don Quixote*, race and class have no higher an order of significance than, say, a hidalgo's typical weekly diet, or the noise produced by a textile mill: aspects of an undocumented historical present. What was missing from the older literary forms, in other words, wasn't social justice, but the passage of time—a dimension the novel was specifically engineered to capture. The novelistic hero is by definition someone whose life experience hasn't yet been fully described, possibly because of his race or class, but more broadly because he didn't exist before, and neither did the technology for describing him. The durability and magic of the novel form lies in the fact that, having gained a certain level of currency, the latest novel is immediately absorbed into the field of preexisting literature, and becomes the thing the next novel has to be written against. In this dialectic, the categories of outsider and insider are in constant flux. For an outsider to become an insider isn't ironic or paradoxical: it's just the way things work.

The danger of ethnicizing novelistic alienation is that it removes this dialectical and historical element from the novel. Instead of striving to capture real life by describing the disjuncture between pre-existing literature and the historical present, "high cultural pluralism" simply strives to describe the greatest possible disjuncture from some static, imagined cultural dominant. The basic novelistic claim—"my early writing imitated the conventions of earlier literature, and wasn't about my comically mundane and eternally surprising life"—is politicized and dehistoricized: "my early writing imitated the conventions of privileged literature, and wasn't about *my people*, whose sufferings have rendered them more raucous and hilariously alive than the uptight sons and daughters of privilege." We have heard this credo from Cisneros, and we hear it, via McGurl, from Philip Roth:

> It "did not dawn on" [Roth] that the "anecdotes and observations" of his boyhood in lower-middle-class Newark with which he entertained his highbrow friends "might be made into literature." Instead, the "stories I wrote, set absolutely nowhere, were mournful little things about sensitive children, sensitive adolescents, and sensitive young men crushed by the coarse life. . . . The Jew was nowhere to be seen; there were no Jews in the stories, no Newark, and not a sign of comedy."

There is no implication that those "highbrow friends" were ever themselves outsiders or made jokes. How could their stories be funny, with "no Jews" and "no Newark"? Eventually Roth's outsider becomes an insider and Zuckerman's literary celebrity becomes a subject for later novels. (This isn't really, as McGurl claims, a sign of Roth's "vertiginously 'postmodern' reflexivity"; Cervantes does the same thing in book 2 of *Don Quixote*, in which Sancho and Quixote have already been made famous by book 1.) There was nothing postmodern about such mobility. Pushkin was initially an outsider because he used colloquial Russian and had an Abyssinian great-grandfather; Dante was an outcast wandering Italy in penury and exile. It's jarring, then, when McGurl characterizes the success and assimilation of Roth and Cisneros as a "phenomenon of American culture," originating in the 1960s university scene, and marked by a "vertiginously dialectical mobilization of the distinction between 'inside' and 'outside.'" In literary terms, the effect of these cultural changes was not so much mobilizing as politicizing, even ossifying.

Historically, this ossification probably originates less in the twentieth century's social advancements than in its worst atrocities. As an example, consider the changing treatment of the Jew in the European novel. At a certain point in the history of the novel, Jewishness, having ceased to be a merely comic or villainous attribute, had come to operate as a reality principle that exposed the machinery of social life. Swann's way—the prosaic way of the narrator's half-Jewish next-door neighbor—revealed the truth about the Guermantes way, and Jewishness became, to an extent, identifiable with the mechanism of the novel itself: the comic, slightly vulgar exposure of the world as a place where would-be knightly heroes have to eat, sleep, and carry money. This identification perhaps goes some way to explain the theory of Cervantes's Jewish converso ancestry, proposed by Américo Castro in 1966. In the wake of the Second World War, the aesthetic imperative to "keep it real" had also acquired an ethical dimension; in 1962 Sylvia Plath wrote "Daddy": "I began to talk like a Jew. / I think I may well be a Jew." If you had to write imaginative literature about your overbearing father, you now had to make him an engine chuffing you off "to Dachau, Auschwitz, Belsen," at risk of falling into the "barbarism" famously decreed by Adorno (who, somewhat less famously, amended this decree in later years:

in light of the continuing diversity of human unhappiness and its inalienable "right to expression," he wrote, "it may have been wrong to say that no poem could be written after Auschwitz"). To justify its perpetuation, the novel itself had somehow to become Jewish. Jewishness, which had once been a code word for the changing of the times, came to represent a kind of tragedy that would never change, no matter how much time passed.

Ironically, a preoccupation with historic catastrophe actually ends up depriving the novel of the kind of historical consciousness it was best suited to capture. The effect is particularly clear in the "maximalist" school of recent fiction, which strives, as McGurl puts it, to link "the individual experience of authors and characters to the kinds of things one finds in history textbooks": "war, slavery, the social displacements of immigration, or any other large-scale trauma"; historical traumas, McGurl explains, confer on the novel "an aura of 'seriousness' even when, as in Pynchon or Vonnegut, the work is comic. Personal experience so framed is not *merely* personal experience," a fact that "no amount of postmodern skepticism . . . is allowed to undermine." The implication is that "personal experience" is insufficient grounds for a novel, unless it is entangled in a "large-scale trauma"—or, worse yet, that an uncompelling (or absent) story line can be redeemed by a setting full of disasters.

This is the kind of literary practice James Wood so persuasively condemned under the rubric of "hysterical realism" ("Toby's mad left-wing aunt was curiously struck dumb when Mrs. Thatcher was elected prime minister"). Diachronicity is cheaply telegraphed by synchronic cues, and history is replaced by big-name historical events, often glimpsed from some "eccentric" perspective: a slide-show-like process, as mechanical as inserting Forrest Gump beside Kennedy at the White House. As Wood points out, the maximalist fetishization of history is actually antihistoric: the maximalist novel "carries within itself, in its calm profusion of characters and plots, its flawless carpet of fine prose on page after page, a soothing sense that it might never have to end, that another thousand or two thousand pages might easily be added."

McGurl's taxonomy includes one group of writers who, though descended from neither slaves nor genocide survivors, are still allowed to write what they know: "lower-middle-class modernists." Neither white nor nonwhite, they "silently aspire to *become* 'white,'" such that Raymond Carver was apparently wont to say, in the early years of his success: "This makes me feel just like a white man." Carver gets away with writing what he knows, partly by not writing very much (minimalism), and partly by not really knowing what it is to be white.

The most exhilarating pages of *The Program Era* sketch a dialectic between Carver, the father of minimalism, and Joyce Carol Oates, the great graphomaniac who "during some periods of her career . . . has produced '40 to 50 pages [of fiction] each day' for a total of 'well over 500 published stories, companion to the 40 or so novels and other books.'" While Carver's stories are characterized by a "relative invisibility of racial self-consciousness," Oates, it turns out, has always manifested guilt about "the unjust advantages of a white skin." The heroine of *I Lock My Door Upon Myself*, walking through a black neighborhood, realizes that the residents' "immediate ancestors had been *owned*. . . . *Like me they are outcasts in this country. Not like me: they are true outcasts.*" In this persecution contest, the winner isn't predetermined. Who is the real outcast? Oates literally dramatizes the contest, which acquires the mesmerizing, morbid fascination of a hot-dog-eating contest between a human and a grizzly bear. Is the real outcast the professor's grieving widow alone in the empty house in the college town, or the paranoid Bosnian graduate student threatened with deportation? Which estranged cousin is the real outcast: the German girl who survived Auschwitz and became a successful but caustic and solitary anthropology professor; or the American girl who narrowly avoided being murdered by her own father, then became a good wife and mother, but ended up getting cancer? Oates is the rare and admirable program writer who never forgets that every unhappy family is unhappy after its own fashion.

The brilliant insight in McGurl's chapter on Oates and Carver is the determining role played in their work by shame. Shame engenders both Carver's taciturnity and Oates's graphomania, which is really a compulsion to restage the outcasts contest, doing everyone justice, and constituting a proof that writing, too, is real work. I disagree with McGurl, however, that the shame shared by Oates and Carver is produced by the writing program in particular, or school in general. "Shame and pride are the affective fuel of the school, the motive force of its everyday machinations," McGurl observes, plausibly enough—except that people were going to school for hundreds of years before the Iowa workshop. In his fascination with the GI Bill, McGurl occasionally conveys the impression that writers didn't go to college before 1945, as when he draws our attention to

the seemingly banal fact that virtually all contemporary American fiction writers . . . have attended college. . . . In previous generations this would not likely have been the case, both because fewer individuals of any kind went to college before the postwar advent of mass higher education and because a college education was not yet perceived as an obvious, and still less a necessary, starting point for a career as a novelist. Rather, as the uncredentialed, or rather press-credentialed, example of the high school graduate Hemingway makes clear, the key supplementary institution for the novel until mid-century was journalism.

The GI Bill dramatically increased the percentage of college-educated Americans, but did it really affect the percentage of college-educated American writers? According to the internet, writers have, in fact, been going to college for hundreds of years.* The claim that the GI Bill produced a generation of unprecedentedly shameful young people, meanwhile, is weakened by the fact that outsiders, from Balzac's parvenus to Proletkult, have been joining the intelligentsia for nearly as long as there has been an intelligentsia to join.

---

* Goethe studied at the University of Leipzig, Swift and Beckett at Trinity College Dublin, Fielding at Eton and the University of Leiden, Balzac at the Sorbonne, Flaubert and Baudelaire at the Paris law faculty, Tolstoy at the University of Kazan, Dostoevsky at the Petersburg Academy of Military Engineering, Chekhov at Moscow State University, Babel at the Kiev Institute of Finance, Solzhenitsyn at Rostov State University, Hawthorne at Bowdoin, Poe at the University of Virginia and West Point, Hardy and Maugham at King's College London, D. H. Lawrence at University College Nottingham, Fitzgerald at Princeton, Steinbeck at Stanford, Henry James at Harvard, T. S. Eliot at Harvard and the Sorbonne, Pound at the University of Pennsylvania, Sinclair Lewis at Yale, Jack London at Berkeley, Dreiser at Indiana, Pirandello at the University of Rome and the University of Bonn, Camus at the University of Algiers, Giovanni Verga at the University of Catania, Kafka at Charles University in Prague, Joyce at University College Dublin, Proust at the École Libre des Sciences Politiques, Mann at the University of Munich, and Musil at the University of Berlin. Byron, Carroll, Donne, Forster, Galsworthy, Greene, Marlowe, Milton, Sterne, Tennyson, Thackeray, Waugh, Wordsworth, and Wilde all attended either Oxford or Cambridge. Many of these writers failed to complete their degrees, but they all spent some time at university. Of writers who *didn't* go to university, many attended elite lycées or secondary schools (Trollope, Pushkin, Maupassant, Melville, Borges). I have been able to find only a handful of famous novelists who, like Hemingway, avoided university in favor of journalism (Defoe, Dickens, Twain). For women, of course, university was a later development.

To my mind, the real cause of shame here is the profession of writing, and it affects McGurl just as much as it does Carver and Oates. Literary writing is inherently elitist and impractical. It doesn't directly cure disease, combat injustice, or make enough money, usually, to support philanthropic aims. Because writing is suspected to be narcissistic and wasteful, it must be "disciplined" by the program—as McGurl documents with a 1941 promotional photo of Paul Engle, then director of the Iowa workshop, seated at a desk with a typewriter and a large whip. (Engle's only novel, McGurl observes, features a bedridden Iowan patriarch "surrounded by his collection of 'whips of every kind,' including 'racing whips,' 'stiff buggy whips,' 'cattle whips,' 'riding crops,' and one 'endless bullwhip.'") The workshop's most famous mantras—"Murder your darlings," "Omit needless words," "Show, don't tell"—also betray a view of writing as self-indulgence, an excess to be painfully curbed in AA-type group sessions. Shame also explains the fetish of "craft": an ostensibly legitimizing technique, designed to recast writing as a workmanlike, perhaps even working-class skill, as opposed to something every no-good dilettante already knows how to do. Shame explains the cult of persecutedness, a strategy designed to legitimize literary production as social advocacy, and make White People feel better (Stuff White People Like #21: "Writers' Workshops").

As long as it views writing as shameful, the program will not generate good books, except by accident. Pretending that literary production is a non-elite activity is both pointless and disingenuous. It's not impossible to be a writer and non-elite; I recently heard a profile on NPR—Stuff White People Like #44: "Public Radio"—of two New York white-collar workers, a Wall Street tech consultant and his best friend, who quit their jobs, cleared out of their apartments, changed their names to Obsidian and Hobo Bob, and lived on the street, just so that they could write poetry full-time. They became known as the Homeless Poets at open-mic nights around the city, where they would read works like the following:

> Waking up achy, and out in the open.
> Guard dogs are barking, before words are spoken.
> Wrought iron benches that cause suffering,
> These are a few of my favorite things.

One admires Obsidian and Hobo Bob for putting their money where their mouths were. But writing, especially nicely turned prose, demands a certain surplus of money and leisure. Very little of it can be done on iron benches surrounded by barking dogs. The best thing about the program is that it frees would-be writers from material lack.

As for the project of redeeming literature as a means to social change, this is a more complicated issue. Despite the recent trend in viewing fiction as a form of empathy training, I'm pretty sure that writing short stories isn't the most efficient way to combat injustice or oppression. In recent years, however, a uniquely ambitious and ingenious attempt to transform literature into a force for public good has been embodied in the career of Dave Eggers. After writing one highly lucrative book about his personal experiences as a White Person, he diverted his wealth and fame to various specifically literary forms of social work, establishing writers' workshops for underprivileged children and oral history programs for the witnesses of human rights abuse. Meanwhile, he began writing books like *You Shall Know Our Velocity!*—which dramatizes the difficulty of getting on a plane to Senegal to give away $80,000 to poor Africans, doubtless an allegory for the frustration of trying to help the persecuted through belletristic writing—and the more successful *What Is the What: The Autobiography of Valentino Achak Deng*. In *What Is the What*, Eggers ingeniously outsources the knowledge part of "write what you know" to someone with a more historically important life than his, removing the offensiveness from the project of virtuosic ventriloquism (not least by diverting the publishing proceeds to a foundation in Deng's name, designed to pay for his college education and to rebuild his village in Sudan). Eggers's *Zeitoun*, similarly, relates the true story of a Syrian-American's experiences after Hurricane Katrina: a character whose fate combines ethnic alienation and world-historical events. Eggers, even more than the Homeless Poets, is admirable for putting his money where his mouth is. Although (or, perhaps, because) he isn't a program graduate, he has found a coherent and satisfying solution to the problem of writing and shame that the program has institutionalized. If writing is what the program says it is, this is how people should write.

But if everyone wrote like Eggers, what would happen to the novel? Eggers's recent books don't read to me like novels. I found the backstory of *What Is the What*—the facts of the collaboration between Eggers and Deng—more compelling and more novelistic than the text itself, which at once omits Eggers and renders him eerily omnipotent. As a counterexample, Christian Jungersen's *The Exception* successfully addresses many of the same problems, but reads like a genuine novel. Set in an office at the fictitious Danish Center for Information on Genocide, *The Exception* explores the psychological affinity between office bullying and genocide, and is based on observations made by Jungersen while working in an office in Copenhagen. Told through the frame of the author's real life as a White Person, it explores and expands the concept of "persecution" to encompass the dynamics among bourgeois Danish government employees. It works as a novel and "bears witness to genocide." Although many American program writers are more stylistically and technically sophisticated than Jungersen (or at least than Jungersen in English translation), I would rather read *The Exception* than the latest technomodernist multigenerational Holocaust novel. This is probably as much a question of personal taste as of literary philosophy, yet it makes me wonder: are Jungersen's strengths inherently less teachable than the skills that are being taught to American writers? In other words, is content less teachable than style?

Many of the problems in the program may be viewed as the inevitable outcome of technique taken as telos. The raw material hardly seems to matter anymore: for hysterical realism, everything; for minimalism, nothing much. The fetishization of technique simultaneously assuages and aggravates the anxiety that literature might not be real work. McGurl writes of the program as a manifestation of "the American Dream of perfect self-expression." Taken as an end in itself, self-expression is surely sensed, even by those who pursue it, as a somehow suspect project, demanding shame and discipline.

The ideal of self-expression also explains the program's privileging of "fiction": where "nonfiction" is burdened by factual content, and "literature" is burdened by a canon of classics, "fiction" is taken to be a pure vessel for inner content. As if the self were a ready-made content, and as if the wish to become a writer—a complicated, strange wish, never fully explored in *The Program Era*—were simply a desire to learn the skills with which to express it. McGurl cites a manual called *The Story Workshop*, by the founder of the Iowa program, Wilbur Schramm, according to whom great stories "are written not because someone says, 'Go to! I shall write a short story. Now—ho hum—let me see.

What shall I write about?' They are written because someone has a story aching to be told." The anxieties generated by this misguided piece of pedagogy are illustrated in Flannery O'Connor's "The Crop," a story about the laughable efforts of an amateur "penwoman" to find a subject for a story: "There were so many subjects to write stories about that Miss Willerton never could think of one. That was always the hardest part of writing a story she always said."

McGurl persuasively suggests that O'Connor wrote "The Crop" as an "auto-exorcism" of her own inner amateur, who must occasionally have wondered what *she* was going to write about. The story had to be disguised as a satire about someone else, because no real writer would admit to such a shameful lack of "creativity." But what is there to be ashamed of? Proust was surely speaking for many of his colleagues when he wrote that the desire to become a writer often comes long in advance of an "authentic" subject:

> Since I wished, some day, to become a writer, it was time I knew
> what I was going to write. But as soon as I asked myself the question,
> trying to find some subject . . . my mind would cease to function, my
> consciousness would be faced with a blank, I would feel either that I
> was wholly devoid of talent or that perhaps a malady of the brain was
> hindering its development.

Writing remains the "invisible vocation" of Proust's narrator, for the greater part of seven volumes. Marcel's desire to write comes not from some inner need to tell the world about medieval churches or his grandmother, but from a love of reading. Many writing students today would be ashamed to admit, as Marcel does, that they long to write a book exactly like *The Arabian Nights* or Saint-Simon's memoirs (or whatever their favorite childhood books were).

Elif Batuman

Might the ideal of "creativity," taken as a supremely valuable, supremely human faculty, be harmful to a writer's formation? It seems ominous that the role of creativity in American education originates, as McGurl observes, in cold war rhetoric: through creativity, America was going to prevail over its "relentlessly drab ideological competitor" and "outdo the group-thinking Communist enemy." The value placed on creativity and originality causes writers to hide their influences, to hide the fact that they have ever read any other books at all and, in many cases, to stop reading books altogether. One telling result of this value is a gap in quality between American literary fiction and nonfiction today. Many of the best journalistic and memoiristic essays in the world today are being written in America. I think of myself as someone who prefers novels and stories to nonfiction; yet, for human interest, skillful storytelling, humor, and insightful reflection on the historical moment, I find the average episode of *This American Life* to be 99 percent more reliable than the average new American work of literary fiction. The juxtaposition of personal narrative with the facts of the world and the facts of literature—the real work of the novel—is taking place today largely in memoirs and essays. This is one of many brilliant observations in David Shields's *Reality Hunger,* in which he argues that we had best give up the novel altogether. But I don't think the novel is dead—or, more accurately, I don't see why it has to be dead. It's simply being produced under the kinds of mistaken assumption that we don't make when it comes to nonfiction. Nonfiction is about some real thing in the world, some story that someone had to go out and pursue. It's about real people and real books, which are, after all, also objects in the world. Why can't the novel expand to include these things, which were once—in *Don Quixote,* for example—a part of its purview?

—

In the greater scheme, of course, the creative writing program is not one of the evils of the world. It's a successful, self-sufficient economy, making teachers, students, and university administrators happy. As for literature, it will be neither made nor broken by the program, which is doubtless as incapable of ruining a good writer as of transforming a bad one. That said, the fact that the program isn't a slaughterhouse doesn't mean we should celebrate, or condone, its worst features. Why can't the program be better than it is? Why can't it teach writers about history and the world, and not just about adverbs and themselves? Why can't it at least try? The program stands for everything that's wonderful about America: the belief that every individual life can be independent from historical givens, that all the forms and conditions can be reinvented from scratch. Not knowing something is one way to be independent of it—but knowing lots of things is a better way and makes you more independent. It's exciting and important to reject the great books, but it's equally exciting and important to be in a conversation with them. One isn't stating conclusively that Father Knows Best, but who knows whether Father might not have learned a few useful things on the road of life, if only by accident? When "great literature" is replaced by "excellent fiction," that's the real betrayal of higher education. +

# Dirty Little Secret

## Fredric Jameson

The secret Mark McGurl discloses is the degree to which the richness
of postwar American culture (we will here stick to the novel, for
reasons to be explained) is the product of the university system, and
worse than that, of the creative writing program as an institutional
and institutionalized part of that system. This is not simply a matter of historical research and documentation, although one finds
a solid dose of that in *The Program Era*: it is a matter of shame, and
modern American writers have always wanted to think of themselves
as being innocent of that artificial supplement to real life which is
college education, to begin with, but above all the creative writing
course. Those who can, do; those who can't, teach. Think of the
encomia of European intellectuals like Sartre and Beauvoir to the
great American writers who didn't teach, didn't go to school, but
worked as truck drivers, bartenders, nightwatchmen, stevedores,
anything but intellectuals, as they recorded "the constant flow of
men across a whole continent, the exodus of an entire village to the
orchards of California," and so on.

Fredric Jameson

There is the real, and then there is the university; and of course in one sense (the best sense) the university is that great vacation which precedes the real life of earning your living, having a family, finding yourself inextricably fixed in society and its institutions. The campus is somehow extraterritorial (McGurl identifies that relatively new genre, the "campus novel"; and he also compares the enclave experience of the university to that now ubiquitous cultural activity, which has itself become an economic industry, called tourism); and the life of the student, when he or she does not have to sacrifice it in finding the tuition fees (the cost of living that life), is one of freedom: freedom from ideology (class interests have not yet come down like an iron cage), the freedom of discovery—sexuality, culture, ideas—and in a more subtle sense, perhaps, the freedom from nationality, from the guilt of class and of being an American. What the "real" writer wants to write about is not that kind of free-floating freedom, but rather the realities of constraint (the campus novel has the vocation of reintroducing that constraint back into the apparent freedoms of university life). So somehow the shame of being "taught to be a writer" (itself a kind of insult) is bound up with the guilt of a freedom your subjects (the "real people" in your novels) are not able to share.

There is more. Those European writers envying earlier American writers who, like Hemingway, were not university students and very far from any thought of writing courses and learning technique—those writers were citizens of societies in which universities were part of the state, and in which attending school was a social activity, sanctioned by society and classified among the official social roles it distributed. But of course in those systems there were no creative writing classes, an invention with which McGurl credits the United States. What the European university produced was not writers but intellectuals, and here we hit on the deeper reason for the American's shame at the country's institutional dirty little secret: American anti-intellectualism.

It is a very old tradition here, which is however not to be explained by some cultural characteristic or peculiarity, since in fact it expresses that most permanent dynamic of all societies—namely, class consciousness. Left intellectuals have the most trouble understanding this, insofar as they expect the content of their ideologies to shield them from the resentment of those with whom they identify. But anti-intellectualism is a form of populism, and it is the privileged position of intellectuals that is targeted and not their thoughts. Universities are part of that target as well, and the writers who feel guilt about their academic associations are also at least symbolically attempting to pass over to the other side, to dissociate themselves from idealism as well as privilege. Indeed, so omnipresent is symbolic class struggle in these matters that we find it at work in all the binary systems that run through McGurl's magisterial book, even though the class identifications shift position according to the concrete national situation. Thus the ubiquitous realism/modernism debate is coded and recoded perpetually, depending on whether realism is identified with bourgeois positions (as in Europe) or with the European colonizer (as in African and many other postcolonial societies). Gender itself is recoded over and over again, depending on whether it stamps literature as feminized and passive (as for the first modernists) or identifies feminism as a militant and oppressed position (as tends to be more the case in many countries today):

> Like the high/low binary to which it is often attached, but even more
> pervasive and various in its uses, the male/female binary floats
> throughout the system of higher education, the creative writing
> program and postwar fiction alike: one can point to the division

between the (hard) sciences and the (soft) humanities, or to the
division between the low-status "schoolmarm" and the high-status
"professor," or, perhaps most interestingly, to the distinction
between feminized "caring" institutions (e.g., the hospital) and
masculinized "disciplinary" ones (e.g., the army). The school is
neither a "feminine" nor a "masculine" institution per se but is
rather the scene of countless micro-struggles between "maternal"
love and punitive "paternal" judgment as two different forms of
institutional authority. This reflects at long distance the advent of
large-scale coeducation in the postwar period, and the related entry
of (some) women into the professional-managerial stratum of the
corporate workforce.

The unavoidable class opposition even recurs within the university;
thus McGurl lets us understand that his restriction of the topic of
American writing to the novel is itself a vehicle of class meaning.
The poets have a nobler calling, and tend to look down on their
lowly storytelling cousins; even theater dissociates itself from this
humbler and more proletarianized vocation, while yet a fourth
alternative—journalism—offers the would-be writer an escape
from literature and its connotations altogether. The judgments of
each of these "specializations" on each other are no less harsh than
that of "ordinary Americans" on the university system in general.
(To which we must add the stifling presence of the university itself as
an institutional actor, within an already ominously bureaucratized
and institutionalized society.)

The point is not so much to argue the "pros and cons" of these
social connotations (which McGurl would like to avoid as much as
possible), but rather to see how for the writers, in their new postwar
situation as inevitable dependents of the university's largesse, the

problem of escaping such coding and such identification is a profoundly formal one, which offers several alternative and seemingly contradictory solutions. It is these solutions and their systemic relationship to each other which *The Program Era* proposes to explore, and it triumphantly does so. It is a complex and dialectical book that practices what McGurl himself identifies as historical materialism and that makes unique demands on the reader, demands which are neither those of traditional literary history (even though the story wends its way from Thomas Wolfe through Nabokov and John Barth, Philip Roth and Joyce Carol Oates, all the way to Raymond Carver), nor those of traditional aesthetics and literary criticism, which raise issues of value and try to define true art as this rather than that.

The dialectical problems come in the reversals of class coding I have already mentioned. Whatever we think of Wolfe today, he not only invented an influential solution to the dilemmas McGurl lays out, but was once (by Faulkner, for example) considered the greatest American writer of his time, and there are reasons for that evaluation which have considerable historical and structural interest for us still. As for the theoretical problems the book poses for the reader, they result from what I will call the practice of transcoding implicit in McGurl's remarkably capacious topic. Transcoding presupposes an allegorical structure, a system of levels, in which we find ourselves obliged to translate from one to the other, inasmuch as each of these levels speaks a different language and is decipherable only in terms of a specific code. So it is that even in these opening paragraphs we have found ourselves moving from the economic situation of the writer to his or her aesthetic, from the status of the university—enormously enlarged since the Second World War and the very symbol of a new and enlarged democratic populace—to its class meaning for the immigrants and racial and gender underclasses who find themselves excluded from it, or on the contrary obliged to use it as a class ladder. We have had to invoke anti-intellectualism (and even to suggest the issue of the difference between America and Europe, and perhaps even, in globalization, between America and the rest of the world).

McGurl's argument makes its way sinuously among a number of different discourses: the history of writing programs and the mentality of their teachers, the way in which these professional developments are related to the evolution of late capitalism, the meaning of multiculturalism, the reevaluation of the central role of New Criticism after the war, the "hidden injuries of class" and the meaning and function of the Jamesian "point of view" (now rebaptized "focalization"), and so on. The text is itself experimental writing, and we have to learn how to shift gears and yet keep the thread, how to remain equal to its demands and to appreciate the originality of its historical judgments and the new system of American literature it proposes, as well as the originality of its method and form.

The book sets out a system in which two triads are coordinated (it will be their interrelationship which poses the most interesting problems for theory). The first of these tripartite systems is that of the teachings and doctrine of the creative writing programs introduced after the war. It can naturally enough be assumed that these literary and formal injunctions reflect significant changes in American subjectivity as well as modifications in the class relationships it reflects. They are quickly summarized: write what you know, show don't tell, find your voice.

In their form, these injunctions constitute an attempt to resolve a dilemma, or better still a contradiction: how can that very personal and individual practice that is writing, and in particular the writing of the novel, be taught? Remember that the novel, for Bakhtin and

Lukács and so many others, is the very expression of modernity as such, and thereby transcends and annuls all the older fixed forms which presumably in one way or another could be taught: epic, drama, the various forms of the lyric, et cetera. The novel is in that sense always "lawless," as Gide liked to say, and we may have to raise some questions when someone like Henry James comes along and offers to codify its new "laws" in doctrines like "point of view." Even though he is virtually absent from this book, for reasons I will come to, Faulkner offered his own useful tripartite formula for what the novelist's practice presupposed: experience, imagination, observation—any two of which will suffice in a pinch (only Wolfe had all three). Maybe observation can be taught, as Flaubert tried to do with Maupassant; unfortunately, the other two are not available in the classroom.

McGurl's three injunctions try to address this difficult problem in a historically new way. (1) Write what you know. This emphasizes experience, in a way that tends to bracket "imagination" and to turn the writer's attention to the autobiographical, if not the confessional. It will be focused and intensified by the next injunction: (2) Find your voice, which perhaps begins with the premium placed by modernism on the invention of a personal "style," and develops into a virtuoso practice of the first person as performance. This seems at odds with the final injunction: (3) Show don't tell, which is the obvious legacy of James's theorization of point of view, and most directly reintroduces "craft" or technique, a set of rules (drawn from drama) that would seem to be more teachable in the context of a writing program than the two other (negative and positive) recommendations.

The attention to craft is thus the trickiest of these formulas, as its ultimate tendency is the despised return to genre and subgenre

Fredric Jameson

(and the loss of any claim to genuinely "literary" prestige, unless the genre is handled reflexively, as pastiche). But it is clearly also the disciplinary component, without which all the excesses of narcissism and verbiage are potentially released. Thus, in a way, "craft" tends to connote not merely discipline and self-discipline, but a kind of restraint that will eventually be identified as minimalism, in another thematic opposition, never theorized directly, which runs centrally through McGurl's book. From this perspective, maximalism is rhetoric and self-expression, and its most distressingly monumental prophet is Thomas Wolfe, while in the contemporary moment the extraordinary productivity of Joyce Carol Oates will come to embody a different but no less troubling and potentially noncanonizable excess. The maximalist impulse will then tend to find its confirming ideology in the (relatively modern) notion of genius, which Kant saw as the eruption of the natural into the human, while its most congenial plot formation will be the novel of the artist.

This is not to suggest that minimalism finds its realization in the repudiation of the category of expression as such. On the contrary, the inaugural model of minimalism, Ernest Hemingway, simply opened up another alternative path to expression, one characterized by the radical exclusion of rhetoric and theatricality, for which, however, that very exclusion and its tense silences and omissions was precisely the technique for conveying heightened emotional intensity (particularly in the marital situation). Hemingway's avatar Raymond Carver then learned to mobilize the minimalist technique of "leaving out" in the service of a rather different and more specifically American sense of desolation and depression—of emotional unemployment, so to speak.

This is the point at which Faulkner's near-absence may be illuminated, for Faulkner is the very locus, one would think, of a

270

maximalism that runs from the full-throated deployment of an expressive outpouring of language to the overweening ambition of the creation of a world extending from a tragic Southern past to a degraded commercial present. The Faulknerian long sentence is then the paradigm of a maximalism that remains high art, but it certainly cannot offer the craft and the tools for pedagogy available in minimalist discipline. I think that leaving Faulkner out of the picture (it is true that, virtually alone among modern American writers, he never had anything to do with writing programs) allows McGurl to avoid embarrassing questions of value that risk disrupting the magnificent and unique theoretical construction he has achieved in *The Program Era*.

I have been emphasizing the subjective turn in postwar American aesthetics which the writing program's theory and practice symptomatizes and reinforces, at the same time as it reveals and satisfies profound changes in the American psyche after the Second World War. The three injunctions are thus a precious clue for exploration both of the new postwar society and economy, and of the evolution of that subjectivity so often loosely identified as individualism. McGurl offers a few sociological references (Wright Mills, Pine and Gilmore, Thomas Frank), and even a few socioeconomic ones (Ulrich Beck, Anthony Giddens). The point is, however, not necessarily to endorse these (many are standard culture critiques), but rather to indicate the direction in which literary theory opens onto other disciplines. Class analysis is meanwhile omnipresent, and plagued as usual by the sometimes involuntary, sometimes intentional and strategic American habit of calling everything "middle class," so that what might once have been called the working class is now some form of lower middle class along with the others. But perhaps it is characteristic of American society today in late capital-

Fredric Jameson

ism, and of the literature that expresses its realities and its ideologies alike, that working-class realities somehow reach classification only via stories told in terms of race and gender, rather than in terms of work, outsourced and famously transformed into so many "service industries." Still, the transformations of subjectivity in this postwar period are necessarily dependent for their inspection on the kinds of narrative available, which McGurl codifies according to class terms.

There is one further observation to be made here: the increasingly self-centered and obsessively reflexive cast of this literary production, which seems to be implied in McGurl's injunctions (write what you know, find your voice), is not to be understood in an exclusively negative or critical way. "Write what you know" and "find your voice" can also be understood as the exploration and opening up of wholly new areas of experience: a naming of new findings, as with the model of the body so influentially pioneered by Foucault, which can now, for good or ill, be adapted to a kind of generalized colonization of subjectivity, its transformation into new experience(s). This process is radically different from the psychic "discoveries" and inventions we associate with the late nineteenth century, with Dostoevsky and James, George Eliot and Pontoppidan; those drew on the openings and possibilities of a competitive capitalism, in which robber barons and monopolies signified an expansion of individual and collective power. This American version, in the late twentieth century, signifies instead the constricted spaces and constraints of an already bureaucratized society, in which the "individualism" of the now lower middle classes is increasingly, as in Carver, the experience of impotence and vulnerability.

In fact, one of the more productive developments of the "postindividual" lies in its gradual allegorical transformation into group identities. This begins with the dialectic of the outsider and the rebel, who gradually—as McGurl demonstrates, relying on a notion of Walter Ong's—become the insiders of new collectivities, the small groups and new ethnicities of multicultural late capitalism. Meanwhile, the emphasis on the individual voice now slowly develops into militant ideologies of difference (which, as McGurl remarks, moves an otherwise distant High Theory such as Derrida's back into closer contact with, and increases its usefulness for, literature and creative writing).

So it is that what initially looked like a "culture of narcissism" now unexpectedly begins to generate new social formations and a new kind of non-introspective literature to express them. Thus McGurl's other tripartite system, which maps the literary forms of the novel into which contemporary production falls. Once again, it is important to remember that while arising as responses to a common situation and a common dilemma, the three tendencies or modes are also antithetical to one another aesthetically, experientially, and in their class connotations: it is here, indeed, that the antagonisms of high and low literature, of the realism/modernism opposition, of art versus life, are played out. But our deeper theoretical question has to do with the relationship between this second tripartite schema and the three writing program injunctions I have laid out. Here it is better to quote McGurl himself:

> Venturing to map the totality of postwar American fiction, I
> will describe it as breaking down into three relatively discrete
> but in practice overlapping aesthetic formations. The first,
> "technomodernism," is best understood as a tweaking of the term
> "postmodernism" in that it emphasizes the all-important engagement
> of postmodern literature with information technology; the second,
> "high cultural pluralism," will describe a body of fiction that joins

the high literary values of modernism with a fascination with the experience of cultural difference and the authenticity of the ethnic voice; the third, "lower-middle-class modernism," will be used to describe the large body of work—some would say it is the most characteristic product of the writing program—that most often takes the form of the minimalist short story, and is preoccupied more than anything else with economic and other forms of insecurity and cultural anomie.

In the first triad, it was easier to see what united the three injunctions than what divided them; here it is the reverse, and unless we somehow identify the aesthetic of production all three classifications share (their "autopoiesis"), the system, however useful or satisfying it may be, will risk breaking down into a series of empirical traits and characteristics.

One has to begin with their differences. Thus so-called "high cultural pluralism" turns out to comprise various kinds of ethnic literature, which unite the particularity of their races, genders, and ethnicities with the universality of a literary modernism which has come in our time to stand for Literature itself (Toni Morrison becomes the exhibit here, whose *Beloved* McGurl ingeniously converts into a kind of schoolroom drama). But now the universalism of these multicultures is rather startlingly contrasted with a "lower-middle-class modernism" (I would have preferred the word "realism"), which is white and thus in this case not only unmarked but also particular rather than universal. This is the textuality and the world of Carver's loners and losers, and it is also the place in which regionalism is suddenly activated as a term: the presumably Northwest regionalism of Carver Country, marked by subalternity and economic marginality, is confronted with the transcendental regionalism of a now truly universal South (indeed, a fascinating part of McGurl's research details the struggle for form and universality between Midwest and South in the early University of Iowa workshops).

There is therefore a struggle for literary status or universality or class prestige involved in these antagonisms (I have already identified such struggles as symbolic class struggle), but in this case what seems to be excluded is "technomodernism." One can once again quibble about the terminology, but much as I would like to I will limit myself to its translation into the single popular term "reflexivity," in particular as it concerns communication, information theory, and language, along with its cybernetic extensions and protensions. At stake here, perhaps, is the distinction between modernism and postmodernism, insofar as the reflexivity of the modern tends to turn merely on writing as such (as in *Pale Fire*), while the postmodern kind (as in the expression "postmodern novel," which seems by now to have become a genre) involves informational technologies that lie beyond old-fashioned language.

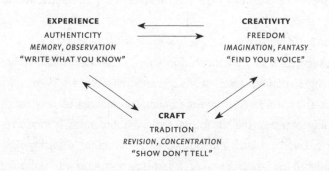

Fredric Jameson

Indeed, this distinction can clarify the presence of the idea of the modern in the adjacent category, "high cultural pluralism," where "high cultural" can be supposed to mean not a periodization but simply an ensemble of now codified and socially accepted techniques that did not exist in the realist era. These techniques can now be used for a range of materials, such as race, which used to be class-marked and thereby automatically registered in the realist category (where they scarcely fit, as with Jean Toomer or Zora Neale Hurston); and now are transmogrified into Literature as such (another sign of this process being the authorization from High Theory to translate race and ethnicity into the concept of "difference").

If we then assume that the two sets of circles are "the same" in the sense of forming a homology, and that it is the implementation of the three writing injunctions which, according to emphasis, projects each of the respective literary areas or categories, we would presumably be reasoning as follows. Writing what you know becomes, reflexively, writing itself, in its multiple and reflexive technologies and communicational manifestations. It probably also means emitting a scent of origins (much like Barth's *Giles Goat-Boy*), in this case the university, making the campus novel (beginning with Nabokov) a favored vehicle. But by now the campus has become the world:

> John Barth began to write *Giles Goat-Boy* at Pennsylvania State University, a land-grant institution where, as he later explained, "in an English department of nearly one hundred members" he taught his classes "not far from an experimental nuclear reactor, a water tunnel for testing the hull forms of missile submarines, laboratories for ice cream research and mushroom development, a lavishly produced football program . . . a barn-size computer with elaborate cooling systems . . . and the literal and splendid barns of the animal

husbandry departments." Massively infused with federal funding for
the support of Cold War weapons technology and other scientific
research, but still catering to a regional and state economy (and its
large football fan base), the secular university has become, for Barth,
comically expanded and diversified in its worldly pursuits, nothing
like the pious gentleman's college of yore.

As for high cultural pluralism (sometimes called multiculturalism),
it too has acquired the status of universality or of Literature (technomodernism already had that, by definition) by way of a category
henceforth excluded by the technology of writing or of High Communication: namely, the humble voice, establishing itself in the
no-man's-land between "show don't tell," where telling is bad, and
"find your voice," where the voice now stands not only for difference
but also and above all for storytelling, and for a new modernist first
person, perhaps harkening back to Mark Twain but now authorizing
new kinds of transformation, such as the one that lifts Philip Roth's
voice out of a narrow ethnic or Jewish literary category into Literature.

I have neglected until now the supplementary complication
resulting from yet a third framework of McGurl's presentation, a
chronology authorized more by the history of writing programs than
the history—yet to be constructed—of American literature itself. The
three historical periods are 1890–1960, covering the founding of
the programs, especially the 47 Workshop, Iowa, and Stanford; their
institutionalization (1960–75); and their omnipresence today in what
remains our contemporary scene of literary production (1975 onward).
Fair enough, and there is rich material here, particularly on the anec-
dotal and biographical level (Wallace Stegner and Paul Engle being
particularly significant figures). But the consequence of this necessary
and even indispensable supplementary framework (which endows a

structural system prone to static and ahistorical cross sections with
a dynamic of metamorphosis and continuity/change which it was
not, according to the critiques of structuralism, supposed to have) is
the illusion that what we have here is a literary history, and in a sense
we do have a literary history, or at least a mapping bound to modify
traditional literary histories. For we do move from Wolfe to Carver,
we take in Barth and Kesey, Oates and Morrison along the way, and
a host of minor writers from yesterday and today. Unfortunately, this
quickly and unconsciously translates back into a canon and questions
of value; and at this point, quite apart from the absence of the poets,
sets off all kinds of idiotic questions about inclusion, principally the
one I have asked throughout: Where is Faulkner?

But now we approach a momentous problem, and it lies in
McGurl's tripartite schema. For it is the fate of any third term to linger
precariously on the margins, disabused of any ambition to become
the synthesis between the two already in place, and thus condemned
to struggle to displace one or other of its opposite numbers to find
its own proper place in the binary system. What McGurl has called
"lower-middle-class modernism" is always on the edge of proletari-
anization, slipping back down into mass culture and the genres still
available as Literature to the nobler modes of technomodernism
and high cultural pluralism in the form of pastiche.

The lower-middle-class mode cannot hope for that distinction,
and so in it the two great tendencies of minimalism and maximalism
fight it out to exhaustion, the former producing Carver, the latter
Oates. Of the two, it may be said that minimalism carries the palm
by way of a genuine high-literary invention—the rebirth of that
quintessential writing-program form, the short story.

Meanwhile, both continue to exude the American misery, and
more authentically than any of the competition convey the shame

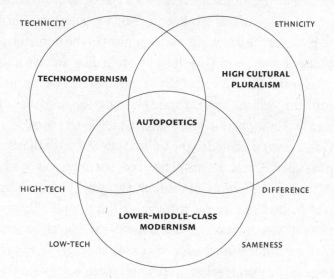

and pride of the human condition as lived by white America. It is a case of winner loses: the closer it is to real life in America, the less it can aspire to the distinction of Literature. At this point, the shame of the writing program joins the shame of America itself, which the other two modes have so successfully disguised.

Unfortunately, every triadic structure tends to fall into a pseudo-Hegelian pattern, and labors mightily to produce a synthesis. McGurl's triad cannot really do that, and so the burden of the operation falls back on the opposition between maximalism and minimalism. McGurl here produces, in the guise of Bharati Mukherjee's concept of "miniaturism," a seemingly satisfying place to stop. Probably the most famous deployment of this term, however, appears in that perverse and dramatic moment when Nietzsche, attacking the Wagnerian "sickness," pronounced Wagner to be a great miniaturist. That startling event should give us pause. Indeed, I want to suggest, following Nietzsche, that only a great maximalist can be a miniaturist (think of Mahler, Proust, even Faulkner); minimalism has no place for the obsessive perfectionism of the miniaturist. So the synthesis won't work (I hesitate before adding my own idiosyncratic feeling that four is better than three, and that we are missing a fourth term, which I would locate beyond the boundaries of the Program Era somewhere in poetry and in individual words).

Is *The Program Era* limited to the United States? It's true that Pascale Casanova's *World Republic of Letters* is evoked, but only so as to adapt it to the "inner globalization" of the multiplicity of literary modes and forms of distinction surveyed throughout this complex history. But American literature and the English language can scarcely be assumed to stop at our borders: for Casanova, consecration by Paris was a crucial stage in the world reception of non-French writers (to that we must also add translation into English, for world recognition today consists in securing this particular green card). Meanwhile, some of our literary positions have also been outsourced; much of what takes place outside can probably be assigned to the lower-middle-class waiting room, and peremptorily classified as mere "realism." Reflexive experimentation has probably long since been played out abroad, but there is one category in which Americans have begun to flag, and that is Faulknerian maximalism, whose interminable voices no longer seem tolerable without their Southern framework. Now, translated into something called "magic realism," this American specialty—whether adopted by Günter Grass or Salman Rushdie or the authors of the Latin American boom—has been promoted into a genuinely global genre, and we glimpse, outside the confines of an American Program Era, the outlines of some wholly different world system of letters coming into being. +

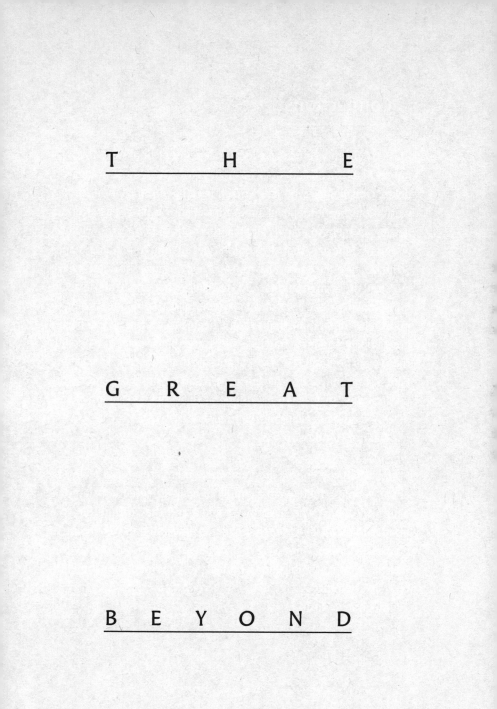

T H E

G R E A T

B E Y O N D

I just taught this course at a local independent bookstore that was mostly made up of students who do not have MFAs, mostly older students. One woman who had worked in refugee camps in Africa had written this beautiful novel about Africa and was having a hard time getting an agent to read it. She had this notion, I don't know if it's a wrong or right one, that she couldn't get anyone to read her manuscript because she doesn't have an MFA and because she doesn't have any short-story publications. And I told her, "That's not true, an agent is just looking at the book and it's wonderful and someone is going to publish it." And I think that to some degree that's true. If you have a great book it's going to find its readers, and that's what I told her. But then I went home and I was sort of not sure that's the case. I mean here I am, I sold a novel after having an MFA and having those short-story publications, so maybe I'm coming at this from a really privileged place and not understanding the true value of my MFA.

**Eleanor Henderson**

I think when you go to a program where there are a lot of really talented people—there were a couple of really talented female poets who were moms who lived in Wyoming and they had gotten to a point with their kids where they had free time and they were trying to go back to writing. They were really talented, and they had no entrée into that New York publishing world. In those moments you think, Oh right, it is helpful.

**Meghan O'Rourke**

# Reality Publishing

## Darryl Lorenzo Wellington

I
-

Go into the magazine section of any bookstore and you'll find professional writers' "trade" journals, imploring your attention with unassailable advice.* The headlines blazon: "Top Ten Tips to Writing Success," "Be a Good Writer in One Month," "How to Sell Your Novel." I don't know how many such magazines exist, but it's more than you'd think. In any issue of a typical writers' journal you'll find exhaustive listings of contests, awards, grant opportunities, and residency opportunities. You'll find a feature on a veteran novelist, or a young one in the first blush of success ("This Could Be You . . ."). And you'll find tips.

Contest listings have an obvious value. But tips? Tips are not information: they're suggestions, approaches, repackaged common sense. Tips make no guarantees, and they have no conceivable end. And so these magazines are crammed with tips. They love tips. They

---

* Part I of this essay was originally published on nplusonemag.com in 2009.

Darryl Lorenzo Wellington

swamp their readership with tips. The joy, or the misery, of tips is their endless repetition.

"How to Arm Your Characters," "How to Improve Your Storytelling," "How to Mine Your Novel for Gold," "How to Land an Agent," "Kafka Toiled in Obscurity & Died Penniless: If Only He Had a Website . . ." The jargon is indistinguishable from the self-help lingo of any genre. Car fanzines on the adjacent racks promise secret knowledge and privileged instruction. Lifestyle magazines promise psychological building blocks, step by step toward a healthier, happier, or even impervious psychology. Nearby style magazines give tips on better and better sex. The headlines blur together in a cavalcade of tips—for excellent writing, extraordinary sex, exquisite cars.

Yet sex and car tips differ from writing tips in a crucial respect. Acquiring sexual expertise does not require you to be connected to any particular industry. Retooling your car doesn't depend on bagging a powerful agent. But fiction is ruled by New York publishing houses—and increasingly influenced by association with major MFA programs. People who live in Statesboro, Georgia, rather than New York, and people who lack any higher education whatsoever, may still want to publish books. You could argue that writers' magazines provide a substitute education for thousands of dreamers without access to writing classes or MFA programs. What you see on the magazine racks, however, is a glut of hard-sell techniques. What you see says publishing is all about Winner and Losers. Though tips may mention literary values, the excess reinforces the impression: only the shrewd survive. You're talented. You know it. Losers play fair, however, and lose. Losers listen to the wrong advice. Winners take everything.

—

284

## Reality Publishing

The landscape described above should be familiar to anyone with a passing acquaintance with reality TV and its conventions. On *Survivor* the castaways make deals behind each other's back. Neither athletic ability nor sportsmanship necessarily carries the day. Humiliation is part of every episode, and the humiliated deserve their failure. While the finest singers on *American Idol* may briefly stand out from the pack, public votes decide the winner. A host of reality shows hurry to endorse the principle that winning and losing have less to do with excellence than with captivating spectacle.

It may come as no surprise, then, that a publishing industry facing its own financial terrors should have spawned the idea of staying relevant by copycatting this form of entertainment. Like the amateur contests it was modeled on, the Amazon Breakthrough Novel Award brought the same stew of spectacle, humiliation, and "reality" into the normally private acts of judgment and reactions of a professional world—in this case, the world of book publishing.

The reality TV universe isn't chaos; it isn't godless. But its gods are pagan. The "reality" is that—like life—the shows are unfair. Public votes sometimes matter and sometimes don't, but they do or don't in a structured way, as if the shows followed a logic handed down from Mt. Olympus. Remember *The Apprentice*, wherein the contestants battled to win a job from Donald Trump? His godliness salted the psychological wounds of failure.

In the Amazon Breakthrough contest, there are three resident deities. The first is Amazon.com. Amazon's already weighty influence over unpublished authors' dreams tripled in 2005 when the company acquired BookSurge, which publishes vanity books. For hundreds of dollars (or thousands, depending on the BookSurge package) desperate authors could see their books bound and galleyed and (in the loosest sense of the word) promoted on an Amazon page.

Add in two New York–based deities to complete the trinity: Penguin, the venerable publisher that pioneered the production of cheap, pocket-size paperbacks, and the National Book Critics Circle (NBCC), whose own set of annual awards are widely respected. Penguin offered a $25,000 publishing contract to the winner of the contest; NBCC reviewers were called on to evaluate the semifinalists' manuscripts.*

Having always promoted itself as a company that empowers readers, the Amazon contest appealed to (or manipulated?) a very internet-savvy reading community. A short history: in late 2007 Amazon issued a call for online manuscripts, and from October 1 to November 5 accepted the first 5,000 entries they received. Volunteers from Amazon's interactive community of "Top Reviewers" (self-styled lit-lovers who have written thousands of customer reviews) weeded those 5,000 entries down to 836.

Then the so-called professionals got involved. NBCC critics received truckloads of full manuscripts and browsed them. The critics penned anonymous capsule reviews, following a format

---

* When this essay first appeared on nplusonemag.com, *n+1* received a letter from Jane Ciabattari, then president of the NBCC. Ciabattari noted that no official partnership existed between her organization and the ABNA: "It is true that a former president of the organization, John Freeman, was involved in the contest (as a judge), as is at least one present board member. Other NBCC members may have signed on to help with the culling process. But these are private, remunerated affiliations." I accepted this clarification, but also noted that, at the time of the contest's inception, John Freeman was NBCC president. He promoted the contest enthusiastically, and his name and NBCC affiliation appeared on ABNA promotional materials. The NBCC also assisted in soliciting reviewers for the contest. Though the NBCC was not an official partner, Freeman's highly visible role, and Amazon's frequent use of the NBCC name, gave contestants reason to believe that it was.

provided by *Publishers Weekly*. Amazon created a special web page featuring a five-thousand-word excerpt from each novel, available for download and customer review. The "contestants" were stacked in alphabetical order by their titles, without cover illustrations—like test products without wrappers or packaging. Eventually Amazon added the capsule reviews, thus creating a web page where anyone who wanted to could read mostly negative and occasionally scathing reviews of nearly a thousand unpublished books.

Meanwhile the real drama (and pathos) unfolded on the contest's vigorous discussion boards. The contestants commiserated and conspired. They traded professional secrets and personal stories (including many, many testimonials reflecting on their childhood beginnings as would-be novelists). There were periodic rants (particularly after the posting of the reviews, which the authors referred to as "*Publishers Weekly* reviews"). There were spells in which the writers simply waited for news. "Amazon must love making us suffer," one participant wrote.

Penguin Books editors sifted the manuscripts that had garnered the best reviews. The endgame began on March 3, when public voting began. The grand-prize winner among the ten finalists would be selected by vote—public vote, à la *American Idol*. From five thousand manuscripts to ten. From ten to one "breakthrough" into the real world of publishing. The other nine finalists would receive compensatory awards: vacation packages for four runners-up, home entertainment centers for the five others.


Full disclosure: I am a member of the NBCC. I penned several of the much-contested *Publishers Weekly* reviews, for a $40 a manuscript honorarium. Am I a "professional" reviewer? I am a poet and a human being—and I review books, too. But for the purposes of the Amazon Breakthrough Novel Award (the discussion boards insisted) I was the bloodless professional, the executioner. Over a period of six weeks, some twenty manuscripts arrived at my apartment. The deliveries thumped at the doorstep like children on Halloween, wanting treats. I dispatched them with 250-word critiques—tricks.

I tried to justify the contest and my participation in it. After all, I thought, the public voting at the end might encourage reading in a fun way. Though the contest may not encourage high literary culture, how can anyone be so snobbish as to argue that people shouldn't be the arbiters of their own tastes? However hokey the spectacle, the competition could unearth a notable manuscript, or so I argued to myself. But none of it quite worked; I still felt queasy about participating. It was probably out of guilt that I began to check the message boards.

Before long, I was hooked, visiting the boards every few days, keeping tracks of distinct characters and general turns in the flavor of the dialogue. Initially the posts were characterized by ebullience and a feeling of community. I was taken aback by how often the contestants gushed with gratitude and used the first-person plural, joining their praises in a chorus of thanks. "We want to thank Amazon for doing this." "This is our chance—our shot."

They expressed familial kinship: "I don't believe I have much chance at the final rounds. Still, I'll never forget all the friends and support I've made here." But as in any reality contest, it's the solo pursuit of fortune that drives an ostensible bonding experience. From the very first rounds, contestants laid out plans to plug their novels on their Facebook pages. They questioned other contestants' positive customer reviews. (Later, they would question the professional capsule reviews.) They strategized ahead to the round of public votes, venting suspicions that other, less honorable contestants would garner a majority of votes by appealing to relatives and local writing groups, while simultaneously positioning themselves as friendly and supportive (perhaps so that, if they made the final ten, the 4,990 eliminated contestants would vote for them).

They were playing to win. I searched the message boards week after week for a facetious reference to the second- and third-place prizes, hoping someone saw humor in the notion that their writing ability could win them a Caribbean cruise or a TV. Week after week, the search proved fruitless.

Allow me, in the spirit of literary confessionals (published or otherwise), to make another personal disclosure: a decade ago I spent a summer interning for an agency known as A Rising Sun Literary Group. Defunct since the late 1990s, the agency charged a $350 fee for evaluating unpublished manuscripts, promising that "a staff of professional writers" would provide critiques. The "professional writers" were college juniors and seniors like myself. At the time I suspected A Rising Sun Literary Group was a scam, but I discovered only recently that it was merely one part of a larger scam, orchestrated by a notorious con artist named Dorothy Deering.

A former science fiction writer turned professional spinner of manipulative fantasies, Deering managed a number of so-called literary agencies in the 1990s. Her agencies—plural, because A Rising Sun operated under a variety of names—charged exorbitant fees and wooed clients with the false belief that their manuscripts were on the verge of being sold to major houses or Hollywood. But the various Deering agencies never sold a book. The FBI finally put Dorothy Deering out of business for shady practices and mail fraud.

Darryl Lorenzo Wellington

A former FBI agent wrote a book about her: *Ten Percent of Nothing: The Case of a Literary Agent from Hell* was published by Southern Illinois University Press in 2004.

Until the company's exposure, the daily mailings stacked high. Rising Sun advertised itself as a "sensitive" company; the pose attracted authors of "sensitive" paper-thin confessionals.

One Rising Sun author impressed me in a memorable way by literally forgetting she was writing fiction. The manuscript was a generic romance story. Character X is in love with Character Y. X is a shy virgin. Y is a bad boy with a reputation. Characters X and Y fall in love. They break up and Character X falls into a state of depression. Character X stays in a state of depression. Her depression worsens. She stops eating. She is diagnosed as anorexic. She swallows an overdose. The doctors save her, but she is convinced she wants to die. For a few pages of her death throes, the author of this third-person novel slips up and turns to a confessional first-person mode. Three pages later the third-person narration returns unannounced. For those three pages, the writer had been too overwhelmed and helpless to distinguish between the facts of her own life story and a work of fiction.

I pondered that sad and bizarre memory as I waded through the many confessional Amazon Breakthrough Novel Award entries. There were no hidden masterpieces in my batch of manuscripts. In no less than five of the twenty novels I slogged through, the lead character was a college English major who dead-ended upon graduation and supported him- or herself by working lowly service jobs. Imagining these economically strapped college grads turned carhops, dishwashers, and bartenders, and trying within the limitations of their resources or their talent to create a literary culture for themselves, sapped the fun out of publicly panning their books in 250-word squibs.

The posting of the reviews unleashed a storm of activity on the message boards. By and large, the contestants were pissed off. Some adopted a philosophical attitude, but the majority (aside from the favorably reviewed gloaters) vented and inundated the boards with hysteria and conspiracy theories, claiming that the paid reviewers had mangled the plots of their novels, that the customer reviews were actually very reliable, that they had personally consulted "book doctors" who had in turn assured them the reviews were ludicrous.

Then and only then did the message boards raise the topic of exploitation, usually in ways that addressed contestants' bruised feelings rather than the big picture. The starstruck babble receded long enough for the would-be novelists to reconsider whether the contest might be inherently cruel or unjust: "Egos have been shattered and hearts have been broken here, and I don't think that's what Amazon intended." On February 9, 2008, a contestant began a discussion thread titled "Did They Actually Read Yours?" in which the suspicion and hostility escalated. A mantra caught on: "I call it speculative-extrapolation. They saw some actual words, had a pre-formed opinion and went with that. . . . I had to read the thing 5 times before I realized how little of it was actually factual." "I felt similarly about my PW review (which was truly dreadful). It seems as though the reviewer read the synopsis and skimmed the beginning of the book and then jumped to a great deal of mistaken conclusions." "I agree that odds are most of the entries are probably unpublishable at this point and that many deserve tough criticism. But . . . I have taken issue with my PW reviewer to the extent he or she simply misrepresented my work."

A great novel—particularly an experimental one—would have a hard time succeeding in any reality book contest, much less the Amazon Breakthrough Novel Award. To impress first the Amazon

Top Reviewers, and then the overworked professional reviewers (who had to read ten to twenty books in six weeks), it was probably best to have written a quick, readable novel that was accessible in a state of distraction. To this extent, the concerns expressed on the message boards—that the standards were ambiguous, the contest was hurried, and the reviewers hadn't read the submissions carefully enough—were legitimate. Even if the bulk of the manuscripts didn't warrant lengthy consideration.

Eventually, the postings began to exhibit healthy doses of cynical wit: "I'm ready to sell out. Yes, I'll do commercials in Japan, whatever it takes. Already I have all but donned a pink skirt and boob tube in my efforts to get passing traffic to my novel. If they want me to write, I can do that as well." And outright hostility: "I have to say this thing with reviews and the visibility of the entries is a farce." The catty sniping—and the emotional high-wire acts—indirectly posed reasonable questions: Were there instructions to the reviewers? What kind of books was Penguin interested in? *And why was Penguin interested in doing this?*

The ten finalists were allowed to make a "plea" for themselves. Their manuscript excerpts were posted alongside photos and autobiographical statements—beauty-pageant-style effusions of passions and dreams, stories about pets, et cetera, worthy of a runway walk finale. The three top vote-getters were flown to New York, where the winner was announced. Congratulations to Bill Loehfelm, author of *Fresh Kills*—a mystery thriller I have never read and probably never will.

The 2008 Amazon Breakthrough Novel Award will be followed by a 2009 contest and so on, possibly forevermore. The *American Idol*–

style format of the contest will come to seem inevitable, as opposed to optional.

The contest was intended for writers at the bottom of the literary food chain and cynically directed at the section of the public most susceptible to the culture of hype. Remember the (extremely American) ethos of the reality-show world: reality contests reproduce "reality" by intentionally making the contests less than fair. The final round in which the public demonstrates its critical acumen (which the contest has done nothing to sharpen) amounts to a sarcastic egalitarian sham. *American Idol* is watched by millions of viewers. The Amazon Breakthrough Novel Award will never attract millions of readers, nor justify the fun and games by popularizing literacy, nor resolve the issue of savvy contestants racking up dubious votes.

Near the very end, a discussion-board thread queried the bumped authors: "Why Are You Still Here?" The answers were unusually reconciled. They planned to purchase the winning book. They were here to support the community. They were still participating out of loyalty and curiosity. They knew they could write a better novel. They appreciated the contest for providing insight into the publishing industry, however arbitrary the judging process appeared to be. They were still here for this noble reason, or that personal motive, or the opportunity to fight another day. Or this unforgettable response: "Cause I like it here. I belong in a way I've never belonged in my real life."

I won't be visiting the ABNA website this year because I can't think of the contest without reflecting on that comment. Whoever wrote this intuitively understood that reality shows depend on feelings of worthlessness. A public that felt empowered would demand more from its contests; a disenfranchised public will easily slip into the role of the buffoon, and even arrogantly demand the privilege of playing the buffoon. Reality-show success is all about childish self-promotion. To mature, or to begin to speak maturely, will usually get you voted off.

II
—

The Amazon Breakthrough Novel Award is still going strong. The reality-show format and gimmicks remain intact, though the entertainment centers and vacation packages were eliminated in the contest's second year. Beginning in 2010, two winners were chosen for publication, one in the General Fiction category and the other in Young Adult Fiction. The advances were lowered from $25,000 to $15,000. (Why not publish two books—or promote two breakthroughs—for the price of one?)

In December 2012, Amazon announced that their partnership with Penguin had been severed; contest winners would now be published by Amazon Publishing, in Kindle and print editions. If there was anything surprising about this change, it was that it took so long: in recent years, Amazon had established several editorial imprints, as part of its ongoing effort to vertically integrate the publishing business. It's almost hard to believe that Amazon and Penguin survived five years of partnership, despite the ever-escalating tensions between Amazon and the Big Six (now Five, with the recent creation of behemoth Penguin Random House) publishers.

The updated, Amazon-only contest will begin with a splash, awarding prizes in five categories instead of two: General Fiction, Young Adult Fiction, Mystery/Thriller, Sci-Fi/Fantasy/Horror, and Romance. Each category champion will receive a $15,000 publishing contract from Amazon; the grand-prize winner's advance will balloon to $50,000. "The Amazon Breakthrough Novel Award has helped thousands of authors realize their dream of writing a novel," announced an Amazon spokesman, setting the dream-bar low. "We're excited to evolve the contest this year to recognize talented aspiring authors in even more genres, with bigger advances, more winners, and quickly bring the winning novels to readers around the world."

After the first part of this essay appeared online, I received a caboodle of responses from Amazon Breakthrough contestants. They were irate that I'd quoted their message-board chatter for the purposes of my piece, and so I won't quote their emails here, but the general tenor was spiteful. The invective they'd hurled at Amazon during the latter stages of the contest they now hurled at me.

I also received comments that challenged me more intelligently. These writers argued that while there was a good deal that was silly or even dismaying about the contest, I had underestimated, or failed to appreciate, how the self-publishing phenomenon spearheaded by Amazon represented a revolution. Self-publishing, they argued, was leveling the playing field, taking absolute authority away from the New York publishing houses. And the most sophisticated made very good arguments that this revolution would not be without the aesthetic merits of a radical, challenging break with the past.

Six years and eight winners later, the jury is still out on how radical this break really is. Bill Loehfelm, whose thriller *Fresh Kills* won the inaugural contest, has since produced three more thrillers, *Bloodroot*, *The Devil She Knows*, and *The Devil in Her Way*, published by Berkley Trade, Picador, and Sarah Crichton Books, an imprint of FSG. The next year's winner, *Bill Warrington's Last Chance*, by James King, was a novel about a family trying to work through their troubles that was more along the lines of conventional literary fiction, though written somewhat

Darryl Lorenzo Wellington

loosely. Each winner was dutifully published by one of the Penguin imprints (Berkley Prime Crime for *Fresh Kills*; Viking for *Bill Warrington*; Riverhead for Patricia McArdle's *Farishta*, about a woman who helps refugees in Afghanistan; Dutton for Gregory Hill's *East of Denver*). None appear to have sold many copies. Each received reasonably positive reviews from the trade publications. None did well enough to paper over an awkward marriage of sensibilities, and one suspects Penguin was not sad to see the partnership dissolve.

Penguin Books and its whiff of the classic hierarchies of old-school publishing are out. But the contest, and Amazon Publishing, and all its accompanying ideological mystifications, soldier on, tapping into the common sentiments of an ocean of unpublished and—more importantly—unconnected authors. They repeat the word "community" like a mantra, because relative to writers with New York agents, New York careers, or even just New York addresses, as well as to writers and students insulated (however temporarily) within the walls of academia, they lack it. They hunger for the insulations of "community"—a word that connotes a sense of belonging, dignity, respect. They easily confuse what they pine after for personal gratification, but what the unconnected truly long for is a sense of belonging to a common culture—a culture both fluid enough to absorb their individual eccentricity, and stable enough to provide standards by which to validate judgments. A literary world exists, and most people—most writers, even—exist outside it. The Breakthrough contest, and the rise of the culture of self-publishing in general, makes them feel like they're on the inside, however long the odds of success.

Call me a utopian, but I believe every entrant to the Amazon Breakthrough Novel Award would chuck the contest, the reality-show format, and all the tips on how to hype your book for a sense of cultural belonging. The Amazon "community" suggests a world in which everyone can publish a book, within a public space that may lead you belatedly to a special destiny. Of course, this community isn't unionized, socialist, or cooperatively owned: far-reaching powers of inclusivity (a community anyone can join) often seem synonymous with far-reaching powers of exclusivity (be with Amazon or be alone). For the time being, the Amazon Breakthrough Novel seems less a promotion for the entrants than for the corporate sponsor, and the winner each year, no matter who wins the contest, is Amazon.com. This hints at a publishing revolution, though like many revolutions before it, it doesn't look to be the one the revolutionaries truly needed, or sometimes thought they were fighting for. +

# Lessons

I probably learned a lot more than anybody else who was in that program for those two years, because I was the only one who hadn't studied creative writing before. So I was learning from them, sucking them dry of all the information they had accumulated. Like, "Oh, yeah that's how you make something move faster, that's how you do dialogue," stuff like that. I got more out of it because I had more to learn, further to go.

I also learned from things I disagreed with, which is key. If you're going to stand out as a writer, you can't just write the way everybody wants you to write. Everybody kept saying "Why, why did this character do this, what's the motivation here?" But the idea that I was going to explain the motivation of my character just didn't resonate with me. You know, the quickest way to be wrong about anybody is to assume their motivations. Motivations are a combination of so many different things—the weather, how much the person slept the night before. People make these consequential decisions based on tiny factors. I felt like it's something people in workshops say when they don't have anything real to add, but feel like they should participate. So they go, "Why does this character do this?" When I saw people trying to compensate for that, overexplaining their character's actions, it usually slowed down the story. It was just boring. So I decided I wasn't going to tell the motivations and I wasn't going to have any backstory.

**Stephen Elliot**

After I was done at the workshop I spent six weeks in Iowa City, living in someone's attic. I walked like ten miles a day and read *Underworld*, some Philip Roth books, things like that. Going back and reading the things I really love, you know, and seeing how they were totally unworkshoppable, each totally its own individual thing that could not be broken down. I think that was probably the best lesson I had during the whole workshop—the six weeks of reading afterward.

**Lee Klein**

# A Partial List of the Books I've Written

## Eli S. Evans

When I was in the MFA program at the University of Arizona, I sent a story to *The New Yorker*, and they didn't publish it but responded with a handwritten note, and I sent a different story to *Esquire*, and they didn't publish that one, but also responded with a handwritten note. When you're doing an MFA these are things you're really excited about. Now they don't seem so important. But at the time I was pretty proud.

By the time I finished at Arizona, I'd signed with an agent who was theoretically representing a novel of mine called *The Alliance*. It's about 260 pages long, and I wrote it in a week, in a kind of rapture. I still think it's the best thing I've written. It was about a group of people—their names were Cocteau, Cousteau (the only woman), Martín, Jacksonian, and Lorenzen Wright—who'd secured a grant for an art project that entailed living together for a year and not doing anything in particular. The place was indeterminate, but it resembled Milwaukee's Third Ward, during its transitional phase, and they were living in one of these old warehouse buildings that by now have all been converted into cheesy condos (a lot of which have subsequently been repossessed or gone delinquent). The book was written in the first-person plural, and it ended sadly when Martín, who was the kid of the group, offed himself, but then there was an uplifting coda in which Jacksonian clipped a pigeon with his car and thought he'd killed it, but then saw it in his rearview mirror ascending skyward, shedding feathers because of the impact. Then came a second coda that took place in a neighborhood coffee shop called the Comic Explosion Café, where the two proprietors had closed for business and entered this hermetic life together in the building basement. At the very end of the novel the building burned down—there were bad economic times and then (maybe), "Better times. Another building was erected in its place."

I had this agent for about a year, but we were not exactly on the same page. He thought I was going to revise the novel, which in fact I needed to do, but instead I put my head in the sand and moved to LA and kept hoping one day he'd email me to say that he'd sold it for $100,000, even though I don't actually think he was showing it around at all. Finally toward spring, with everything in LA having worked out pretty lousily, I had my roommate proofread it for grammar mistakes and sentences that randomly turned into other sentences, and sent it to my agent saying it was "revised." In return, I was promptly informed that he was "trimming his list" and I hadn't made the cut. This was devastating.

Then I wrote a very bad novel, about five hundred pages long, called *Dreaming of Heidegger*, that I don't even want to talk about.

By that point I was well into my second year in Los Angeles, living in a big warehouse space on the corner of Pico Boulevard and Fourth Avenue, in a desert of poverty and tire shops that were fronts for underground economic activity. I started a new novel, which would take me the next two years to write. It ended up being 2,424 pages long. The novel was about a kid named Engelbert—after Engelbert Humperdinck—who has an identical twin but his twin is a heart-throb, a confident guy, a lawyer in San Francisco. Engelbert is not a heartthrob. He lives in LA and works at a video rental store, and his best friend is a lesbian, but then his lesbian best friend falls for his brother, and upon finding this out Engelbert drives home and gets pulled over for making an illegal left turn. The police officer decides to let him off the hook using what he calls the "diarrhea excuse"—the idea being that since for safety purposes the officer has to call in the stop before he even gets out of his car, he can't just pretend it never happened, so it's the unwritten rule among police officers that when you want to let someone off you say they had a bad case of diarrhea. I had a last sentence in mind, which I had had in mind for a really long time: "Here seems like the kind of place people will come a thousand years from now, as I have come to it tonight, to contemplate a world that never was, and the future as it might have been." "Here" was the intersection of the 405 and the 110, near LAX, which I would pass beneath on my way home from Orange Coast College after teaching evening classes. It looked, without traffic, skeletal and ghastly.

I finally arrived at that sentence, after putting it off for more than two thousand pages, and then I went to the Hollywood YMCA and, true story, played pickup basketball with, among other people, Jus-tin Timberlake. I called the novel *A Man Without Love*, which is the title of an Englebert Humperdinck album you'll find if you paw through the records at any Goodwill or Salvation Army.

All throughout the writing of *A Man Without Love* I was really staring into the abyss—I had no prospects, no agent, and my aspirations to write successfully, to publish work, to eventually pay off my parents' love and faith and pay back all those fuckers from high school by giving a reading at the local Harry Schwartz Bookshop, were in great peril of going unfulfilled. When I started the novel, the truth is that deep down I didn't want to finish it, because as long as I continued writing I didn't have to confront all those extraliterary things, didn't have to query agents or publish excerpts in obscure online journals. So the novel was basically a symptom of a kind of pathological desire to not get to the end, and what I wrote, and the way I wrote, was not an effort to get closer to the end, but to push it further away. And then I reached that last sentence, a million words later, and went and played basketball with JT. A short excerpt of *A Man Without Love* was published online, thanks to the sympathies of the editor of a small literary journal (he had previously declined a novella I'd written called *Here Comes Truman Freeman*). I sent other excerpts to assorted literary agents who seemed too confused by what I was trying to offer them (*how* many words?) to even decline coherently.

Meanwhile, I was driving out to Orange County twice a week to teach community college, for which I was paid a little less than $2,000 a month. I was carrying $10,000 of credit card debt, incurring endless fees and penalties, and I spent all my time writing and anyway had no money to go out. After three years of this, I couldn't take it anymore. I decided that the best thing would be to find a way to go back to school, because then I wouldn't have to make payments on my student loans, and I could take out a new student loan to pay off the credit card debt that had become such a torment. I wasn't really committed to pursuing an academic track, because I wanted to be writing novels and other narrative forms, so I applied for and was accepted with a scholarship to a nontraditional MA program in theory and criticism at the Art Center College of Design out in Pasadena.

A Partial List of the Books I've Written

The program was kind of cool—Chris Kraus and Sylvère Lotringer, I believe, had been on board at its inception, and the people teaching in it had a lot of freedom, and it was oriented toward a critical *writing* practice. (It went out of business a year after I finished.) I moved all my credit card debt to student loan debt, and completed an MA.

In off-hours during those years, when I wasn't working or writing fiction, I'd started writing essays, one of which, "The Television Diaries," was eventually published in *n+1*, and honestly that small success did a lot to pull me out of the abyss. Then, the summer after I finished at the Art Center, an editor from Rodale Press contacted me. She'd heard me read from "The Television Diaries" at an event in LA and loved it. She was in charge of a new Rodale imprint that planned to publish fairly heady books—some by recognized names, but they also wanted to develop a stable of young writers. On the basis of what she'd heard me read, she saw me as a younger, more intellectual David Sedaris, and was interested in a book of essays along those lines. I had written a lot of essays over the previous couple of years, but most were pretty rough, and I'd never conceived of them as a book. I cobbled together a manuscript as quickly as I could, because I didn't want the window to close, and she turned the project down. I believe she said that I was more of a David Foster Wallace type than a David Sedaris type, which I took as a compliment, but also that the essays often slipped into an unrewarding solipsism, which I didn't take as a compliment.

But I'd foreseen her response, so instead of dealing with Rodale directly I'd involved an agent with whom I'd been in touch the year before. That happened in part because a girl I had a crush on suggested I write an essay for the *Vanity Fair* Essay Contest, the topic of which was what it means to be an American. I wrote an essay that was double the word limit, and more intended to impress my crush than to win the contest, but it came out pretty well. The girl and I got together for a while, and I published the essay on a literary website called Eclectica. Because it was so long and more a mockery of the topic than a sincere engagement with it, I titled it "Second Place in the *Vanity Fair* Essay Contest," which led a lot of people to believe that I'd won second place in the *Vanity Fair* Essay Contest, including this agent, whose initial inquiry came with congratulations, and who seemed to continue to believe that I'd finished second in the *Vanity Fair* Essay Contest even after I told her I had not. It's weird—my own aunt is still convinced I won second place in that contest because on the internet my name is attached to that phrase. Anyway, I sent this agent some work when she contacted me, including another novel I'd written called *Limbless*, and she was nice but *Limbless* was alas too "quiet" for her. But when I called a year later and said an editor at Rodale had solicited a book from me, she was naturally very eager to be involved.

Having an agent now—she worked at one solid agency when I signed with her and subsequently moved to a better one—I decided that I should get the hell out of Los Angeles (I rented a renovated barn in the Ojai Valley, on an orange grove owned by the Anderson family for which UCLA's Anderson School of Business is named), and put together a better, more cohesive book of narrative essays, if that's what the world, or the publishing world, was interested in. I also decided that this was (at least temporarily) my last best chance to publish a book through an agent with a real press. If it didn't work out, if I worked on the book for six or eight months and nobody bought it, I didn't want to start at zero again. I'd been pretty poor for a number of years, and on occasion what the kids call "hood rich," meaning you spend everything you get right away in a conspicuous fashion, and I felt exhausted. So I also applied to PhD programs in comparative literature. Having spent a lot of time in Spain, and consequently a lot of time getting familiar with the contemporary Spanish literary scene, I had a place to start with PhD literary studies, plus I had that MA, which would allow me to bypass some of the early coursework. I was not, and still am not, in any way dedicated to the idea of being a traditional literature professor, but I wanted to do something that in principle could end in a job, and regardless would put me in a meaningfully different situation in the world.

Well, the book didn't sell. I have plenty of rejection notes indicating that it almost maybe could have, but I also think it was pretty flawed, that though it contained some great pieces it wasn't all in all my best work, and was a performance oriented by a certain idea I had of what I might be able to get somebody to publish. My agent was still sending it out to the end of our list of publishers at the beginning of my first year as a PhD student. If it had sold, even for a very modest sum, I do believe I would have dropped out promptly.

What was it like, during those years in the desert, as I now think of them? (And really, that warehouse on Pico and Fourth was in what they now call an "urban food desert," and I always thought of the area as desertlike. I once found a baby rattlesnake strangled with electrical wire and tied to a signpost across the street.) In short, it fucking sucked. It sucked because I was poor. It sucked because I would throw these bits of writing out into the void. I didn't even have internet in my building, so I'd go to this joint in Koreatown, a couple miles away, that was mostly for Korean teenagers playing war games, and rent internet time by the hour, and send bits of writing to journals and query agents, and I knew it was all ending up in the slush pile. It sucked because I had no friends, really, and just wrote all the time and didn't really even have anyone to show my work to. It sucked because there wasn't a parking lot in the LA metro area where, unless I was actively shopping, I was permitted to park.

Mostly it sucked because there had been a moment in my life, I suppose as a younger person, when I knew that I aspired to be a writer. This is not the same as feeling at home writing, or feeling the need, the compulsion, to write, which I also felt. But there was this moment when I spied an image of myself as a writer, whole and intact and accomplished, and recognized that image as me—as who I needed to be in order to be me. As to the question of exactly what that image looked like, I really do think it involved coming home to Milwaukee and reading at Harry Schwartz, and my parents there proud, and the teachers who supported me and cared for me and encouraged me when I was completely and utterly alienated from my peers being there, and then maybe some of those peers as well, and me harboring no ill will toward them but instead being very charitable and forgiving in my success. And instead you find yourself in this beat-up old building in the middle of nowhere Los Angeles with no heat and holes in the walls and cracks in the windowpanes, teaching two days a week at a community college in Orange County and the rest of the time writing less to accomplish something than to avoid failing at it, and you see that image fading, and as it does being alive starts to feel haphazard and purposeless, not like destiny but like some unfortunate accident that has befallen you for no good reason at all. +

# Advice

If I were speaking to an eighteen-year-old, I'd say, "Don't worry. Don't be precocious." But the flip side of that is, this is the only life you'll get, and it won't come again. So, I don't think you should be precocious, and I don't think you should beat yourself up for not having published a book at the age of twenty-eight, but I think that a young person should keep a journal, and read seriously, and, you know, think about everything that happens.

**Caleb Crain**

My advice? Oh God, does anyone really want it? "Do this," "don't do that." You spend your whole life as a writer trying to get at something deeper and then you wind up sounding like the back page of *Glamour*. The best advice I ever got about writing was from my undergraduate writing professor, Blanche Boyd. She just said, simply, "You don't have to wait to be great." But that's more of a much-needed ego boost for when you're twenty years old and feeling down on your own abilities. It's more of a piece of inspiration. I suppose my advice would be: Read, practice, have faith, be prepared to write for free if you have to, don't give too much thought to your generation, find the balance between cynicism and compassion and don't move, read some more, take notes, finish what you start, remember what you love, say "thank you," set the table.

# Lessons

When I was deployed to Iraq in 2010, I wrote an essay called "Something on Something That's Something Like Disillusionment" for a nonfiction seminar. It was very self-effacing, purposefully ironic, kind of jokey, laden with footnotes and obscure references, and it basically talked about how even guys who blow stuff up for a living can get bored, worn out, and jaded even while things are blowing up all around them. It contrasted the older guys who don't even turn to face an explosion with the new guys who still get excited and amped up every time. A day or two before it was due, we were doing a detonation on the range and a rogue piece of fragmentation from a detonation missed me by inches and struck a young man right in front of me in the chest. He died instantly. When I returned to the essay to look it over before turning it in, I wanted to throw up. Not a word of it seemed true. It didn't seem funny, like it did when I wrote it. It didn't seem like it was written by the same person. Because it was due, I didn't have much choice but to turn it in, but I sent a cover note to my professor saying it may as well have been titled, "Something on Something That's Something Like a Bunch of Bullshit." I would imagine most writers go back and see things they've written that no longer seem true or that they've "grown out of," but I don't know how often the shift happens so quickly and so violently, in a matter of days or hours or even seconds.

# Contributors

**Maria Adelmann** is a writer, painter, teacher, and card maker. She lives in New Jersey.

**Elif Batuman** is the author of *The Possessed: Adventures with Russian Books and the People Who Read Them*. She went on to teach a nonfiction workshop at Koç University in Istanbul.

**Eric Bennett** is an assistant professor of English at Providence College. His book on creative writing and the cold war, *Workshops of Empire*, is forthcoming from University of Iowa Press.

**Carla Blumenkranz** is an editor of *n+1*.

**Alexander Chee**'s second novel, *The Queen of the Night*, will be published in fall 2014.

**Caleb Crain** is the author of the novel *Necessary Errors*.

**Sloane Crosley** is the author of *I Was Told There'd Be Cake* and *How Did You Get This Number*.

**Mark Dintenfass** is the author of *A Loving Place* and *Old World, New World*.

**Stephen Elliot** is the author of seven books, none of them written in, or about, New York. He doesn't have an MFA. He founded the literary website The Rumpus.

**Eli S. Evans** is currently at work on a dissertation, a collection of short, sentimental poems composed at odd hours, and a novel. He works as a lecturer in the Writing Fellows Program at Tufts University.

**Melissa Flashman** is an agent at Trident Media Group.

**Kathleen French** is an MFA student in fiction at NYU.

**Keith Gessen** is an editor of *n+1* and the author of *All the Sad Young Literary Men*.

**Emily Gould**'s novel *Friendship* will be published in July 2014. She is also co-owner of Emily Books and the editorial director of 29th Street Publishing.

**Chad Harbach** is an editor of *n+1* and the author of *The Art of Fielding*.

**Matthew Hefti** is an explosive ordnance disposal technician at McConnell Air Force Base in Wichita, Kansas, and has served four tours of duty in Iraq and Afghanistan. He recently completed his first novel.

# Contributors

**Eleanor Henderson** is the author of *Ten Thousand Saints*. She is an assistant professor of writing at Ithaca College.

**Fredric Jameson** is the William A. Lane Professor of Comparative Literature and Romance Studies at Duke University. His most recent book is *The Antinomies of Realism*.

**Lee Klein** has edited the semi-literary site Eyeshot.net since 1999. *Thanks and Sorry and Good Luck*, a collection of performative and/or helpful rejection letters he has sent over the past dozen years, will be published in 2014.

**Ellen Litman** is the author of *Mannequin Girl* and *The Last Chicken in America*. She is an assistant professor of English at the University of Connecticut.

**Jynne Martin** is the director of publicity at Riverhead Books.

**Kristin McGonigle** is currently at work on a nonfiction book about emigration.

**Meghan O'Rourke** is a poet and critic living in New York. She is the author of two books of poems, *Once* and *Halflife*, and the memoir *The Long Goodbye*.

**Kaitlin Phillips** is a writer living in New York.

**Jim Rutman** is an agent at Sterling Lord Literistic.

**George Saunders**'s most recent book of stories is *Tenth of December*. He is a professor of English at Syracuse University.

**Tom Spanbauer**'s fifth novel, *I Loved You More*, will be published in April 2014.

**Lorin Stein** is the editor of *The Paris Review*.

**Astri von Arbin Ahlander** is an agent at Ahlander Agency in Stockholm. She is the editor in chief of *The Days of Yore*, an online interview project.

**Diana Wagman**'s fourth novel, *The Care and Feeding of Exotic Pets*, was published in 2012. She lives in Los Angeles and teaches screenwriting at California State University, Fullerton.

**David Foster Wallace** is the author of three novels, including *Infinite Jest* and *The Pale King*, three story collections, and several works of nonfiction. He died in 2008.

**Darryl Lorenzo Wellington** is a poet and culture critic living in Santa Fe. His work has appeared in *Dissent*, *The Nation*, *New Politics*, *The Washington Post*, and *The Progressive*.

**Ben White** lives in New York and works in publishing.

# Permissions Acknowledgments

Grateful acknowledgment is made for permission to reprint the following material:

Chad Harbach's "MFA vs NYC" was first published in *n+1*, issue 10 (Fall 2010), © 2010 by Chad Harbach. Printed by permission of the author and *n+1*.

George Saunders's "A Mini-Manifesto" is adapted from "You Are Not the Only One Writing About Moldavian Zookeepers," edited by Chloé Cooper Jones and first published in *The Faster Times*, www.thefastertimes.com. Printed by permission of the author and *The Faster Times*.

David Foster Wallace's "The Fictional Future" is excerpted from "Fictional Futures and the Conspicuously Young," © 2012 by David Foster Wallace Literary Trust. That essay is collected in *Both Flesh and Not* (New York: Little, Brown & Co., 2012). Excerpt printed by permission of Little, Brown and Company. All rights reserved.

Lorin Stein and Astri von Arbin Ahlander's "People Wear Khakis" is adapted from their interview in *The Days of Yore*, October 2012, www.thedaysofyore.com. Printed by permission of the participants and *The Days of Yore*.

Keith Gessen's "Money (2006)" was first published in *n+1*, issue 4 (Spring 2006), © 2006 by Keith Gessen. Printed by permission of the author and *n+1*.

Elif Batuman's "The Invisible Vocation" is adapted from "Get a Real Degree," published in *London Review of Books*, vol. 32, no. 18, September 2010, © 2010 by Elif Batuman. Printed by permission of the author and *London Review of Books*.

Fredric Jameson's "Dirty Little Secret" was first published in *London Review of Books*, vol. 34, no. 22, November 2012, © 2012 by Fredric Jameson. Printed by permission of the author and *London Review of Books*.

Interviews with Sloane Crosley, Eli S. Evans, Eleanor Henderson, and Ellen Litman were conducted by Kathleen French.

Interviews with Matthew Hefti and Meghan O'Rourke were conducted by Kaitlin Phillips.

Interviews with Mark Dintenfass, Stephen Elliot, Lee Klein, Kristin McGonigle, and Tom Spanbauer were conducted by Ben White, and are excerpted from "Workshop Workshop," first published in *Vice*, vol. 16, no. 1, January 2009, © 2009 by Ben White. Printed by permission of the interviewer and interviewees.

## Permissions Acknowledgments

The interview with Caleb Crain was originally published in *What We Should Have Known: Two Discussions* (New York: n+1 Research, 2007). Printed by permission of Caleb Crain and *n+1*.

Quotations from Paul Engle's letters in "The Pyramid Scheme" are printed by permission of Hualing Engle.